Who Murdered Mary Rogers?

by
Raymond Paul

PRENTICE-HALL, INC.
Englewood Cliffs, New Jersey

For Champagne Annie
with love

———◆—◆◆◆—◆———

Design and decorations
by Linda Huber

Who Murdered Mary Rogers?
by Raymond Paul

ISBN 0–13–958306–8
Library of Congress Catalog Card Number: 76–145464
Printed in the United States of America T
Prentice-Hall International, Inc., London
Prentice-Hall of Australia, Pty. Ltd., Sydney
Prentice-Hall of Canada, Ltd., Toronto
Prentice-Hall of India Private Ltd., New Delhi
Prentice-Hall of Japan, Inc., Tokyo

Foreword

The murder of Mary Cecilia Rogers is a tragi-comedy of human frailty, of duplicity and betrayal, of corruption, incompetence, insanity, and of death. Told against the background of violent lawlessness which scarred New York City in the mid-nineteenth century, the saga of the "Beautiful Seegar Girl" adds its fragment of evidence in corroboration of Nathaniel Hawthorne's belief that "Life is made up of marble and mud," a "sphere of strangely mingled elements" in which "so much of the mean and ludicrous [is] hopelessly mixed up with the purest pathos. . . ."

The Rogers murder also marks one of the most explosive eras in the history of American journalism. The broad coverage given the case by James Gordon Bennett, Benjamin Day, Horace Greeley and other pioneers of "The Front Page," "stop-the-presses" school of newspapermen not only widened the concept of what news was "fit to print," but enlarged the role of editor from recorder and essayist to reporter, investigator, reformer, and gadfly.

"The Mystery of Marie Rogêt," Edgar Allan Poe's sequel to "The Murders in the Rue Morgue," was the second detective story written by the creator of that popular genre, and as it was based on the facts of the Rogers case, and as Poe later publicly claimed to have solved the real murder in the pages of his fictionalized account, the tale may also be considered the first specimen of the "true crime" story. Recent scholarship has shattered Poe's reputation as a "detective," but no one has ever realized how close he came to making good his boast or understood the ironic trick of fate which cheated him of the honor he coveted. A study of the crime requires a study of Poe's tale and provides, perhaps, the best means of examining the creative methods of story-wrighting employed by the author whom Henry James called a great genius and great charlatan. Included in this volume is an edition of "The Mystery of Marie Rogêt" which, for the first time, fully annotates Poe's sources and revisions.

At its core, the murder of Mary Rogers is a whodunit. The case provides a classic mystery puzzle for the connoisseur of premeditated mayhem. The suspects are both unsavory and bizarre: John Anderson, the merchant who held seances with the ghost of Garibaldi and amassed a million-dollar fortune on the stock market tips of a dead girl; Ann Lohman, the Queen Mother of abortionists, whose unique home for unwed mothers was dubbed "The House Built on Baby Skulls," and against whom suspicion ran so high that her life was threatened by a vigilante mob; Daniel Payne, the alcoholic fiancé who staged one of the most elaborate and theatrical suicides on record; Alfred Crommelin, the rejected suitor, whose pose of pious respectability seemed strangely at odds with his natural talent for perjury; Joseph Morse, the greenhorn gigolo who took it in bad part when a lady resisted his not inconsiderable charm; Frederica Loss, the tavern keeper whose house concealed so many obscene mysteries; and the strange "tall, swarthy man," the shadowy, unnamed figure seen with the victim on the day she disappeared, at whom Poe pointed the finger of guilt.

One of them murdered Mary Cecilia Rogers.

"Here are they all," says Nathaniel Hawthorne's Satan. "This night it shall be granted you to know their secret deeds."

TROY HILLS, NEW JERSEY   R. P.

An Acknowledgment

The author of a "first book" incurs more debts
than a gambler (whom he largely resembles), and
certainly more than he can honorably repay. Only
in retrospect can he begin to appreciate the
good will and many kindnesses of friends who
listened to his troubles, read his copy, and patiently
perjured themselves to ease his doubts.

Asking pardon of those whose names I omit,
I offer special thanks to these friends of many
years: Scott and Henrietta Welch; Rich and
Barbara Ross; Al and Joyce Tomlinson; Howard
and Jane Farrands; Bill and Marie Goione.

My thanks to my family.

And to Anne, who mixes the drinks and heroically
corrects the spelling, to whom this volume is
affectionately dedicated.

Contents

Corroboration will rise
upon corroboration, and the murderer
will be traced.

———◆—◆◐◆—◆———

EDGAR ALLAN POE

Prologue

In the summer of 1841 a beautiful, and notorious, young girl named Mary Cecilia Rogers was brutally murdered in Hoboken, New Jersey, initiating one of the weirdest and most tangled mysteries since Cain took a club to Abel.

The official investigation, launched in a chaotic witch hunt and sunk in an abortive and illegal hearing, stands as a tarnished monument to police ineptitude and magisterial malingering. The unofficial investigation, passionately conducted by a circulation-crazed press which considered slander the foundation of journalism, firmly established the gentle practices of the yellow press twenty-two years before William Randolph Hearst first nestled at his mother's breast.

Many great names, Edgar Allan Poe, James Gordon Bennett, William Seward, Horace Greeley, tiptoe in and out of this strange case like restless spirits; and ever behind the eerie events stands the beckoning ghost of the lovely victim, the ghost which drove her young lover to take his life, annihilated the sanity of her greatest benefactor, and haunted the dying hours of a raving woman.

The facts of the Mary Rogers affair must be sought in the files of the New York and New Jersey newspapers of 1841, for official records were taken carelessly or not at all, and have not survived. Any investigation of the murder must therefore be prefaced by a discussion of the conditions which prevailed among New York journalists in the mid-nineteenth century.

Had Mary Rogers been murdered a decade earlier we would have little or no knowledge of her death, for the press of the early 1830's would hardly have stooped to notice her sordid little tragedy. In those days New York journalism was dominated by dreary six-penny "blanket sheets," four or six pages, each ten columns of infinitesimal type, and two-thirds or more consumed with advertising. What "news" there was appeared on the second, or editorial page, and consisted of minutes of Congress and the State Legislature, items clipped and quoted from English journals or the papers of the South and West as they arrived in the mail, and labored articles on questions of politics, economics, or public morals.

The sole exception was the *Sun*, a little scandal sheet founded in 1833, whose publisher, Benjamin H. Day, had proven the potential of the penny press and prospered by ignoring world and national news and filling his paper with the fascinating sludge dredged from the proceedings of the police courts. But, though the *Sun*'s circulation grew to surpass the combined total of its rivals, its filthy little light continued to shine alone out of a tedious and verbose darkness.

Not that the publishers of the time were not colorful. Ironically the only drab one seems to have been Benjamin Day. Colonel James Watson Webb might attack rival editors in the street with his cane and get himself imprisoned for dueling, but his *Courier and Enquirer* was deadly dull. William Cullen Bryant might horsewhip an enemy in public, but his *Evening Post* sagged under the weight of scholarly poems and free-trade editorials. Major Mordecai Manuel Noah might rescue American slaves from the Barbary Coast and write a dozen successful dramas, but his *Evening Star* put readers to sleep. The Wall Street fourth estate, as a whole, exhibited all the energy, liberalism, and verve of a Presbyterian college. A gigantic gap existed between the *Sun* and

2

its six-cent competitors. Into this breach, on May 6, 1835, sailed James Gordon Bennett like a fresh breath of foul air.

Bennett's *Herald* deliberately courted, and thrived on, controversy. Tall and gaunt, with a face like a whiskered feed bag and a nose like a meat hook, the editor launched his fourth desperate attempt to establish a solvent daily, armed only with five hundred dollars, a monumental ego, and a conviction that a newspaper universally denounced will also be universally read. The sizzling pages of the *Herald* offered something to offend everybody.

For the Protestants: "A more corrupt, infidel, and rotten race of clergy than the clergy of the present age has not existed since the time of Caiaphas and Ananias, the high Priests and high scoundrels of Judea, in the time of Augustus Caesar."

For the Catholics: "If we must have a Pope, let us have a Pope of our own—an American Pope, an intellectual, intelligent, and moral Pope—not such a decrepit, licentious, stupid, Italian blockhead as the College of Cardinals at Rome condescends to give the Christian world of Europe."

For the Jews: ". . . I don't think much of Moses. A man who would take forty years to get a party of young women through a desert is only a loafer . . . Moses himself, according to the best biblical critics, was the first white man who married a Negro woman, and thus gave a sanction to amalgamation and abolition."

For those who complained that he spoke flippantly of the Virgin Mary: "Indeed, I care for nothing in this world or out of it, but the Holy Virgin and the blessed petticoat, to both of whom be all honor, glory, delight, and happiness, now and forever more. Amen."

For the Scots, in whose country he had been born: "They are a damned scaly set, from top to bottom, and when I pass them in the street, I always take the windward side, and avoid shaking hands as I would the itch."

Politically, Bennett bragged that his paper was independent of the influences of either the Democrats or the Whigs, and

proved it by his savage attacks on both. He loved to annoy
the prim and proper journals which flinched at words like
petticoat and trousers and called a leg a limb. When a Mrs.
Gove delivered a lecture series on anatomy to the young
ladies of New York, the *Herald* reported her remarks, carefully censored to avoid shocking the squeamish.

> I now come to the most important part of all,
> the proof of the virginity in a female—there is no
> proof—no infallible test—I know of my own
> knowledge this to be the case—I had no such
> test—know not what is meant *** I first mar-
> ried *** When *** consummation *** these
> were generally thought to be sure signs, but
> it is not so. I know by dissections of female
> infants *** could not by any means *** the
> Jews thought *** some have quoted the 22nd
> Chapter of Deuteronomy to contradict what I
> can prove *** from personal experience ***
> verses 13 to 52. (We cannot give the passage
> from Deuteronomy, alluded to by Mrs. Gove;
> it is unfit for our columns.)

Bennett's most vicious diatribes were reserved for his fellow
journalists, particularly Colonel Webb and Major Noah,
former employers, and Ben Day, who had refused to hire
him. Noah, who in addition to his journalistic activities was
also a justice of the criminal courts, fought Bennett with libel
suits and won. Webb, a man of action, twice flogged the
Herald's editor in the public street. Such attacks against
Bennett were common for obvious reasons. Day, whose *Sun*
was called "our highly respected, dirty, sneaking, driveling,
contemporary nigger paper," preferred to fight Bennett in
his editorial columns. He took special pleasure in reporting
the first of Bennett's encounters with the fiery Webb:

> As the story is told to us by an eye-witness,
> the colonel met the brawling coward in Wall
> Street, took him by the throat, and with a cow-
> hide striped the human parody from head to

4

foot. For the space of nearly twenty minutes, as we are told, did the right arm of the colonel ply his weapon with unremitting activity, at which time the bystanders, who evidently enjoyed the scene mightily, interceded in behalf of the suffering, supplicating wretch, and Webb suffered him to run.

In spite of it all, Bennett continued his assaults against his better known rivals on the theory that each time they returned his insults in print, it would boost his circulation. He was right and the *Herald* sprouted like a fungus. The volume of advertising rose correspondingly, and the paper carried such notices as: "TRY THEM: And You Will Be Sure to Recommend Your Friends To Buy Them—DR. GOODMAN'S ANTI-GONORRHEAL PILLS!" or "LEECHES! LEECHES! A Lot of Very Superior Leeches just received." The *Herald's* advertising rate went up. More and more copies were sold daily. In vain did the *Sun* sneer that Bennett's only chance of dying an upright man "will be of hanging perpendicularly from a rope." James Gordon Bennett was clearly becoming the most universally denounced, and universally read, editor in New York.

———◆◆◆———

On April 10, 1836, at three o'clock in the morning, Mrs. Rosina Townsend smelled smoke in one of her upstairs bedrooms. She dragged herself out of a bed she was sharing with a gentleman with whom she had merely a passing acquaintance, and climbed slowly to the second floor. She paused before one of the doors, sniffed again, tried the lock, and shoved the door open. The room was a shambles of scattered bedclothes and assorted lady's garments. The bureau had been rifled. On the bed, already seriously charred by the small, smoky fire that smouldered there, lay the once beautiful body of Miss Ellen Jewett, alias Maria Benson, alias Helen Mar, alias Dorcas Dorrance, known to a goodly portion of the

5

gentlemen of Manhattan, married or otherwise, as the undisputed Queen of the Pave. Her lovely forehead bore the scars of what looked very much like a couple of good blows with an ax.

———————◆•◦•◆———————

Ellen Jewett's career had been brief but busy. Born in Augusta, Maine, she had, when only eleven, "given her budding body" to a boy named Sumner who would live, and die, to regret he had ever met her. Her alcoholic father, dismayed that he had sired a child prodigy, placed her in the home of a Judge Weston where the girl received an excellent education. But Sumner rematerialized after a stint as a seaman, and a series of surreptitious midnight rendezvous were held until Judge Weston found out and, like the villain of a contemporary melodrama, kicked Ellen's rosy body out into the slush. She groped her way to Portland and found lodging at a local brothel. She soon found herself the sweetheart of a young banker who established her in an elegant house and presented her with the duplicate key. Hers might have been a Cinderella story if, like the proverbial counterfeit copper, Sumner had not once again appeared. The outraged banker caught the pair together and beat Ellen's perennial paramour into a very dead pulp. Ellen fled to Boston and eventually to New York where she soon established herself as the premier attraction of Rosina Townsend's thriving little hotel. She made many friends, but the closest, it was whispered, was a handsome nineteen-year-old boy named Richard Robinson, alias Frank Rivers, who now found himself charged with her murder.

Here was the perfect newsbeat: A gorgeous young prostitute foully slain with a hatchet; a chance to expose the nefarious, and fascinating, night life of the great metropolis; a marvelous opportunity to sermonize interminably on the fate of promiscuous youths and fallen women. Naturally the six-cent journals ignored the story. The stuffy *Statesman* spoke for its brethren. The practice of reporting sensational items, it said, "does not meet with our approbation, on the score of either propriety or taste. . . . We deem it of little benefit to the cause of morals thus to familiarize the community, and especially the younger parts of it, with the details of misdemeanor and crime." While the blanket sheets remained aloof, James Gordon Bennett, struggling to recover from a financially crippling fire which had destroyed his office and his press, poised himself on the diving board of his *Herald* and did a graceful one and a half gainer into the muck and mire of the Jewett murder case.

Within twenty-four hours Bennett had published the story of the murder and Robinson's arrest. Within forty-eight hours he had personally visited the murder scene and reported his findings to a panting penny-press public:

> I could scarcely look at [the body] for a second or two. Slowly I began to discover the lineaments of the corpse as one would the beauties of a statue of marble. It was the most remarkable sight I ever beheld—I have never, and never expect to see such another. "My God," exclaimed I, "how like a statue! I can scarcely conceive that form to be a corpse." Not a vein was to be seen. The body looked all white, as full, as polished as the purest Parian marble. The perfect figure, the exquisite limbs, the fine face, the full arms, the beautiful bust, all, all surpassed in every respect the Venus de Medici according to the casts generally given of her.

The respectable press was scandalized at such shameless sensationalism. So were the vast majority of people who bought out the *Herald*'s printing and clustered at its office, clamoring for news. Bennett dug into Ellen Jewett's sordid past and revisited Rosina Townsend's house, interrogating the flustered madam and publishing the first newspaper interview on record. He prowled through the dead girl's effects and announced that her reading material had included Scott, Dryden, Byron, Bulwer, Shakespeare, and Lady Blessington's *Flowers of Loveliness*. Church groups and ladies' societies

7

mobilized behind the memory of the murdered whore, and Bennett made another wonderful discovery, one that was to stand the press in good stead fifty-six years later while covering the story of Miss Lizzie Borden. The pious public, although abhorring newspaper accounts of sensational events, nevertheless will avariciously swallow all seamy details if they are flavored with a healthy dose of moralizing. With the fury of an Old Testament prophet, Bennett attacked the world's oldest profession, the dissipation of the city's youth, and the general condition of New York's morals, while the rest of the town's journals attacked Bennett.

The *Herald*'s editor was disgusting and debauched. His inspection of the murder scene was the action "of a vampire returning to a newly found graveyard—like the carrion bird to the rotten carcass—like any vile thing to its congenial element." The *Sun*, in particular, called Bennett every name it could think of; denied the truth of his reported interview with Mrs. Townsend; intimated that Bennett had been a regular customer at that lady's establishment. The *Herald* went blithely ahead, now tantalizing its readers with Ellen Jewett's ample and torrid correspondence, typical of which was one letter from a character who signed himself Wandering Willie:

> I shall never forget the moment I saw your fair form in the Police Office. You are fit to be a princess—a very queen. What a prize the villain had who seduced you at the Boarding School! Yet you are as sweet a companion now as ever. Oh! lovely creature, what a form! what a figure! what a fine bust! Your lineaments ****** rich lips, *** full bust, *** Your mind too, is of the first order.

The police, the public, and the vast majority of the press were convinced of Richard Robinson's guilt. As the case neared the courts, Bennett made still another discovery. A newspaper need not simply report an infamous murder; it can also investigate it. His examination of Rosina Townsend, the editor wrote, did not somehow ring true. Whose testimony placed the Robinson boy at the scene of the crime? Only Rosina's. Who professed to see the lad in Ellen's room before the murder? Only Rosina. Who fingered Robinson for the police? Only Rosina. Who was thought to be jealous of her star boarder and was known to owe Ellen a large sum of money which she was unwilling or unable to repay? One guess. The *Herald* labored mightily to cast doubt on Mrs. Townsend's character, testimony, and innocence. The *Sun*, working in collusion with the authorities, shot back with portions of Robinson's letters which proved him a wild and profligate individual. It insisted on the youth's guilt and charged that Bennett had been bribed to divert suspicion from the defendant. When Robinson was acquitted, Ben Day implied that only the fact that the boy found the money to retain a trio of crack lawyers had saved him from his deserved fate: ". . . Our opinion, calmly and dispassionately formed from the evidence, is that Richard P. Robinson is guilty of the willful and peculiarly atrocious murder of Ellen Jewett. . . ."

Both Robinson and Rosina Townsend soon left town and the Jewett mystery was never solved. But New York's fourth estate had learned a valuable lesson. Never again would any of the press be able to avoid covering a major crime story. Most of the six-cent sheets soon began carrying columns of police court news. The city's next big murder was to be the case of Mary Rogers, and the lead in reporting that sensation would once again be taken by James Gordon Bennett, still at the helm of the *Herald*, and Benjamin Day who, having sold out the *Sun* to his brother-in-law, Moses Y. Beach, would be striving to regain a foothold among the penny press with a new rag christened the *Evening Tattler*.

———◆◦◆◦◆———

In late May of 1840, the *Evening Signal* hit the streets with the most scathing castigation of Bennett to date. Nor was this an isolated attack, but the opening shot of a full scale war against the *Herald* in which almost every journal in the city was to join in what Bennett sneeringly dubbed a "Holy

Alliance" aimed at driving the hated "polluter of the press" out of business. Impossible though it seemed, Webb, Noah, Beach, and their pack had finally found a subject on which they could agree: James Gordon Bennett. He was: "a daring infidel, habitual liar, moral leper, venal wretch, double apostate, blasphemous monstrosity, pestilential scoundrel." Dictionaries in a dozen editorial offices were thoroughly ransacked; a boycott was established of every advertiser who dared to hawk his wares in Bennett's columns and of every hotel or club whose lobby was contaminated by a copy of the infamous sheet. The "stigma of the city" was denounced from every lectern and pulpit within thirty miles.

The *Herald* returned the fire. Mordecai Noah was "half Jew, half infidel, with a touch of the monster"; the physical handicaps of Park Benjamin, editor of the *Signal*, were "a curse by the Almighty." The Holy Allies, taken separately or together, were the most unsavory pack of chiselers and liars who ever filched an inkpot. The conflict raged for months: the Wall Street press roaring their epithets, the *Herald* surrounded but coiled and spitting. When it burned itself out in the political furor of the Tippecanoe campaign, Bennett was bloody but still on his feet. The Allies had failed to achieve a Carthaginian Peace, but they had scored more than a few points. Though it bayed that its circulation had risen during the Holy War, the *Herald* was hurt. Its pages never again carried the kind of outrageous items which had scarred them in the thirties. The violent battle had cleared New York's journalistic air. Though editors sporadically let loose with brief volleys of venomous flap, the press settled down to coexistence in a simmering stalemate. The way was clear for a relatively calm, impersonal, and dispassionate coverage of the murder of Mary Rogers.

The state of New York's law enforcement agencies in the summer of 1841 was a sorry one. The police were separated into a day force and a night force, the former called roundsmen and the latter watchmen, known to the populace as "leatherheads" since they wore leather helmets. Along with a cloak, this helmet constituted the only uniform. The watchmen were required to varnish the hats twice a year and, from all accounts, this seems to have been the most exhausting of their duties. Their nights were whiled away drinking in the taverns or catching a little shut-eye in one of the watchboxes, where more than once they might be ambushed by the gangs of young toughs who prowled through the slumbering city. If they were lucky, their helmets were stolen. If they were not, a rope would be looped around the box and the whole affair, leatherhead and all, dragged triumphantly through the streets.

The roundsmen were plainclothesmen but scarcely detectives. No training was required in criminology or, for that matter, in anything else. No physical or written examinations were given and few of them were particularly imposing or athletic. They were enlisted, primarily, from the ranks of unemployed stevedores, porters, and laborers; they were political appointees and their jobs were always just as safe as the next election.

No regular salary was paid. The officers subsisted on what they received for serving warrants and on witness fees of a dollar a day. The bulk of their income resulted from the collection of rewards offered by victims of theft for the return of their pilfered possessions. Collusion between the police and the underworld, therefore, was not uncommon. The thief would steal some valuable, and its owner would offer a reward for recovery of the item. The officer sought out his confederate, returned the hot goods, and split the reward. The widespread corruption reached as high as the justices. Obviously this system did not make for a preventive police; it was in the interest of the officers to promote crime rather than prevent it. Just as obviously the puny witness fees hardly made it worthwhile for the leatherheads to risk their necks chasing young punks without prices on their heads, and the city's seamier sections were terrorized nightly by packs of soap locks and butcher boys, their jackets marked by painted insignias, their shirts open to the waist.

Ultimate responsibility for keeping the peace rested with six special justices who presided from dawn to sundown at the police office at Third Street and the Bowery, and in the Halls of Justice fronting on Centre Street. The law provided that the Court of Special Sessions convene "on every judicial day in each month, during the time the General Sessions is sitting; and on Tuesday and Friday during the vacation." One of the six justices was to preside, assisted by two aldermen who served without extra pay. But in May of 1840, the ordinance was amended by the passage of the "Act for the better organization of the Criminal Courts in the City and County of New York," by which the aldermen were removed as judges and two new associate justices of the Criminal Court were created. The regular judges were incensed and one alderman, Elijah Purdy, immediately sought to prove the act illegal. The move was a Whig ploy and the two newly created judgeships went to two members of that party just before Robert H. Morris, a Democrat, took office as Mayor. James Gordon Bennett, who posed as a neutral but had been a political hack for the Jacksonians and continued to lean editorially in their direction, was up in arms, the more so because the appointments had been awarded to two of his oldest and dearest enemies, Henry Lynch and Major Mordecai Manuel Noah, late of the *Evening Star* and well scarred veteran of the great Holy War.

The *Herald* screamed relentlessly against the appointments and savagely ridiculed the qualifications of Lynch and Noah. When the first grand jury sat, the new justices regaled the jurors with undisguised attacks on Bennett and his paper. Bennett replied in kind:

> During the last two terms of the Court, Lynch and Noah each addressed the Grand Jury for the first time since their illegal appointment. It was their debut as Judges, and such a debut! We shall republish these charges in a few days, with suitable note and comment, as specimens of courtesy, dignity, learning, and propriety.

12

Meanwhile we ask—we beg—we entreat Recorder Tallmadge to deliver the next charge to the Grand Jury himself, and to give an example of learning, sagacity and knowledge to his assistants, in order that they may learn the extent of their duty. The newspaper press in a free country is a part of the administration of justices —a part of the police system—a part of the social system—a part of the legislative system. Neither executives, legislators, nor judges are hedged round with the mystery of kings or privileged classes, as in Europe. They are all servants of the public here—amenable to public opinion—to public praise and public censure, when they deserve it.

No man has the mind to comprehend this more than Judge Tallmadge—no men less so than Lynch and Noah.

When the case of Mary Rogers broke, the New York press was unanimous in its call for a complete overhaul of the city's polluted police system, the *Herald* loudest of all. But Bennett had another ax to grind. His entire staff would be dedicated to gathering proof that the girl had been assaulted and killed by a street gang. Once it could establish this fact, the *Herald* would declare total war, not on the police alone but specifically on Noah and Lynch for busying their court with petty offenders, deliberately refusing to involve themselves in the murder investigation, and encouraging lawlessness by dealing entirely too leniently with the thugs and ruffians who did appear before them. Bennet had a point. An examination of the police reports in any newspaper during the height of the Rogers affair shows that, while every element of law enforcement in the city was supposedly mobilized in the search for her killers, the court of Lynch and Noah was methodically handing down diminutive sentences for pig stealers and wife beaters. The following is typical:

John Williams, a very decent looking lad, apparently a waiter by profession, was put on trial

13

for biting off the ear of a big, hulking Negro
loafer. The accused told a rhodomontade story as
to how he bit off the Negro's ear to save his own
nose. The Jury, however, found him guilty, and
the Court adjudged him to stay in the Tombs for
thirty days.

Through August and September Bennett wielded the
Rogers case like a club against the two judges. Noah read
the *Herald*'s police reports minutely and brought suit for
any discrepancy. Smarting under one such suit, Bennett let
fly with a steaming editorial:

> . . . (the judges) exhaust their efforts and fac-
> ulties—all their law and half of their gospel—in
> procuring the indictment of a newspaper for the
> horrible offense against society, of making an in-
> correct report of a trial for stealing three pounds
> of pork—or a pilfering of a few bags of coffee—
> but for the taking away the honor and the life
> of a virtuous, respectable, lovely young woman,
> the only daughter of an aged mother, Judge
> Noah has no time to attend to such trifles—and
> Judge Lynch is so much engaged in granting
> writs of *habeas corpus* (fees in each case from
> $10—15), permitting the escape of undoubted
> malefactors, that he is equally unable to call the
> attention of the police or the Grand Jury, to the
> mere violation and murder of a young woman in
> the lower ranks of life.

Bennett's claims could be taken more seriously had he not
followed them with the statement that the administration of
justice in New York had been going from bad to worse since
"the escape of the murderer, Robinson," a reference to
Richard Robinson, a clear case of libel had that acquitted
gentleman been in the vicinity to press charges, and, moreover, an incredible piece of hypocrisy for the journal that
had doubled its circulation by arguing Robinson's innocence.
Nevertheless, it is evident that there was shameless competition among the magistrates for habeas corpus fees and that
on at least two occasions Justice Robert Taylor, one of the

major figures in the Rogers investigation, was beaten out of the fees by the sleight of hand maneuvers of Judge Lynch.

Three officials headed the inquiry into the death of Mary Rogers. Along with Robert Taylor of Manhattan and Gilbert Merritt of Hoboken, the triumvirate included New York Mayor Robert H. Morris, a seemingly competent man, qualified by his experience as a lawyer and judge. It is therefore probably unfortunate that Morris was away from the city during most of the month following the murder. On the seventh of August, while attending a fire, he had been thoroughly wetted down by several malicious constituents who commandeered one of the engine pumps. His Honor had immediately left the city, presumably to dry out, while his duties were fulfilled by Alderman Purdy. There is a noticeable improvement in investigative procedures after Morris' return on the twentieth.

Here then were the conditions extant on the eve of Mary Rogers' murder: a police system gutted with corruption and incompetence; a judicial system torn by opportunism, partisan politics, and internal strife; a press barely beginning to recuperate from the wounds of a violent war of words; a public incredible in its lawlessness, incredible in its naivety.

Almost buried on the third page of the July 28 issue of the *Sun* appeared the following notice:

> Left her home on Sunday morning, July 25, a young lady; had on a white dress, black shawl, blue scarf, Leghorn hat, light colored shoes, and parasol light-colored; it is supposed some accident has befallen her. Whoever will give information respecting her at 126 Nassau shall be rewarded for their trouble.

The following morning the *Sun* commented in its news columns:

> The body of a young lady some eighteen or twenty years of age was found in the water at

Hoboken. From the description of her dress, fears are entertained that it is the body of Miss Mary C. Rogers, who is advertised in yesterday's paper as having disappeared from her home, 126 Nassau Street, on Sunday last.

The stage was set. New York and New Jersey were about to launch one of the most bizarre and mystifying murder investigations in history.

Mary Rogers

Madame Restell

Edgar Allan Poe

MANHATTAN

1 Hoboken Ferry dock
2 Mary's most direct route from her home to the ferry (dotted line)
3 The Dead House behind City Hall
4 Anderson's tobacco store on Broadway
5 Mary's house on Nassau Street

The Hudson from the Elysian Fields

Ferry to Hoboken

NORTH RIVER

EAST RIVER

BATTERY

LEONARD
ANTHONY
DUANE
READE
CHAMBERS
MURRAY
PARK R.
CHURCH
BARCLAY
VESEY
FULTON
DEY
WEST
WASHINGTON
GREENWICH
BROADWAY
NASSAU
JOHN
ANN
CITY HALL
ROW
ELM
PEAR
CENTRE
CHATHAM
FRANKFORT
SPRUCE
BEEKMAN

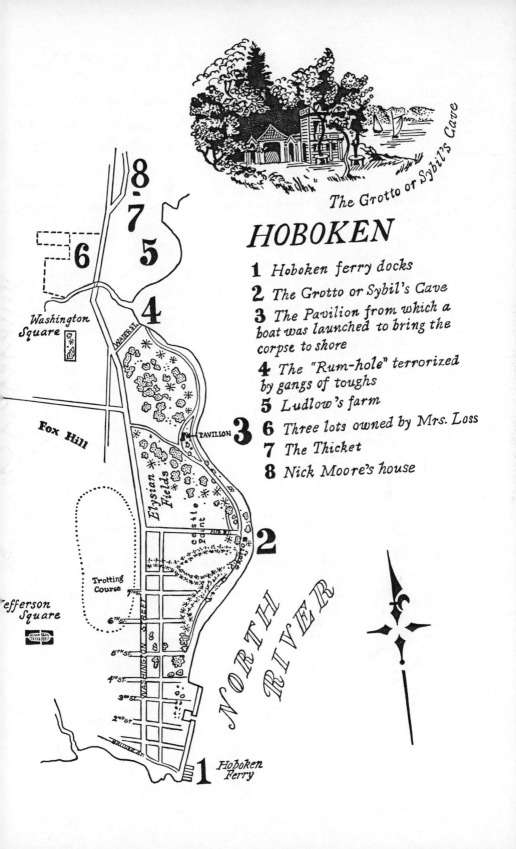

The Grotto or Sybil's Cave

HOBOKEN

1 Hoboken ferry docks
2 The Grotto or Sybil's Cave
3 The Pavilion from which a boat was launched to bring the corpse to shore
4 The "Rum-hole" terrorized by gangs of toughs
5 Ludlow's farm
6 Three lots owned by Mrs. Loss
7 The Thicket
8 Nick Moore's house

Washington Square

Fox Hill

WATER ST.

Elysian Fields

Castle Point

PAVILION

Trotting Course

Jefferson Square

7TH ST.
6TH ST.
5TH ST.
4TH ST.
3RD ST.
2ND ST.
TRINITY ST.

WASHINGTON STREET

NORTH RIVER

Hoboken Ferry

Horace Greeley

Moses Y. Beach

James Gordon Bennett

Benjamin Day

One

Oh! If there be a spot on earth for
*   contemplation made,*
Hoboken, 'tis thy fairy land, thy shore of poplar
*   shade;*
Where no intrusive voice may break the calm of
*   thy retreat,*
Save the sweet swan-like waves that die in music
*   at our feet.*
                    ANONYMOUS (wisely) 1830

Murder, if we are to believe the Bible, was the second thing man learned to do after his expulsion from the Garden of Eden. But the New Yorker of the midnineteenth century viewed the peaceful village of Hoboken as a modern Paradise, and for those who dwelt east of Eden, murder in Paradise was unthinkable.

On Wednesday, July 28, 1841, Henry Mallin, a Broadway vocalist, decided to take a holiday in Hoboken. Today, for those who are familiar with the filthy little city that nestles in the center of New Jersey's violent Barbary Coast, and have sniffed the pungent aroma of the Hudson's "sweet swan-like waves," it is difficult to believe that in the 1840's Hoboken was New York's rustic playground. Her shaded paths, picnic groves, and pleasant taverns attracted thousands of visitors each year. Edgar Allan Poe went there. Charles Dickens made a pilgrimage in 1842. Martin Van Buren, Daniel Webster, William Cullen Bryant, Washington Irving, Robert Fulton, all had preceded Mr. Mallin to Hoboken's beautiful Elysian Fields, a sylvan park which stretched along the river shore from Tenth Street north to the Weehawken line. What Mallin expected to find in Hoboken is hard to guess. A quiet stroll beneath the famous poplars, a relaxing day of sailing or fishing on the Hudson, a beer in the tap room of the Mansion House—any of these pleasures might have been in his mind. Horse races and bareknuckle fights were held in the Fields. Once the incredible P. T. Barnum promoted a buffalo hunt. It is safe to assume that, whatever his plans, Henry Mallin did not expect to discover a corpse in Paradise.

At about three o'clock in the afternoon Mallin debarked from the Hoboken ferry and began walking north toward the Elysian Fields. With him were four friends from New York: H. G. Luther, James M. Boullard, a Mr. Thornton and a Mr. Kavanagh. At Fourth Street they entered a wooded path that would lead them the final six blocks to the beginning of the park. Steep marble cliffs loomed on their left, bare in most places, overhung with the deep green of the groves of trees that lined the top. A few feet to their right, the waters of the Hudson lapped against the shore. The river was dotted with colored sails. It was an extremely hot day. At the foot of Seventh Street they stopped for a cool drink of water at the Sybil's Cave. The cave had been formed by making an excavation in the rock at the base of Castle Point where that promontory jutted out farthest into the river. A stream of fresh water flowed steadily from a spring deep within the cliff. The local Chamber of Commerce had been known to claim miraculous powers for the spring. As a joke it was sometimes said that the Sybil's Cave emitted the elixir of life.

Having refreshed themselves, the five men rested for a few moments before walking on. A couple of small boys in a rowboat were fishing two or three hundred yards off shore.

Suddenly one of them stood, stared at something floating near the boat, and then shouted, "There's a dead body!" Immediately the other took up the cry. Mallin rose, jumped down from the bank, and went to the water's edge. The thing lay on its left side, rolling between the tides with the gentle motion of the river. The waves alternately washed the long black hair up from the forehead and smoothed it back over the face. The boys were still shouting.

Mallin, with Luther and Boullard, raced to the Elysian Fields' dock for a boat. Taking a wooden plank with them, they rowed out to the body, but all were reluctant to touch it with their hands. Two or three times they tried to hook the dress with the plank but succeeded only in ripping it. Finally they fastened the stern line under the chin and towed the corpse close to the shore where, with the aid of William Waller, one of the crowd of curious that had begun to gather near the Sybil's Cave, they managed to drag it up on the bank until it was half out of the water. The rope was removed from the throat and tied about the waist, the other end being secured around a rock so the river could not reclaim the corpse. The spectators edged up to it in a silent circle.

It was the body of a young woman in her late teens or early twenties. The face was somewhat discolored and bloated; there was an ugly bruise near the left eye and a deep scratch on the left cheek that ran down to the shoulder. She was fully clothed. A bonnet was on her head and her hands were covered with light kid gloves which exposed long dripping fingers. She wore no jewelry.

It was now three-thirty. Someone was sent for the physician, Dr. Richard F. Cook of Hoboken. New Jersey law made her justices of the peace responsible for the investigations of all violent or sudden deaths. The nearest J.P. was in Secaucus, the Hon. Gilbert Merritt, and he, too, was summoned. He would not make an appearance until after seven o'clock. Henry Mallin and his friends had no intention of allowing one unpleasant incident to spoil their entire afternoon. They went on toward the Elysian Fields.

Until sunset the corpse lay uncovered, the face slowly blackening into a condition that would make identification impossible except by the clothing. At one point in the afternoon the body was hauled out of the water and up to the footpath. Along that path the word was passed from those leaving the cave to those approaching it. People clustered into small, quiet groups, waited their turn, and then moved forward to stoop awhile over the remains. The more courageous grabbed at the dress or poked the body. One young man lifted the dead girl's leg and made a crude remark.

Mary Cecilia Rogers was born in New York City in 1820, the child of her parents' old age. Her father died when she was five, leaving her mother, Phoebe, to raise the girl alone. The only other offspring, an older boy, had joined the merchant marine while Mary was little more than a child. Her mother was in chronic ill health, and Mary was put to work early as a milliner to aid in the support of the family.

John Anderson had come to New York from Boston while still a young man and worked as a wool-puller and a bricklayer before getting financial backing for a small tobacco store on Wall Street. Business was good and in 1836, when only twenty-four, Anderson was already on his way to the tremendous fortune he would eventually amass. It was in the early spring of 1836 that Anderson decided to move his shop into larger quarters on Broadway near Pearl Street, and it was about the same time that he first saw Mary Rogers.

The girl was sixteen and very beautiful, if we are to credit contemporary accounts. She was tall with a figure "exquisitely symmetrical," features "regular," complexion "good," and "a wealth of jet black hair." The enterprising Anderson would hire this charming young girl as a salesclerk, and lure every gentleman in New York with a healthy imagination or a good memory to his counter. This seemed the perfect promotional stunt for his new store. The plan succeeded wonderfully. The profits in snuff alone were not to be believed.

Phoebe Rogers was reluctant to allow her daughter to be exposed to the leers and rough vocabularies of the denizens of Broadway, but Mary was excited by the job, and the salary offered was too good to refuse. Mrs. Rogers permitted Mary to accept the position on condition that Anderson make sure the girl was never left alone in the shop, and that he or one of his employees would see her safely to her mother's door each evening. The tobacco business was soon booming. Anderson's emporium became the favored hangout for every stud and dandy on Broadway. It is said that many famous figures also came to his door, among them Washington Irving, James Fenimore Cooper, and Edgar Allan Poe. Many of those who haunted Mary's counter were reporters for the city's press who quickly dubbed her the "Beautiful Seegar Girl." A strong affection grew up between Mary and Anderson's wife which ultimately resulted in the Rogerses, mother and daughter, moving into the Anderson home. At the same time Mary was swiftly becoming one of the town's most popular and well-known celebrities. Then, in October of 1838, she discovered the price of fame.

On the evening of Thursday, October 4, a woman named Mrs. Hayes, a cousin of Mary's, went to the coroner's office in New York with a letter purported to have been written by Mary to her mother and left on the girl's dressing table that morning. The letter was apparently a suicide note in which, it was said, Mary had taken an affectionate farewell of her mother, begged her seagoing brother to care for the old lady, and announced her intention of doing away with herself. The cause of this desperate plan was reported with a sneer by the *New York Times and Commercial Intelligencer*:

> It seems that Miss Rogers was employed in Anderson's seegar store, in Broadway. There she met and fell in love with a gallant gay Lothario whose name did not transpire. After a month's course of billing and cooing across the counter of Anderson's store, which ended like the smoke of one of that gentleman's seegars (not, however, to

speak disparagingly of their deported worth), in
thin air. The Lothario was found one morning
missing, and that was the reason why Miss Rogers
is now missing. When she left, she took with her
a shilling, as it is supposed, with the intention of
purchasing poison.

Within twenty-four hours after this story appeared, letters
had arrived at the offices of all the newspapers which had
printed it, letters from someone identified by the *Times* only
as "a correspondent who says he is well acquainted with the
parties in the 'love and suicide' affair published yesterday. . . ."
This mysterious "correspondent" wished to inform the press
that the entire incident was a hoax "got up by some evil-
disposed person, who addressed a letter to the mother of Miss
Rogers, amounting in substance to that published yesterday."
The Rogers, it seemed, had simply been the victims of a
cruel joke played by one of Mary's girl friends. Mary, herself,
had actually been visiting relatives in Brooklyn, had been
absent only five hours, and was now safely back in her
mother's arms. The *Times* printed this retraction on October
6, the same day that similar articles appeared in the *New York
Herald* and the *Journal of Commerce*. It seems evident that
the "correspondent" had determined to squelch the suicide
story wherever it had been reported, and equally evident that
the letters were written anonymously, since the journals of
that time never withheld names "upon request," and always
published the names of correspondents when known.

Someone wanted it believed that Mary's disappearance
had not occurred. But the fact was that a note did exist and
that Mary was gone. How long she was gone cannot be said
with certainty; it was at least six days and perhaps longer. Nor
did the correspondent's denial of her absence gain credence
since the girl was obviously AWOL from her accustomed
position behind Anderson's counter. The rumors were many
and each found its way into the public prints, not unusual for
that time. New York was still a small town with too many
newspapers, long on gossip and short on news, where a six-
month-old item on a fire in Pittsburgh or a lynching in

Tennessee could be certain of a spot on the second page. Among the stories that circulated, one held that Mary had been seduced and kept at Hoboken for two weeks; another suggested that the whole thing was the invention of two malicious reporters who had printed the false story as a prank. At least one paper charged that the affair was a publicity stunt engineered by Anderson. "After the smoke of the extra seegars sold during the excitement had cleared away," growled the *Commercial*, "the young woman returned as good as new."

When she did return to the city, Mary was horrified at the public interest aroused by her vanishing act. One journal, the *New York Sunday News*, recorded that she fainted at the tobacco shop upon first seeing the stories and had to be carried home. By afternoon she felt well enough to return to work but by then the tale of her reappearance had spread, and a crowd had gathered before Anderson's establishment in hope of getting a glimpse of the notorious "Beautiful Seegar Girl." Frightened and in tears, she dashed back to her mother's rooms and took to her bed for three days with a bad case of nerves. Only a great deal of soothing from Anderson and a handsome salary raise induced her to reassume her perch behind the "seegar" counter.

At about the same time, her brother sailed as first mate aboard the *Josephine* out of Rio, bound for New York. En route, the vessel's captain died and young Rogers took command. On arriving, he learned of his sister's difficulties, determined that a tobacco store was no place for a young girl, and put his savings into the purchase of a building at 126 Nassau Street in lower Manhattan which could serve as an office building and boardinghouse, and provide Mary and her mother with both a residence and an income. No amount of pleading from the desperate Anderson could prevail this time. No promised pay hike was enough, although the tobacconist upped the ante to the princely rate of $400 a year. Within six months of her strange disappearance, Mary and her parent had set up housekeeping in what was to be the last home either one of them would know. Rogers, satisfied that his sister was now safely settled, returned to South America. Mary began taking in boarders.

Alfred Crommelin moved in on December 7, 1840. He was young and single, apparently attractive to his youthful landlady, and certainly attracted to her. His occupation remains a mystery (quite possibly it was the law), but he seems to have been successful at it. For nearly six months he tried to court Mary but his efforts were wasted. Mary had her cap set for another of the inmates at 126 Nassau Street, a cork cutter named Daniel Payne, a gentleman of irregular habits whose affection for John Barleycorn was at least as ardent as his love for Mary. The girl's affair with a man who infinitely preferred opening corks to cutting them disturbed both Phoebe Rogers and Crommelin who, with his romantic advances rebuffed, puffed himself up and assumed the pose of her moral guardian and protector. Things came to a head around the first of June, 1841, when Mary announced her engagement to Payne. A stormy session ensued between Mary and Crommelin in which he denounced Payne as a dissipated wastrel, but the girl's mind was made up. The erstwhile suitor packed his bags and moved out, but not before making a final noble gesture. To both Mary and her mother he proclaimed grandly that if either was ever in trouble she should not hesitate to call on him. Then Crommelin and Archibald Padley, another boarder with whom he had formed a friendship, took rooms on the same floor of a house at 19 John Street.

But Phoebe Rogers did not give up so easily. On or about July 23, the old lady had a final, serious conversation with her daughter concerning Payne. Possibly some difficulty had occurred between Mary and her intended since their engagement. Possibly her mother's arguments against Payne were at last beginning to take effect. Whatever the reason, Phoebe obtained from the girl what she later confided to the colored servant woman to be "a positive promise" that the marriage to the cork cutter would never take place.

It was also on July 23 that Mary first tried to contact Alfred Crommelin. On that day, a Friday, he received a note signed with Phoebe's name but written in Mary's hand, asking him to call at the rooming house. No reason was given for the invitation and Crommelin was still sulking over the argument they had had seven weeks before. He showed the letter to Archibald Padley. When they returned to Crommelin's office, they discovered a second note written by Mary, this time on the slate which hung next to his office door, again asking him to call. The girl had also left a red rose in his keyhole. He decided to go to Nassau Street the next day. On the morning of Sunday, the 25th, however, he changed his mind again. His final break with Mary had left a bad taste in his mouth, and he was reluctant to face Payne, who still boarded with the Rogers. He spent the day in his rooms, a decision he would bitterly regret, although in fact his visit on Sunday would have served no purpose. It was already too late.

The last person to see Mary alive, according to his later deposition, was Daniel Payne. Payne testified that he was shaving in his room at about ten o'clock on Sunday morning when Mary knocked at his door. When he opened it, she said she was leaving to spend the day with a cousin, Mrs. Downing, at 68 Jane Street, Manhattan, and would return by omnibus that evening. He replied, "Very well, Mary, I will look out for you." She appeared, he said, "cheerful and lively as usual." Three or four times she had visited the Downings, and on two previous occasions he had waited for her omnibus at the corner of Broadway and Ann Street and walked back with her to the house. This was again to be their arrangement, but a sudden and severe rainstorm hit the city on Sunday afternoon and Payne decided his fiancée, unwilling to venture out in such weather, would spend the night with her cousin. Payne did not meet the omnibus. Instead he went out for a drink. Mary did not return that night.

Phoebe Rogers was sick with worry. On Sunday afternoon she told the servant woman that she feared she would never see Mary again. Toward evening she left the house and went to the home of another cousin, Mrs. Hayes, to see if Mary had gone there. She had not, but Mrs. Hayes walked back to

Nassau Street with the old lady to comfort her. When Payne came in about nine that evening, Mrs. Hayes asked if he had any information about Mary's latest escapade and he recounted the morning's conversation. Apparently Mary had told no one except Payne of her plans for the day. "Oh well," sighed Mrs. Hayes, who had been through all this with Mary before, "she'll probably be home in the morning." She took one look at the frightened mother and prepared to spend the night. Payne went up to his room. Mary did not return on Monday morning.

Mrs. Hayes left before Payne came down to breakfast. She had gone to her own house to see if Mary had been there or had left word during the night. Phoebe explained that she would return immediately with word for Payne. Payne didn't wait. He went to work, assuming that if all was not right the women would contact him. At dinner he learned that Mary had not been at either Mrs. Hayes' or Mrs. Downing's. The Downing family had, in fact, been away all day on Sunday and had no idea whether Mary had called or not. Mrs. Downing had had no knowledge of the girl's intention of visiting her. The entire family was now thoroughly alarmed. Payne decided to institute a search. Instead of going to the police, he went to Mrs. Pitcher's in Harlem, the only friend of Mary's that he knew outside the family, but without success. At a loss, he tried Williamsburg next, questioning people at random, learning nothing. Tuesday he repeated the same pattern at Hoboken and Staten Island. No one he spoke to had seen Mary. That evening he inserted an advertisement in the *New York Sun*, which had the largest circulation in the city, promising an unspecified reward for information concerning the girl and giving the Nassau Street address, but not mentioning Mary by name.

Alfred Crommelin had heard of Mary's disappearance on Monday but presumed she was simply visiting relatives. Payne's ad in the *Sun* disturbed him, however, and on Wednesday morning he went to Nassau Street. Both Phoebe Rogers and Payne were in the parlor when he entered, but the fiancé got up at once and left without speaking, Phoebe explaining rather feebly that he was going to inquire at Bellevue. In fact Payne headed for a tavern on William Street to investigate an anonymous letter, the first of dozens which would be received by the family, the newspapers, and the police. A young girl had been at the tavern, but the description of her did not fit Mary. The cork cutter then retraced his steps to Hoboken and approached strollers on the path between the ferry and the Elysian Fields, passing the Sybil's Cave where, within an hour or two, a dripping corpse would be dragged onto the bank. Between one and two o'clock he took the ferry back to New York and worked at his shop until seven.

Crommelin, meanwhile, was convinced of foul play. He went to the police station in lower Manhattan, asking for a particular officer named Jacob Hays whom he knew by reputation, but was unable to find him. He tried to run down another anonymous tip, this one suggesting that Mary had been seen at a tavern near the Shakespeare Hotel, but again it was a wild goose chase. Rounding up his friend Padley, he reported back to Phoebe Rogers, and then crossed the river to Hoboken. Walking up the path toward the Fields, they noticed a large crowd gathered near the Sybil's Cave. Someone told them that a young girl had drowned and her body had been washed ashore. Crommelin rushed forward, shoved his way through the ring of onlookers, and knelt beside the corpse. He brushed the long hair away from the blackened and swollen face. He examined the clothing. Then he looked up at Padley, and Padley nodded slowly.

At seven o'clock, the evening of Wednesday, July 28, John Anderson was at work in his tobacco shop, unaware that an event had occurred which would cost him his peace of mind, his political ambitions, and eventually his sanity. Daniel Payne was just entering his rooming house. He had not yet been told that he was no longer engaged. In her tavern in Weehawken, Mrs. Frederika Loss was serving ale to her customers. No one had yet heard of the widow Loss but they would, they would.

27

Dr. Richard Cook was examining the victim of a brutal murder, ignorant of the fact that within a few weeks he would be a medical laughingstock, his professional reputation in ruins. Mr. Joseph Morse, a New York engraver, was hiding out from an assault charge brought by his wife, unconscious of the far more serious charge he would soon be facing.

It is safe to say that if the Hon. Gilbert Merritt, justice of the peace of Hoboken, had known the troubles and aggravations that lay ahead of him that hot July day, he would have stayed in his bed, or perhaps under it. As it was, shortly after seven o'clock Justice Merritt began presiding over the inquest into the death of Miss Mary Cecilia Rogers. The inquiry was brief and it was hurried, partially because it was late and partially because in the terrible heat the deceased was commencing to get a bit gamey. Merritt called only five witnesses, chief among them, Alfred Crommelin, whose major function was to establish positive identification of the body, and whose major concern seemed to be protection of the dead girl's reputation. Deceased was "the officiating manager of the family," Crommelin deposed, "the main support of an infirm and aged mother—with the whole charge of conducting the boardinghouse." She had, during the time he had known her, "borne an irreproachable character for chastity and veracity. She was amiable and pleasing, and," added the rejected suitor, "rather fascinating in her manners." Further, he had "never heard her virtue questioned in the least." Crommelin's intentions toward Mary's memory were, no doubt, admirable, but, in view of subsequent revelations, it might have been well for him to remember that he was under oath.

The most important, and ultimately the most controversial, part of his testimony lay in his identification of the corpse. The girl's face was, by the time Crommelin reached her, too blackened and disfigured to be recognized, and the identification was made entirely from the clothing and the size and shape of the body. He emphasized the smallness of the feet and lower part of the body, particularly noting the fact that clips had been used to take in the dead girl's garters. He ripped open the sleeve and rubbed the arm, looking for identifying "marks" which seem to have been certain formations of hair on the arm rather than skin blemishes. He examined the clothing carefully. He was positive. When the identification had been made, Dr. Cook gave him some articles to take back to Mary's mother. These included a part of the skirt of the dress and a piece from the sleeve, the flowers from the girl's bonnet, a garter, the bottom of her pantalette, a shoe, and a lock of her hair.

Archibald Padley was sworn in to corroborate Crommelin's testimony, which he did with respect to both her identity and her character. Two witnesses to the discovery of the body were heard: one, John Bertram, had simply watched the remains being towed to shore; the other, William Waller, had aided in tying the body to a rock near the Cave. The final witness, Dr. Cook, was sent with three of the jurors to conduct a thorough examination of the body, to write out his findings, and to read them to the jury. Unfortunately no record of his testimony now exists; however nineteen days later the physician was again questioned, this time by the mayor and coroner of New York after the city authorities had taken up the investigation. A substantial portion of his evidence was printed in the *New York Herald* from the shorthand notes of one of its reporters and has survived.

Were there "marks of violence upon her person, sufficient to cause death?" Cook was asked. The doctor "certainly should say there were." The specific instrument of death was a strip of lace trimming from an underskirt which had been torn off and tied round her throat with a hard knot under the left ear, tied so tightly that it was hidden from sight in the flesh of her neck. Cook had found it by accident when, passing his hand behind the ear, his fingers had felt the knot. His theory: The girl had fainted and before she could regain consciousness, the piece of lace had been employed to guarantee that she never would. Cook's examination had convinced him that "for all practical purposes" she had not been smothered. He stated that "at the time she was found and under the circumstances, it would have been impossible" to tell whether Mary had been drugged or not.

What was the condition of the body? "The face when I examined it was suffused with blood—bruised blood. There was frothy blood still issuing from the mouth, but no foam, which issues from the mouth of persons who die by drowning." The doctor was positive she had not drowned. "Her face was swollen, the veins were highly distended. If she had been drowned there would not have been those particular appearances that I found in the veins. The blood was so much coagulated that it was with difficulty I could get it to follow the lancet at all. If she had been drowned the discoloration would have been in the cellular tissue and not in the veins." He had found a bruise about the size and shape of a man's thumb on the right side of the neck, and two or three others on the left side which might have been made by a man's fingers. This led him to believe that "she had been throttled and partially choked by a man's hand."

Both arms had been bent over the chest, and were so tight and stiff that force was needed to straighten them. The right hand was clenched while the left was partially open but rigid. The position of the arms indicated, he said, that her wrists had been bound together and that she had raised her hands "to try to tear something from off her mouth and neck, which was choking and strangling her." The position of her arms was further evidence against drowning, he maintained, for he had attended sixteen or seventeen cases of drowning and invariably found the arms not bent, but extended.

There were abrasions on the left wrist "in the form of two circles around it, as if a rope had been tied around it once or twice." The right wrist bore similar marks but only on the upper side, confirming Cook in the belief that the wrists had been lashed together with the bottom of the right wrist pressed against the top of the left. The girl had been raped, the physician thought, the hands being tied while she was violated and the cords removed before she was thrown into the river. He had found additional abrasions at the top of the back, across both shoulder bones and at the bottom of the back, caused, he surmised, "by the young girl struggling to get free, while being brutally held down on her back, to effect her violation." These excoriations must have been made before her death because coagulation had been found in the cellular tissues. She had been laid on a hard substance, "a hard board floor, the bottom of a board, or something similar." He was positive "the outrage was not effected on a bed."

The girl's outer dress had been badly torn in several places, in part as a result of Henry Mallin's attempts to hook it with a plank. But a strip about a foot wide had been ripped by the murderer from the hem to the waist, and then not torn off but wound three times around the waist and fastened at the back "by a sort of hitch," apparently to be used as a handle in lugging the body to the water. The dress immediately beneath the outer frock and the upper petticoat, of a fine muslin material, had a piece twelve to eighteen inches wide completely removed. It had been torn evenly and with great care from the bottom of the garment and tied across her mouth with a hard knot at the back. Cook's explanation: "I think this was done to smother her cries, and that it was probably held tight round her mouth by one of her brutal ravishers." The muslin was still on the body when it was found, no longer covering the mouth but still knotted and hanging loosely about the throat. Over this the bonnet had been tied on the head with "a slip knot, not a lady's knot . . . a sailor's knot," in the ribbons beneath the chin, leading the doctor to conclude "that her hat was off her head at the time of the outrage, and that after her violation and murder had been completed, it was tied on."

Cook did not think she had been struck with a blunt or sharp instrument. In his opinion the body had been in such a state when he first saw it that recognition was possible and added that "Mr. Crommelin appeared to recognize it immediately." This last statement and several others of the doctor's opinions would become highly controversial in the weeks ahead.

The doctor's evidence that rape had been committed was considered by the *Herald* as of "so delicate a nature" that it did not belong in the columns of a family newspaper. His conclusions, however, were published and they amounted to this: that "bruises about the head and face" and other appearances of the body enabled him to be positive that she had been ravished; that "previous to this shocking outrage, she had evidently been a person of chastity and correct habits"; that she had been violated "by more than two or three persons"; that "there was not the slightest trace of pregnancy." Such was the testimony of Richard Cook.

The coroner's jury reached an obvious conclusion. Mary Cecilia Rogers came to her death by evident signs of violence on her body committed by person or persons unknown.

The inquest adjourned at nine o'clock. The body was hastily buried in a double coffin covered with only two feet of dirt. Henry Mallin and his friends had returned in time for the inquest but stomped back to New York in a huff when they learned that Justice Merritt had no intention of hearing their evidence. One of them, H. G. Luther, had the decency to go to the rooming house in Nassau Street and inform Daniel Payne and the family of the discovery of the corpse and Crommelin's identification. This was at seven-fifteen and there was yet time for the girl's lover or one of the relatives to go to Hoboken, but strangely, no one did.

It was nearly eleven before Crommelin and Padley reached the Hoboken pier and found the ferry no longer running. They walked to Jersey City but there also the last boat of the night was gone. They went to a hotel.

The sickly heat of the July night settled over the little village of Hoboken and her Elysian Fields. Perhaps somewhere along the shaded paths, the lovely arbors, the spirit of Mary Rogers wandered, the ghost that would lure a lover to his death, destroy an old friend's mind, and haunt a woman's dying hours.

For four days the murdered girl's family would keep silent. For four days Gilbert Merritt would make no effort to uncover her killer. For four days the New York authorities would not be officially informed of her death. Then the newspapers would get wind of the tragedy, and all hell would break loose.

Two

The *New York Sunday Mercury* assumed, and was generally conceded, credit for being the first journal to bring public attention to the murder in a brief, error-filled item published on August first, although the *New York Herald* had printed a more accurate account the preceding evening. By Monday, August 2, the entire fourth estate was baying in full pursuit of the story, the authorities on both shores of the Hudson were being prodded into action, and the city was jumping with rumors.

Hoboken was a boom town. Mobs of the ghoulishly curious jammed her ferries, crowded her paths and arbors, prowled about the Sybil's Cave and the road where the body had lain. For the saloons it was a wondrous windfall. The bars were packed, and the name of Mary Rogers was on every smacking lip. The Elysian Fields, the Grove, Castle Point, the winding shore, all were crawling with parties, picnics, groups of strollers. From the fashionable boarding schools in New York, flocks of young ladies were herded to the Sybil's Cave and subjected to long sermons on the inevitable fate of bad little girls.

A "public outcry," largely generated by the press, was raised against the lagging magistrates and police who had not yet run down the "brutal ravishers and murderers." There were rumors that Mary had been seen at Theater Alley, a few blocks from her home, being accosted by a youth whom she "apparently" knew. A "well known" young man was suspected and had fled the city. A break in the case was expected at every issue.

Gilbert Merritt came in for a healthy share of abuse. He was charged with mismanaging the inquest, with attempting to allow the investigation to drop, with malingering and incompetence. On August 2, the justice dashed off an angry note to Colonel Webb at the *Courier and Enquirer.* "In consequence of the great, though just excitement" in Hoboken over the murder of Miss Rogers, and "in answer, once and for all, to the many inquiries" he had received, he must say that it was far from his duty as a magistrate to give information or to answer questions of idle curiosity. However, he deemed it the duty of every individual with "the least regard for the well-being of society," who had any information about the case, however remote it might seem, to communicate with him; this evidence to remain confidential "until after an interview, or until restriction is withdrawn." Merritt interrogated three suspects. He came to New York to confer with officials there. Still the newspapers continued to take his name in vain.

Reports persisted that Mary had been observed arguing with a gentleman from Manhattan whose identity was known and who had left the city with the police on his heels. The "responsible" journals denounced this idle tale though it was rooted more deeply in fact than they supposed.

On the fifth, the first important arrest was made. A seaman, William Kukick, was dragged out of his bunk on the S.S. *North Carolina* and booked on suspicion of murder. Kukick had boarded for a time at the Rogers house, leaving on the previous July third, and his brother had stepped out with Mary on occasion. On the evening of the day when the girl was sighted in the river, Kukick had hurriedly signed on his ship, appearing nervous and in a sweat to get aboard. And the corpse's bonnet had been fastened with what Dr. Cook called a "sailor's knot." But the young tar insisted on his innocence. He had not seen Mary since he moved out of her house and he had never dated her. He had been in Boston on the day of her death, had not returned until two days later, and he could prove it. Witnesses who had seen a girl they thought was Mary with a youthful escort could not identify Kukick. The seaman's alibi was checked and he was released.

With the absence of any genuine clues to the killer the investigation took on aspects of a witch-hunt. Stymied, the magistrates groped through one tedious and fruitless examination after another and seized hungrily at any thread of a lead. It was a golden opportunity for dozens of New Yorkers to settle old grudges, and the mail was filled with anonymous letters implying the guilt or guilty knowledge of someone or other. Typical of these vicious notes is the following:

> *E. Keyser, 43 Washington Street, knows something of the murder of M. C. Rogers. Anonymous letters speak the truth sometimes. You would do well to examine him.*

Mr. Keyser, and many other innocent unfortunates like him, were harassed, but the solution to the Rogers affair remained elusive.

One such letter, however, proved to be of more substance. Addressed to the *New York Tattler*, and dated August 7, it reported that two gentlemen had been in Hoboken on July 25 when a rowboat containing six boys and a dark-haired girl reached the shore. The seven had walked into the woods, the girl apparently going unwillingly. This epistle was signed only "T.D.W." and the two gentlemen in question were unnamed, but the *Tattler* "put all the force in our office on the trail," and dredged up the mysterious witnesses.

The pair were a Mr. Fanshaw and his son-in-law Mr. Thomas. Their story was essentially as stated in the letter. Speculation was high that the young woman was Mary Rogers, but when she came forward she proved to be a child of fifteen who had journeyed to Jersey that Sunday with her parents and her boyfriend. The lad had taken her for a rowboat ride, and they had been overtaken and boarded by a gang of teenage toughs who had slapped the boy around and pirated his date. The little girl was forced into the woods and mistreated, though not violated. Later she was put in the gang's scow and piloted, unharmed, to Manhattan. The police had run into another dead end.

In the face of official silence the newspapers busily invented their own theories of the crime. James Gordon Bennett declared that it was obviously the work of a gang of young hoodlums; Ben Day's *Tattler* prepared to suggest that Mary Rogers was, in fact, not dead at all. At least one publication, the *New Era*, advanced the idea that Mary was a suicide, but, as the paper could not explain how she had tied her own hands together, knotted her torn lace collar around her neck, died, then untied her hands and thrown herself into the river, no one listened too carefully to this solution.

A prime suspect, of course, was the dead girl's fiancé, Daniel Payne. Youthful, fashionably dressed, about five feet, seven inches tall, brown haired, Payne appeared at the Halls of Justice on August 12. He explained his relationship with Mary and described the scene at his bedroom door on the last occasion that he, or anyone, had seen her alive. He deposed as to his movements on that Sunday. He had left his rooming house at eleven A.M. and walked to his brother John's home in Warren Street. He'd remained in his brother's company all morning, much of the time at a place called Scott's Bazaar in Day Street, from which they had hiked up Broadway to Saint Paul's Church and parted at one o'clock. Payne had strolled to a Mr. Bickford's and read the newspapers for an hour, then eaten dinner at Goslin's restaurant in Fulton Street before returning to his room for a three-hour nap. At six he went down to the Battery for a drink. There he again encountered his brother and they spoke for a moment. He next walked up Broadway, noticed the rainstorm approaching, decided Mary would not return that evening, thought it was too early to go home, and waited out the tempest at Bickford's tavern. At a little after nine o'clock, he went home to bed. At the Rogers house he discovered Mary's worried mother and aunt, and the rest of his actions were as has already been described. At the conclusion of his testimony he was taken to the Dead House to identify the girl's remains.

The New York authorities, pressured by the papers and dissatisfied with the identification made at the time of the Hoboken inquest, had arranged to have the corpse brought to the city where a second autopsy had essentially confirmed the findings of the first. Portions of the clothing had been examined by Phoebe Rogers, Mrs. Hayes, and a girl friend of the deceased and had been positively identified. The mother had specifically recognized a rip in the girl's dress which had been mended the day before she disappeared. Now Daniel Payne was led into the morgue, confronted with the cadaver, and asked to make final identification. The scene is colorfully recounted by a reporter from the *New York Journal of Commerce*:

> The body of this unfortunate girl was, yesterday, at the request of our city authorities, disinterred and brought from Jersey to this city, and deposited in the dead house in the Park. And difficult would it be for the most imaginative mind to conceive a spectacle more horrible or humiliating to humanity. There lay, what was but a few days back, the image of its Creator, the loveliest of his works, and the tenement of an immortal soul, now a blackened and decomposed mass of putrefaction, painfully disgusting to sight and smell. Her skin which had been unusually fair was now black. . . . Her eyes so sunk in her swollen face as to have the appearance of being violently forced beyond the sockets, and her mouth, which "no friendly hand had closed in death" was distended as wide as the ligaments of the jaw would admit, and wore the appearance of a person who had died from suffocation or strangulation. The remainder of her person was

37

alike one mass of putrefaction and corruption on which the worms were revelling at their will. And as if nothing should be wanting to send the moral home to men's hearts, and render it more painfully impressive, the young man who was to have been, in a few days, married to her, now stood beside the rough box in which all that remained of her he loved was lying. Her whom but a few days back, he had seen, "exulting in her youth," filled with life, hope and animation, whom he so ardently wished to make his wedded wife, to fold to his bosom, to press to "his heart of hearts," now lay before him an inanimate mass of matter, so hideous, horrible and offensive that the bare idea of coming in contact with it was almost sufficient to make the gorge rise.

Unsavory as this episode must have been for Payne, his troubles were only beginning. A substantial segment of the press openly questioned and ridiculed his testimony. The *New York Times and Evening Star* led the attack. Why, they wanted to know, had Mary told no one except Payne, not even her mother, that she meant to go to Downing's? Why, when he had promised to meet her that evening, had the young man been on his way to the Battery for a drink at the precise moment when her omnibus would be arriving at Ann Street in the opposite direction? (The omnibuses in fact did not even operate on Sundays, but Payne was unaware of this.) Why had the cork cutter gone to Goslin's to eat when he might have walked one block less and dined at his own boardinghouse? During the time he had supposedly napped at home, had he been seen by any resident of the house? Was there any witness who could place him at Bickford's? Why had he consulted none of Mary's intimates during his search for her? Why, after he had been told of her death on Wednesday evening, had he made no effort to attend the inquest or to make a subsequent trip to Hoboken? The newspaper was suspicious and the questions were echoed by the *Herald*, the *Commercial Advertiser*, and the *Tattler*, which called for Payne's arrest.

The harried gentleman rushed to defend himself. On the thirteenth he penned a letter to the *Times*: Since the editors had calculated "to throw a doubt on the mind of the public" as to his whereabouts on the day of the murder in spite of his deposition, he begged them to suspend further comment until he had produced affidavits which "will entirely exculpate me with regard to this horrible affair." Three days later Payne entered the *Times* office armed with seven sworn statements from Bickford, Goslin, brother John, a Battery barkeep, and Goodwives Rogers, Hayes, and Downing which accounted for every step he took and every breath he drew on the sabbath in question. The paper was satisfied. "No one can read the affidavits," it stated, "without feeling that Mr. Payne stands exonerated from even a shadow of suspicion."

The incredible clumsiness with which the early investigation was conducted must stand as a monument to police ineptitude, even for those lawless times. They waited twelve days to question Payne and then seemingly would have been content with his unsupported word had the papers not pressed for proof. It was eleven days before they disinterred the body and moved to verify its identity, thirteen days before they examined Crommelin, and they appear never to have searched Mary's house in Nassau Street. Almost every important step they took was forced by the criticism of the newspapers. A running battle existed between the officials and several of the dailies, the former pleading for a hiatus in press coverage, insisting that premature disclosures of clues were defeating the purposes of the inquiry, while they continued operating as much as possible in secret. The latter blasted these Star Chamber tactics and castigated the authorities for their blundering. A number of journals including the *Sun*, the *Tribune*, and the *American* defended the magistrates but the *Tattler* trumpeted: "It is certain that the public look more to this paper now, than to the Police, for an elucidation of the mystery." And the *Herald* moaned: "Really—really, the newspapers are becoming the only efficient police, the only efficient judges that we have."

What chiefly annoyed the press was the failure of the

authorities to offer a reward for Mary's killers. Since the police did not receive salaries, were required to pay their own expenses, and subsisted only on rewards, it was illogical to expect any officer to exert himself while success held no hope of remuneration, yet the family could not, and the government refused to put up the necessary funds. At the beginning of August, Gilbert Merritt had written to New Jersey Governor William Pennington, requesting that a sum be proclaimed. The answer was a simple and final no. Trenton apparently felt that the dead girl was a New Yorker and the fact that her body had washed up on the Jersey shore was no proof that it had been lobbed in from the same side of the stream. Any question of reward was strictly New York's problem.

City officials were equally convinced the crime had been committed in Hoboken. The law authorized the Mayor "to issue his proclamation, whenever he may deem it necessary, for the apprehension of any murderer, and offer such reward as he may think proper, not exceeding the sum of $500.00," but, since Mary had gotten herself throttled out of town, the Mayor did not "deem it necessary." The reward issue precipitated not only an interstate conflict but a similar tug-of-war between New York City's Democratic mayor and council and the Whig governor, William Seward, in Albany. Each side held that any responsibility which might exist for offering a reward lay with the other. The newspapers howled but nothing was done.

Finally, on the evening of August 11, a citizens' committee met at Stonehall's Hotel in Manhattan, largely at the instigation of James Gordon Bennett, to protest the official inertia. The thirty-five "outraged" gentlemen who attended adopted a stinging document denouncing the police and magistrates, a statement which bore strong evidence of Bennett's fine hand and acid pen, and they raised a reward of $300. The most generous contributions, each $50, came from the *Herald*'s publisher and from John Anderson. By the end of the month the sum had doubled so that, when Governor Seward finally surrendered on September 3, and agreed to offer $750 in state money, the total value of a solution to the Rogers mystery was $1,350.

The committee accomplished more than one of its aims, for it stimulated one of those bitter, personal exchanges between Bennett and Moses Beach of the *Sun* on which the penny press thrived. The *Sun* deplored the group's charges against New York's finest and piously avowed that, reward or no reward, it was almost sacrilegious to imply that every effort was not being made to run down the heinous villains. The *Herald* raked Beach for his "savage attack" on public-spirited citizens whose only concern was for law, justice, honor, and virtue. Bennett slyly noted that Beach had made a magnificent contribution of two dollars and wondered, "Who did the fellow cheat out of that sum?" Beach angrily denied contributing anything and sailed into Bennett with charges of organizing and using the committee for publicity and self-aggrandizement. And so the battle raged for three or four issues, the *Sun*, secure in its omnipotent virtue, inscribing its MENE, MENE, TEKEL, UPHARSIN with a fiery finger on Bennett's wall, while the *Herald* bobbed, weaved, and, following its unerring instincts, went for the groin. The circulation of both papers soared.

The inquiry into the fate of the Beautiful Seegar Girl continued at a snail's pace. The justices heard testimony from Crommelin, Padley, Cook, Henry Mallin, Phoebe Rogers; the parade of witnesses was endless but there was nothing new to be learned. Then, in mid-August, the case broke wide open. The mysterious young man whom early rumors had placed with Mary a few hours before her death and who had fled the city on the very day her body was found, had been finally unearthed, cowering in a Worcester saloon. He was being shipped home from Massachusetts in chains. The New York press selected a sturdy tree, made certain the noose was tight, and eagerly awaited his arrival.

Three

Joseph Morse was an engraver, and from all reports he was a good one. He'd been born in Nantucket, Massachusetts, and like many boys in that great whaling town he had spent time at sea. Later he'd sold newspapers, pamphlets, and almanacs on the New York streets before becoming apprenticed to an engraver. By the summer of 1841, though not yet thirty years old, Morse had acquired a good reputation in his trade and a prosperous shop on Nassau Street. Somewhere along the way he had also acquired a wife.

The domestic life of the Morses had all the characteristics of a pitched battle. The engraver, who had been something of a slob in his dress and manners at the time of his marriage, underwent a wonderful metamorphosis in 1840. He began affecting the attire of a Broadway dandy, his trademarks being a Panama hat and a fine Prince Albert coat. He took to wearing gloves and carrying a monocle, and his wild bush of a black beard was carefully trimmed down into a set of immaculate side-whiskers, of which he was particularly proud. Thus neatly wrapped in his new finery like a hairy Christmas gift, Morse considered that altogether he was much too splendid a specimen to be wasted on one woman alone. He commenced spreading his charms around. Mrs. Morse commenced sleeping solo.

43

The marital skirmishes burst suddenly into full-scale war in late December of 1840, and Morse moved out of his home on Green Street and into the back room at his office. He returned to his wife's bed periodically, however, and on one of those occasions, the evening of Wednesday, July 21, 1841, the reunion ended in a violent quarrel and Mrs. Morse was badly beaten. The next morning she issued a complaint against him with the police, and an officer Hilliker, armed with a warrant, went hunting for the wayward engraver at his office, where the elder apprentice, a boy named Edward Bookout, denied knowledge of his employer's whereabouts. Had Hilliker searched the shop he would have found the fugitive sleeping soundly in the back room, and thus saved both Morse and himself a great deal of subsequent time and trouble. But he merely left a note asking Morse to stop in at the station house.

The bewhiskered dandy had not expected his irate spouse to involve him with the law. Facing the alternatives of prison or wedded bliss, he chose the lesser of two evils and went home on Friday evening. There he remained until Sunday morning, the twenty-fifth, when, at the same moment that Mary Rogers would have been rapping at the bedroom door of Daniel Payne, Morse told his wife that he had an important engagement in Hoboken and left the house. In fact the engraver did have an engagement, a date with a pretty young dark-haired girl he had met near his shop on Nassau Street, a girl whose name he did not know.

(That afternoon two gentlemen from New York were strolling along the shore in the Elysian Fields when they noticed a young couple seated on a bench near the river, involved in a loud argument. The man wore a Panama hat and a Prince Albert coat, and had black side-whiskers. The girl was quite pretty in a light frock and long, dark hair beneath a flowered bonnet. Both seemed greatly agitated. One of the two strollers smiled. "Looks like a lovers' quarrel," he said to his companion.)

Joseph Morse did not come home until ten-thirty on

Monday night. He was obviously tired and he was in a black mood. In answer to his wife's probing, he said that he had been forced to spend Sunday night in Hoboken by the severe thunderstorm. He appeared more excited and irritable than was usual even for him and cut short her questions by announcing he was going to bed. She went out to the pump to get a pitcher of water for the morning and then climbed the stairs to the bedroom. But her husband was not in his nightshirt. He was changing his clothes and preparing again to leave the house. Where the hell was he going this time? And while they were about it, where had he really spent Sunday night? That, he snarled, was none of her business. He was going out and that was that. If he left the house again she would follow him! If she dared to follow him, he could positively promise she would be rewarded for her efforts with a punch in the mouth. He stalked out of the house and she stalked out after him. One block from his door he wheeled, waited for her to catch up with him, and made good his promise. Then he roared off into the darkness.

Officer Hilliker was upset. A full week had passed since his visit to the engraving shop, and Morse had not replied to his note or made an appearance at the station. Mrs. Morse had reappeared, however, on Tuesday morning to swear out a second assault complaint before Justice Taylor to which she had added, at the suggestion of the Justice, the charge of abandonment. Two days later Hilliker again presented himself at Morse's establishment. The apprentice Bookout said that his master was out of town. He didn't know where. Neither did a neighbor named Ireland, but Mr. Ireland did know one thing. Morse's baggage had been removed from the shop forty-eight hours before.

Hilliker ran down the lead. The luggage had been shipped to Boston on Tuesday afternoon and presumably its owner had followed. Morse had been born in Nantucket and his mother still lived there. To the officer it seemed obvious. A married couple had had a row and this time the husband had gone home to mother. Pursuit was out of the question. Hilliker would have had to pay his own expenses and with no reward being offered he stood no chance of reimbursement. He abandoned the chase and reported back to Justice Taylor. Morse had a good business in Manhattan. No doubt he'd come sneaking back when his wife cooled down.

The following day, Friday, the officer was present when two gentlemen of the city appeared before Taylor with an interesting story. They had read a brief account of an inquest held in Hoboken on the body of a young girl supposed to have been murdered the previous Sunday in the Elysian Fields. They had remarked on the coincidence that they, too, had been at the park on that very afternoon, and then one of them remembered the couple he'd seen quarreling on the bench. They described the pair and the girl's appearance did seem similar to that of Mary Rogers. But it was the description of her escort, the Broadway dandy with the side-whiskers that set Hilliker's suspicious mind to work. When his duties permitted, he paid a return visit to Mrs. Morse. From that lady he learned the details of her husband's last stormy night at home. Convinced he was on the right track, the officer went to Nassau Street to talk with Mary's cousin, Mrs. Hayes. Her description of the dead girl tallied with that given by the two strollers. Hilliker took some pieces of the sleeve of Mary's dress from her mother and returned to the station. There one of the witnesses made positive identification of the dress as that worn by the young woman he had seen in Hoboken. Hilliker laid his findings before Justice Taylor, and a warrant for Morse was immediately issued. It was decided that Hilliker must leave at once for Nantucket by the Boston boat, taking one of the witnesses with him to identify the suspect. But the officer did not have the funds to finance his investigation. Justice Taylor fished $80 out of his own pocket and handed it over.

Hilliker was a good cop. In the midst of the official blundering, procrastination, bickering, and incompetence that confused the entire Mary Rogers affair, his orderly and dogged pursuit of Joseph Morse stands out as a masterful piece of detection. Though convinced that the engraver was hiding out with his mother in Nantucket, Hilliker decided to double check his theory and had Edward Bookout hauled in for interrogation. Under heavy questioning the apprentice broke down. He wasn't certain where Morse was holed up, but the suspect had directed him to write to a post office box in Worcester when it was safe for Morse to return. Bookout, in fact, had already mailed a letter advising Morse that the heat was still very much on, and that he must alter his dress and make an Abraham's sacrifice of his magnificent beard. Hilliker's problem was simplified and yet difficult. He must reach the Worcester post office before Bookout's letter did.

But the boat for Worcester had already sailed, and the detective was forced to board a ship headed for Boston. It was the fourteenth of August, a Saturday, before he could arrange overland transportation to Worcester. Arriving at three P.M., he headed for the post office. No mail had yet come for Joseph Morse. Hilliker left orders to detain any letters so addressed and then, knowing the suspect's habits, he began making the rounds of the Worcester saloons. At a tavern on the city's outskirts the break came. Someone remembered a Mr. Morse who answered the description. Those whiskers were unforgettable. But this Morse did not live in Worcester but at Holden, a small town seven miles distant.

At Holden the officer easily learned where his quarry was staying. Leaving his witness at a back table in a nearby bar, Hilliker took up a post near Morse's door. At nine-thirty the engraver emerged from the house. Hilliker approached him and, without identifying himself, invited Morse to have a drink. The two men had never met and Morse was not suspicious. From his back table the witness studied the suspect's appearance and listened to his voice. Then he looked at Hilliker and made a sign. "Your name, sir, is Joseph Morse, I believe," said the policeman, "and you are under arrest." Morse demanded to know the charge. "On the complaint of your wife," Hilliker answered. Morse seemed greatly relieved. "Oh! Is that all?" "Yes," said Hilliker, "and for the murder of Miss Mary Rogers."

Morse refused to submit to the arrest until he was threatened with extradition. Then, however, he went quietly enough back to Worcester where Bookout's letter had arrived. The envelope was given to Morse who opened it and turned its contents over to Hilliker. The next day, August 15, the officer returned to New York with Morse in custody and delivered him to Taylor. The accused, with his jowl shrubbery still intact, was placed with a dozen other men in a room where the second witness, who had not accompanied Hilliker, picked him out and made a positive identification. He was then locked up and denied a lawyer.

Slowly Justice Taylor was collecting witnesses to account for Morse's movements on the fatal Sunday. He had been seen at 10:30 A.M. in the area of Mary's home. One of his friends deposed that he had met the engraver on Sunday morning and that Morse had said he was going to Hoboken. The suspect himself seemed incapable of telling the same story twice. At times he would admit he had been in Hoboken, and then insist he'd gone to Staten Island. He had spent the day alone. He had spent the day with a woman, but he didn't know her name. More and more entangled in his lies Morse became, while the newspapers, jubilant at his capture and for the most part convinced of his guilt, howled for his blood, and Taylor gradually tightened the noose of damning affidavits around his neck. At last on Wednesday evening, the eighteenth, the prisoner announced he was ready to tell the "truth."

He had left his home that Sunday to rendezvous with a young girl whom he had seen a few times near his office but whose name he did not know and had never learned. He took her on the ferry to Staten Island and bought her refreshments at a local spa called the Pavilion. Ever so cleverly the crafty idiot had maneuvered the hands of his watch back until the last boat for the city had debarked, forcing them to spend the night. Morse had bought her dinner and then sought to establish a beachhead in a Staten Island hotel room, but the game little lady had withstood all assaults and successfully defended her chastity through what appears to have been an all night siege. In the morning he had accompanied her back

48

to New York and left her on the corner of Barclay and Greenwich at between ten and eleven. He had never seen her again. The decision to go to Massachusetts was made on Monday night, after he had struck his wife, out of the fear of another assault complaint. But later he had learned of the death of Mary Rogers and, with typical egotism, had assumed that the deceased was the same girl he had seduced and that her shame had driven her to suicide. Through the entire affair Morse seems to have been far more terrified of his wife than of the murder charge. This new story, however, was no more convincing to Taylor than any of the others Morse had told, until, on Thursday morning, the lady in question came forward.

In tears and escorted by her mother, she arrived at the station. She was a pretty little thing, no older than sixteen, and the tale she related was pathetic. She had been deceived into remaining at the Pavilion with Morse until it was too late to return. On his promise of separate rooms and "a female of the house" to sleep with her, she had agreed to go with him to a hotel. When it became obvious that these promises would not be kept, she tried to force him to leave her room, but the gentleman dissuaded her "by dint of threats that he would expose and hold her name up to odium." They retired to the room's one bed near midnight; "he kissed me and hugged me a good deal." She could not say that he tried to use force. She lay on the bed with him for a few hours, "partly" undressed. At last his attentions became unbearable. She rose, wrapped a sheet around herself, threatened to scream if he approached her, and sat staring out of the window until daylight. Morse, who had no knowledge of her testimony, was reexamined and his story agreed with hers in all particulars. Moreover, four men, that afternoon, appeared before Taylor and swore that they had seen the engraver and the girl on Sunday. All four knew Morse on sight and two were acquainted with the lady. The authorities' case against the little dandy was coming apart at the seams.

To be absolutely certain, Taylor and the acting mayor,

49

Alderman Purdy, crossed to Staten Island and verified the engraver's alibi with employees of the hotel. There could be no question. Whatever else Joseph Morse was, he was not a murderer. The charges were dropped.

The newspapers reacted typically. The *New York American* clucked: ". . . will not the decent press take a hint from the false scent upon which, in this case, they have opened, with such wide-mouthed and cruel alacrity? Will they not see that common fairness and justice require that names and pretended circumstances of character and alleged antecedent misconduct, should not be trumpeted forth against a man arrested only on suspicion, and who may, as in this case, be wholly guiltless of the crime imputed?"

The *Herald* sneered: "Morse is to keep clear of Staten Island and of young ladies in black especially, for the future. Thus ends that nine days wonder."

The *Sun* pontificated: "Morse has a reputation for industriousness and is a fine artist . . . and we leave him with those kind words which our Savior spoke to fallen man—'Go, and sin no more.'"

The girl whom Morse had lured to Staten Island was so shaken by the ordeal of her examination at the hands of Justice Taylor, who had required from her every minute detail of the unpleasant evening, that she purchased poison and prepared a suicide note. A member of her family accidentally discovered her intention and prevented her from carrying out the deed.

The engraver's troubles were not yet over. The charges of assault and abandonment brought by his wife still had to be faced. He had by now acquired an attorney who, on Saturday morning, arranged for bail and Morse was released. Simultaneously Mrs. Morse was visiting a lawyer and consulting on divorce proceedings. She made an appointment to continue the discussion at two that afternoon, but it was never kept. While her attorney waited for her return, the amazing woman appeared before Taylor and dropped all charges against her husband. The bail was released, the prisoner discharged, and hand in hand the battling Morses walked off into the sunset.

Four

Ben Day of the *New York Evening Tattler* had a theory. Perhaps the reason why the murderers of Mary Rogers remained undetected was that Mary Rogers was, in fact, not dead. Oh, granted *some* young female had been savagely attacked and brutally murdered, but what evidence actually existed to connect that unfortunate with the Beautiful Seegar peddler? When you looked closely at the affair, damn little.

To argue this idea successfully, the *Tattler* had to make four major points: (1) that Mary had not been seen by anyone after she left her mother's house on Sunday morning, implying that she had taken pains to avoid recognition which, in turn, suggested a premeditated disappearance rather than murder; (2) that no corpse would rise to the surface after being immersed in water only three days, the maximum time that Mary could have been dead; (3) that Alfred Crommelin's identification of the body was highly questionable; (4) and that the indifferent attitude of the connections, including Payne, toward the deceased was explained only by the fact that none of them truly believed the dead girl to be Mary.

On the first issue, the paper contended that Mary was so much a local celebrity that "if she had gone to Hoboken, or if she had passed the length of three blocks in Broadway, there would be, probably, hosts of witnesses." On the second, they held that "all experience has shown that drowned bodies, or bodies thrown into the water immediately after death by violence, require from six to ten days, for sufficient decomposition to take place to bring them to the top of the water." But Mary could have been dead for only three days, and the probability that she could not have been dumped in the river unobserved until after dark reduced that time to about sixty hours. That she would surface so quickly was "a doubtful point," and besides it was "exceedingly improbable that any villains who had committed such a murder as is here supposed, would have thrown the body in without weight to sink it, when such a precaution could so easily have been taken." The *Tattler* failed to note that the last fact would argue against *any* corpse being submerged without weight, though that was precisely what had been done to whomever Henry Mallin had fished out of the Hudson.

On the question of Crommelin's identification the editors were expansive. Since water retards decomposition, they said, how was it that the features were so obliterated that he could recognize Mary only by other means, and not very certain means at that? The markings on the arm were merely *hair*! The similarities of build and apparel were inconclusive. (Here the *Tattler* ignored or was ignorant of the fact that the body had been exposed to dry air and ninety-degree heat for three to four hours before Crommelin saw it.) Rather, the journal suggested, Crommelin had been prepared to learn the worst, and naturally he had looked "not for appearances to show who the drowned person was, but for facts to strengthen his own preconceived opinion, that he had found the murdered body of Mary C. Rogers." The *Tattler* had every confidence in the gentleman's integrity, sincerity, and "self-denying perseverance," but his evidence amounted "*to nothing at all.*"

Furthermore, the relatives and friends of Miss Rogers had received the news of the floating cadaver with incredible apathy. Not only had none of them made the effort to go to Hoboken or aid in the investigation; not only did they fail to notify the police or even the tenants of offices in the Rogers house who learned of the murder from the newspapers; but in addition they allowed the girl to be buried by the city and refused either to attend the funeral or to permit her to be interred in the family cemetery plot.

> Now we ask the reader:
> If the friends of Mary Rogers can be supposed to believe the body found was hers, under these circumstances?
> If the proof of the identity of the body amounts to anything, when analyzed?
> Why did the mother think on Sunday before tea, that she "should never see Mary again"; when she had repeatedly before stayed at her aunt's overnight?
> Why has "the public" done all the investigation, and why have the connections, including Payne, held back?
> Would you, reader, dare to offer $500 for the production of Mary Rogers, alive and well, unless fifty thousand cents were put in your hands to meet the contingency? We should not.

(The *Tattler*'s third question concerning Phoebe Rogers is particularly interesting, because it belies ignorance of the fact that, at the time Mary's mother made this dire and often quoted prediction, she was not aware that Mary had gone to Downing's or that she might remain the night. What did the old woman know that gave rise to this fear?)

This then was the *Tattler*'s theory as it appeared in their issue of August 23. The reaction from Alfred Crommelin was swift and angry. He immediately stormed into the offices of the *New York Courier and Enquirer* to plant a story stating his dissent from the *Tattler*'s "long and labored" article. He was certain of his own identification, and the clothing had been positively recognized by Mrs. Hayes, a close friend of Mary's, and the girl's mother; the last "even pointing out some particular repairs done on the Saturday previous to her leaving home." The *Tattler*'s answer was essentially a rehash of its earlier position. It continued to state erroneously that Payne had not learned of Mary's death until Thursday morning, July 29, when he had actually heard of it from Luther the previous evening, in time to attend the Hoboken inquest. This fact would have strengthened its argument, had it read the cork cutter's deposition carefully. For the first time the *Tattler* contended that, as Crommelin had not seen Mary since the first of June, he could not have recognized her dress, a patently ridiculous idea since the garment had been worn long enough to require mending, the Rogers were not in a financial position to purchase new frocks every month, and the identification of the dress by the female relatives rendered Crommelin's unnecessary in any case.

On August 25, another penny paper, the *New York Planet*, released a letter purported to be from Pittsburgh to the effect that Mary was alive and well in that city. The young lady had left home to visit a maternal uncle in Milwaukee after an angry fight with Daniel Payne and with her mother, who had urged her to marry Payne in spite of the fact that "her heart was possessed by another," a Mr. Getchell, whom she was now preparing to wed. She had left her mother a note full of "bitter reproaches" which, since it had not been produced, she assumed the old lady had destroyed. The whole story was so obviously a phony that even the *Tattler* refused to credit it.

Also on August 25, Mr. Edward B. Hayes made an appearance at the offices of the *Tattler*. He was the son of Mary's cousin, Mrs. Hayes, and, with the exception of Mrs. Downing's husband, the dead girl's only male relative in the city. Cousin Edward seems to have been a rather delicate creature. He had visited Hoboken, but his stomach did not permit him to view the body and so he could not support Crommelin's identification. He was prepared to swear that Crommelin had been the principal cause of the family's apparent apathy. That gentleman had gone to Hayes on the day following the inquest and said that Daniel Payne had to be prevented from going to Hoboken, that the cork cutter was "a madman." On Crommelin's instructions, Hayes had convinced John Payne that his brother must be taken out of the city. Crommelin had, moreover, prevented the female relatives from crossing the river. He had urged that the family remain quiet about the murder "giving as a reason that it would lead to the detection of the perpetrators of the deed," and on one occasion insisted that the women must not speak to the police but must "let the matter be for him" to deal with.

It was untrue, said Mr. Hayes, that Mary had been buried in Potter's Field at the taxpayer's expense. Mr. Downing had paid for the funeral and both he and Payne had been present at the ceremony at the Rogers' family plot. Within twenty-four hours a letter had arrived from Payne announcing that Hayes' story was "strictly true in every particular."

All this was finally too much for Alfred Crommelin. He did some investigating of his own and fired off a communique to the *Tattler*:

> Having by the advice of my friends and the often repeated assurances of the gentlemen connected with the Police, which has as yet never been complied with, allowed a certain class of the penny press to go on from day to day to calumniate me, without their asking for one moment on what grounds, whether slight or sufficient—And supposing their vituperation to be well spent—as it is now mere repetition—now to show my fellow citizens that I fear no questions and wear no mask, I in the most public manner demand, wish and expect an open investigation of all and every part of my conduct in relation to the inquiries respecting the murder of Miss Rogers—no secret inquisitorial proceedings—we will have all the forms of law, and in open Court, with the reporters and other members of the press present, and one reporter sworn to report literally as spoken. I also demand that Mrs. Rogers, the mother, Mr. Payne, the lover, and Mr. Hayes, the cousin, shall be present, and also such other persons as I will name as witnesses, shall be summoned, and that they all answer such questions as shall be put to them

by me, or my counsel, on my having sufficient notice, if such investigation is granted for me to ascertain the residences of a few witnesses, say two or three days. To give some little idea of the grounds of slander, and the accuracy of the information of the papers before alluded to, it was near six o'clock before I made up my mind to differ from my friends, and make any reply whatever in the papers. In twenty minutes I ascertained the remains of Miss Rogers was not interred at the expense of the family, as Mr. Hayes states, confirmed by Mr. Payne, but by the city. Mr. Callender, Clerk of the Police, paid the undertaker the whole of the expense, $29.50; also, it was not at the early hour he states, but quarter to 12 o'clock, at noon; further, no person followed, but a stout man in a brown coat, took a cab, and went to the Carmine Street church, where it was deposited. For the accuracy of this, I refer to Mr. McCadden, the Undertaker, who has kindly allowed me to make use of his name. So one story is very good, but there is two sides to it.

A. Crommelin.

This was not the first public harassment Crommelin had suffered. His arrest for the murder had been falsely reported several times and he had been accused, as had Payne, of writing the warning to Morse at Worcester. A week earlier he had complained privately to Gilbert Merritt about harsh and severe treatment by both the New York police and "the lower order of the press," who were "endeavoring to heap odium" on his head. The kindly Justice penned a soothing letter: ". . . Admitting all this, what of it? When you enjoy the proud satisfaction of having performed your duty, as you have faithfully and diligently done thus far, day and night, in endeavoring to ferret out, and bring to justice, the concealed though wretched murderer of Miss Rogers. . . ." And so on and so on. The jumpy Crommelin was flattered. At least one magistrate recognized the great value of his selfless efforts to aid in the investigation, even if the city authorities considered him an irritating pest and the papers attacked his integrity.

It is conjecture, of course, but Crommelin must have bitterly regretted his refusal to respond to Mary's urgent pleas. He had promised to be her fortress in any time of trouble, and yet, the first and last time she had come to him, he had turned a deaf ear to her cry for help. Why had she tried to contact him? It was true that Phoebe Rogers swore that the reason was to sell him a due bill for $52 given in rent by a former boarder. But romantic young girls, engaged to marry other men, do not as a rule leave roses in the keyholes of former suitors when they call on mere matters of business. True, the notes were signed with Phoebe's name, but both were in Mary's writing. Possibly the old lady did not even know that her daughter was trying to reach him. The poor girl must have been in more trouble than $52 could solve. (And yet perhaps not. It was to occur to Gilbert Merritt, if not to Crommelin, that there was one problem a young girl might solve with $52, and that the solution might very well be sought, and bought, in Hoboken. But that idea had not yet entered the Justice's mind.)

Conscience stricken, Crommelin determined he would not fail Mary in death as he had done in life. As for Merritt, attacked by the press for accepting Crommelin's identification rather than postpone the inquest until the girl's relatives could view the body, the Justice had little choice but to defend the erstwhile swain and his testimony. But the New York officials, under no such pressure, regarded Crommelin as an officious aggravation. The would-be Hawkshaw winced beneath their sneers and the irresponsible castigation of a portion of the fourth estate. The false reports he could stand, but the charges against him by Edward Hayes and Daniel Payne came too close to the truth to go unanswered. For the first time Crommelin rejected the advice of his friends and personally entered the public controversy.

More conjecture. It is probable that the statements of Edward Hayes, openly confirmed by Payne, and not specifically contradicted by Crommelin, were true. It is likely that Crommelin did intervene to prevent the women from going to Hoboken, did send Hayes to speak to John Payne about getting his brother out of town, did make himself spokesman for the family as far as possible in their relations with police. It is equally likely that those portions of Hayes' story which Crommelin's letter particularly denied were untrue. The confidence with which the names of Callender and McCadden are mentioned, as if defying the *Tattler* to check out his contentions, argues strongly that Crommelin could prove that the corpse was buried at city expense, not in the family plot, and with the attendance of only one mourner. The last statement is the shakiest. The open letter quotes the undertaker as saying that "no person followed" the body, "but a stout man in a brown coat took a cab, and went to the Carmine Street church, where it was deposited." The phrase is carefully worded so as not to specifically deny Payne's presence at the interment, but only his claim that he followed the hearse. The mourner in the brown coat might have been Payne, who owned such a garment, or Mr. Downing, as the *Tattler* surmised, or even John Anderson. That more than one witness was present at the funeral is possible. Payne, who had been chastised by the newspapers for "indifference" to his fiancée's death, had publicly claimed to have attended her burial. It would require a great fool to make such a claim openly which could so easily have been disproven if false.

None of this, however, explained why the engaged man had failed to attend the inquest or go to Hoboken prior to his removal from the city by his brother. Nor did it clarify why the family had refused to pay for the funeral or allow the body to be placed in the Rogers' plot.

The "open investigation" of Crommelin's conduct, which his letter had demanded, never took place. The *Tattler*, meanwhile, amused itself with a vicious assault on Richard Cook. The doctor's testimony that Mary had been repeatedly violated and the facts offered as proof of this were "disgustingly ridiculous," and "the subject of contemptuous sneers by nearly all the physicians in the city who have heard it." The Hoboken quack was a century behind his time, and it was lucky for his reputation that part of his evidence could not be published, "as its absurdity would make him a byword at once." The poor sawbones was livid. In Hoboken, clutching a glass of gin, he stormed that the *Tattler*'s editors were being bribed by the murderers to slander him and demanded they be arrested.

The editors were not arrested but Archibald Padley was, on August 27, and clapped into the Tombs by Justice Milne Parker on suspicion of the abduction, rape, and murder of Mary Rogers. Held in secret, refused the names of his accusers, denied an attorney, Padley was subjected to a three-day inquisition and released only when the newspapers learned of his imprisonment. The prison keeper received the release order from Justice Taylor on the morning of the 31st and then discovered that Parker had quietly arranged to smuggle the prisoner out of the Tombs fifteen hours earlier and without the knowledge of his jailors. Both Taylor and his head screw were furious, but Parker had other troubles. He faced impeachment proceedings for similar irregularities in connection with another arrest. The magistrate had friends in high places. He would be acquitted. It seems clear, however, that while the New York police might resemble the Keystone Kops, they had all the finer instincts of the S.S.

The *Tattler* continued to insist that the body found was not that of Mary Rogers. They didn't know it but an event had already occurred on the Jersey side of the river which would cast an entirely new light on the investigation, and lob their pet theory into the wastebasket. At last the site where the Beautiful Seegar Girl was murdered had been discovered.

Five

*The most frequent source of false mem-
ory is the accounts we give to others of our ex-
periences. . . . We think of what we wish had
happened, of possible interpretation of acts, and
soon we are unable to distinguish between things
that actually happened and our own thoughts about
what might have occurred.*

WILLIAM JAMES

*In . . . murder cases which have been dis-
cussed excitedly, and minutely reported in the
newspapers, it has been a frequent occurrence to
have some amazing testimony offered by a woman.
Sometimes she appears for the defense, sometimes
for the prosecution, but she is so frequent a phenomenon that I have kept a symbol for her in my
notebook,—for convenience I label her M.F.W.,
—Marvelous Female Witness.*

EDMOND PEARSON

A short stroll north of the perimeter of the Elysian Fields,
at the base of the path that wandered leisurely up to the peak

61

of Weehawken Hill, sat a small picturesque tavern called Nick Moore's House. Mr. Moore had vacated the premises several years before, but the present proprietress, a bouncy little barmaid of about forty named Frederica Loss, saw to it that thirsty visitors were made welcome at her watering hole. Mrs. Loss called herself a widow, though in fact she had been divorced from a man named Kellenbarack with whom she had mated and migrated from her native Prussia. When she shed her husband, Frederica assumed her maiden name of Loss, but her three young sons, who aided in running the tavern, continued to answer to Kellenbarack. By the autumn of 1841, the merry "widow" had done very well for herself. In addition to Nick Moore's House, she held title to three large lots in Weehawken. Business was good. It was about to get better.

On August 25, Mrs. Loss sent her two younger boys, sixteen-year-old Charles and twelve-year-old Ossian, out to collect sassafras bark. What the lads did collect, however, was not bark but something that would explode the Mary Rogers case back into the headlines, ignite a bitter debate between the *Herald* and the *Tattler*, make their mother's name a household word, and set Gilbert Merritt on the trail of what he would ultimately deem the solution of the strange mystery.

Beside the hill road lay a small, dense thicket within which were four large stones that formed, for those with active imaginations, a kind of seat with a back and footstool. The boughs and briar bushes were twined so thickly around and above these rocks that entrance to them was difficult and, once within, it was impossible to stand erect. As he passed this spot, Ossian chanced to look in and noticed a piece of white cloth lying on the largest of the rocks. The boys scrambled in and Charles picked it up. It was a woman's petticoat. On a second stone they found a silk scarf, "all crumpled up [the *Herald* was to suggest] as if torn off forcibly." In a hollow between the seat stone and the trunk of a small tree were a parasol and a girl's handkerchief bearing the initials

M.R. A pair of gloves lay on the ground, torn inside out as if hurriedly drawn from the hands. Hanging on the briars were strips from a woman's dress, one piece so doubled as to have a thorn three times through it. The underbrush was thoroughly trampled down and mashed roots and broken branches showed evident signs of a struggle. Several marks of a man's high-heeled boot were discernible. Tracks led out of the thicket and down to the river bank as if someone had walked to the water while dragging some sort of dead weight. Where the tracks crossed two fences, the rails had been removed and now lay in the grass. The *Herald* described the condition of the articles:

> In order that it may not be supposed that these things were placed there recently, it is proper to state, that from their appearance this could not have been the case. The things had all evidently been there at least three or four weeks. They were all mildewed down hard with the action of the rain and stuck together with mildew. The grass had grown around and over some of them. The silk of the parasol was strong, but the threads of it were run together; within the upper part, where it had been doubled and folded was all mildewed and rotten, and tore on its being opened. The white linen handkerchief had a corded border round it and was mildewed also. So was the scarf. This and the petticoat were crumpled up as if in a struggle. The pieces of her frock torn out by the bushes were about three inches wide and six inches long. One part was the hem of the frock and it had been mended; the other piece was part of the skirt, not the hem. They looked like strips torn off, and were on the thorn bush about a foot from the ground. The petticoat, shawl, etc., were full of little bugs, called by the Dutch, kellerasle, that is, in English, cellar jackass, an insect that always gets into clothing lying in wet places.

The boys gathered up the items and brought them home, but Mrs. Loss held them for seven days before informing the authorities. She would later explain her delay by saying that she thought "something might turn up to make them more useful than if she handed them over at once." To the little woman it perhaps seemed incredible. That poor young girl whose murder had the police baffled, the newspapers agitated, absolutely everyone talking, that unfortunate child had been killed right in that thicket, hardly a stone's throw from her door. Why, she might have heard something, seen something. Of course. There had been a scream. She had thought it was her eldest boy but it hadn't been; it might have been Mary Rogers; it must have been Mary Rogers. And when she walked down the hill that Sunday evening and passed within a few feet of the thicket, the horrible murderers might at that very moment have been committing the foul deed. No doubt they were. Was it possible that Mary had stopped at her tavern? She'd been exceedingly busy that day; it was so terribly hot. And . . . there *had* been a girl, young, pretty and, now that she thought about it, wearing the identical dress, pieces of which she now held in her hands. And there had been a young man, tall, swarthy; it was all coming back to her. Why (land sakes!), she remembered it as if it were yesterday.

On or about the second of September, the widow Loss went to Gilbert Merritt. Dr. Cook was dispatched to the tavern where he received the clothing, and the New York officials were contacted. The Marvelous Female Witness told her story.

It was at four o'clock that the young lady entered Nick Moore's House that fatal Sunday. She was of the age and exact appearance of Mary Rogers, and was dressed as the papers said Mary was dressed. She was "very affable and modest in her behavior," and was escorted by a young man of dark complexion. Mrs. Loss had brought several glasses of liquor into the parlor where the company, five or six young couples, were sitting, and the swarthy man had offered Mary one of the glasses. Mary, being a good girl, had preferred lemonade. They remained only a short time. Then the girl took the arm of her gentleman and, bowing to her hostess, she left and walked up Weehawken Hill. The widow had particularly noticed the frock because it was identical with the dress her sister had worn on a visit just before her death. Mrs. Loss had remarked on this to her eldest son Oscar.

She never saw Mary Rogers again. Soon after dark, she sent Oscar out to drive away a bull which had wandered down the hill road from the house of a neighbor, James Ludlow. A bit later she heard "a frightful screaming as if of a young girl in great distress, partly choked, and calling for assistance, and sounded like 'Oh! oh! God,' etc., uttered in great agony." The shrieks were so loud that another of her sons heard them from her cellar. Fearing Oscar had been gored, she rushed out toward Ludlow's, calling the boy's name. "As soon as she called out," the *Herald* reported her as saying, "there was a noise as of struggling, and a stifled suffering scream, and then all was still." She found Oscar safe at Ludlow's and returned to her tavern. Because several loud fights had occurred that day, she thought no more about the screams. In fact she thought so little of all that stifled suffering that in discussing the bull episode a few days later with a neighbor she failed to mention the screams at all.

The *Herald*, our principal source for the widow's tale, gave the story full play. From the outset Bennett had insisted that Mary had undoubtedly been the victim of an attack by one of the gangs of "fire rowdies, butcher boys, soap locks, and all sorts of notorious miscreants" that terrorized honest folk on both sides of the river. This new evidence could do nothing but confirm that theory. As further proof the paper stated that a greater number of young thugs than usual had crossed the Hudson that Sunday to drink at a rumhole on the mudbank near Nick Moore's House. Two particularly suspicious boatloads of scoundrels had landed and laid siege to the little saloon, drinking their fill, refusing to pay, and threatening all present with clubs. The ruffians, fifteen of them, all armed with sticks, had then left to climb the hill where they prowled until after dark. Then the two rowboats had been observed debarking in a great hurry.

Not all the newspapers were as ready as the *Herald* to

accept Mrs. Loss' saga at face value. Several journals wondered why the clothing had not been found earlier, and suggested that it had been brought recently from New York and planted in the thicket to divert suspicion from the actual murder site. But now a second witness came forward to partially confirm the widow's testimony. Adam Wall, a Hoboken stage driver, had been at the ferry dock at three P.M. with another man when Mary arrived on the boat. She was accompanied by a young, swarthy man. The couple had taken the path to Weehawken. Wall, said the *Herald*, had later seen the body on the shore near the Sybil's Cave and was positive it was the same girl.

The investigators sprang into action. On September fifth and sixth, they inspected the area of the thicket minutely. Also on the fifth, Mayor Morris issued another appeal to the press to hold all stories on the murder, which was, as usual, ignored. On the seventh, Morris published a plea for anyone who had been near Nick Moore's House on the day of the murder to communicate with him at his office. New York was crawling with rumors.

One journal remained for the moment aloof. The *Tattler*, which had argued that Mary was not dead at all, found these new developments seriously detrimental to its point of view. Quietly its reporters went about checking the stories of Wall and Mrs. Loss. On September twenty-fifth, in the columns of its Sunday organ, the *Brother Jonathan*, the paper released its findings. Because the question of the accuracy with which the widow's statements were reported and the equally important issue of the veracity of those statements are at the heart of any attempt to discover the fate of Mary Rogers, it is necessary to reprint the *Brother Jonathan* article almost in its entirety:

> Moved by the wonderful stories and the very connected manner in which the circumstances, real, supposed, and rumored, relative to the Mary Rogers disappearance have been detailed, "one of us" has taken a trip to Hoboken and we propose

to give the results of that jaunt, and the impressions produced by what was seen and heard. If the narrative throws a little discredit on a portion of the chain of circumstantial evidence which has been paraded in the newspapers, we cannot help it. Our object is to tell the truth and nothing more; to sift the evidence and to expose its deficiencies. When the reader has perused our cogitations, he will be compelled to admit that the case remains as mysterious, at least, as ever. The story is far, very far, from being clear in all its particulars.

Mrs. Loss, who is a very clever intelligent little woman of about forty, does not appear to owe the *Tattler* any very good will—a prejudice, we regret to say, very common at Hoboken. However, the establishment may possibly survive the wrath of the united kingdoms of Hoboken and Weehawken, and as we did not take pains to tell the Hobokenites of our connection with the denounced establishment, their wrath did not mislead us. . . .

Mrs. Loss, in her conversation with us, destroyed a great part of the unity of the Weehawken murder narrative. It will be recollected that if it has not been positively so asserted, the inference has been allowed to go abroad that Mary Rogers and her companion, when at Mrs. Loss' house, formed a distinct and separate couple, holding no communion with the others; and that Mary and her companion went alone from the house. Mrs. Loss says that she does not know how the company came, whether altogether, or in successive couples. There were about a dozen couples at the house while Mary was there. Refreshments were ordered, and lemonade and other preparations were carried in on a tea server, and placed upon a table. Mary sat with two other females upon a settee, and when the server was brought in, said "I will take lemonade." No fresh order was given, as there would probably have been, had Mary and her attendant formed a distinct party; but he selected a glass of lemon-

67

ade from the common stock, handed it to her, and resumed his seat.

Nothing particular occurred at the house during their stay. Mrs. Loss remarked upon the peculiar neatness of Mary's dress and form, to her boy; but saw nothing in the appearance of the company generally, which led her to any other observation, or to the suspicion that all was not right, and precisely as it should be. When the company left the house, they all left it together; and at least six couples, including Mary and her attendant, walked up the Weehawken road together. Mrs. Loss thinks that Mary took the arm of the young gentleman who handed her the lemonade, but upon that point cannot be positive, as she did not see his face as he walked away. This was the last time that Mrs. Loss saw Mary.

In the evening Mrs. Loss sent her boy to drive home an unruly bull. While he was gone, she heard one scream, but caught the utterance of no sentence, as has been represented. She did not hear "Oh my God!" or any expression of the kind—nor did she hear the scream repeated—the bull came thundering down the hill at the same moment that she heard the scream, and but for the circumstance, she says it would not have alarmed her. She feared the boy might have been gored, and immediately ran up the hill to Ludlow's house, where she found her boy safe and sound, playing with some companions. In going up she passed "the thicket"—in returning she passed it—and within ten feet of the center of it, too—but she heard no screams or struggles, and saw nothing unusual. At Ludlow's house which is nearer "the thicket" than Mrs. Loss', even the first and only scream was not heard.

Now then for "the thicket" itself. It is between two roads and the distance across is from thirty to forty feet. There are two or three houses within half call of it. It can only be entered on all fours, or on the hands and knees. It requires a man with young limbs to get into the place at all. No girl under any circumstances,

68

could be persuaded to go voluntarily in such a place among the stones, sharp rocks, and dirt—particularly after a rain, when the leaves and earth would be so wet and filthy. There are houses so near that the shelter of a cave would not be thought of in a storm; and were there no houses near, shelter in such a place would be worse than exposure in the open air. A body, dead or alive, could not have been dragged in there without severe laceration, and rending every garment from it. There were no *excoriations* of such description upon the supposed body of Mary C. Rogers.

Arrived at the inside, there is not a flat rock there—not a platform or even surface, a foot in diameter. There is hardly a place to sit down—and no place upon which a person could lie down with any more ease than he could in a barrel with nail points inward through its sides. Such was not only our opinion but that of two or three gentlemen present, strangers to us. The lessee of the property, who has been its occupant thirty years, shakes his head incredulously at the circumstance of the clothes having lain so long in the thicket undisturbed, while he has no doubt, nor indeed has anyone in Hoboken, of the identity of the body found as that of Mary Rogers. He never had heard, 'til he saw it in the prints, of the rails broken down, etc., etc.; and as to struggles or footmarks, they are all obliterated, if they ever existed. The fence is in perfect order now at any rate.

. . . We left the ground, far from satisfied that "the thicket" has been anything more than the depository of the garments, etc., by interested hands, long after the disappearance of Mary C. Rogers. If she went away from the house in company with four or five persons of her own sex, beside the young man, how is it that none of these persons have yet come forward? Who knows that Mary Rogers was at Mrs. Loss' house at all on that day? Mrs. Loss only identifies "the girl" with Mary by the description she has heard—having never, to her knowledge, seen her before. We repeat, this part of the tale throws more mystery over the event than has ever been thrown before. Who were the five or six couples who walked up the hill with Mary and her attendant? Where did they last see her? Who was the young man? And is he murdered too?

Brother Jonathan also interviewed Adam Wall and determined that his testimony amounted to nothing. "He did not remember having seen the girl on that Sunday, until a month afterward. Then being over in New York, at the Hoboken ferry, a coach driver, whose name he does not know—whom he has never seen since, and saw only once or twice before—sang out to him (Adam)—Well, Dutchman, so that pretty cigar girl was killed that day I pointed her out to you. Adam could not at first remember the circumstance of her being pointed out to him at all—and is not very clear upon it now. If this coach driver saw Mary at Hoboken, why has he never come forward amid all the outcry that has been made?"

The *Tattler*'s revelations cast serious doubts on the evidence of both Mrs. Loss and Adam Wall. Neither had ever seen Mary before, and both based their identifications on the vague and conflicting descriptions in the press. The stage driver's story, based on a chance remark by an unknown man made a month subsequent to the crime, was completely demolished. As for Mrs. Loss, all that actually seemed to have happened was that several couples had stopped at her tavern, that one particularly pretty girl had asked for lemonade, and that at dusk she had heard what she thought was a single scream. The *Tattler* implied that the widow's conclusions were the work of an overactive imagination, or perhaps the shrewd inventions of a woman well aware of the benefits all that publicity would accrue to her business.

In trying to debunk the thicket as the murder site, the journal had poorer luck. It argued three major points. First, it stated that, with three houses nearby, no one would use the thicket as a shelter. This was logical but no answer to the theory that she was forced off the road and attacked. Second, it noted the difficulty, but not the impossibility, of entrance and the cramped and uncomfortable nature of the interior, yet concealment and not comfort would be the primary concern of a rapist. Third, it maintained that the briars would have left marks on the body and quoted a juror who had observed Cook's postmortem as saying that no such scratches existed. Yet Cook had deposed to "considerable excoriation" on the back and shoulders. Had the girl been knocked senseless first, and had her attacker crawled into the thicket, dragging her in after him by the feet, those marks might be accounted for.

The *Herald*, whose report of the widow's testimony had apparently embellished it almost at will, blithely ignored its rivals' attempts to discredit its star witness. On September 21, it published a sketch of the thicket. Accompanying the drawing was a fuller description of the spot. It was three to four hundred yards from Nick Moore's House between the mountain road and the path that led down and north to Bull's Ferry. Its entrance was close to an overgrown, unused carriage route, and its back was formed by two beech trees and a stone wall. The paper suggested that Mary had been placed on the stone "seat" and held against the rock which formed the back of the seat. And it reported for the first time that the girl's shoes had been pierced by large thorns "precisely resembling" those found in the thicket.

Three days later another sketch appeared, this one of the entire area of the shore and Weehawken Hill. The *Herald* again insisted that the thicket's interior was sufficiently hidden from the road that the clothing might have lain undetected for a month, and that the area was so isolated and untraveled, especially at night, that the girl could have been murdered, dragged to a boat, and dropped into the river without the crime being witnessed. The article closed with the newspaper's "probable view" of the murder:

> ... that she and the young man who was at Mrs. Loss' with her, were coming down the grassy middle road; that he was knocked down senseless, and she was seized; that she then screamed,

71

and was heard by Mrs. Loss; then was choked 'til she was senseless, and dragged into this thicket out of the way, on the approach of Mrs. Loss. And the body of a man might lay on the grass road at dusk, and a person pass along the lower road, and never notice it, or see it. Or the young man who was with her might on that very road have been attempting to take liberties with her; she resisted and screamed; he choked her, dragged her into the thicket, and there violated and murdered her. Then stayed by the dead and mangled body of his victim in that dark thicket, with no eye but that of God upon the murderer and the murdered maid, until all was still—perhaps 'til near midnight. Then, tying the frock around her to form a handle, he carried her to the river, and hurled her in, and fled, too horror stricken to think of returning to the scene of the murder, to remove the articles found by the boys.

The following morning the *Tattler* hurled down the gauntlet with its attack on the evidence of Mrs. Loss and the coach driver. The *Herald* would undoubtedly have accepted the challenge but, at the same moment that copies of *Brother Jonathan* were being hawked in the streets, police were searching the rooms of John C. Colt, brother of the famous gun manufacturer, and discovering the remains of a printer named Samuel Adams, all crated up and ready to be shipped to St. Louis. New York had another murder to amuse itself.

In the midst of the furor over the Colt affair, one more mild flurry of excitement occurred in the Rogers case. A report came out of Albany that a New York coachman, James Finnegan, had been traced to that city and taken into custody for Mary's murder. Police already had two or three of the coachman's gang, and one of them had confessed the crime and fingered Finnegan as the ringleader. Six or seven thugs were involved, all with records. Two of them had known Mary, had met her as she left her home on Sunday morning, hired a boat and lured her to Hoboken and her death. One of Mary's missing rings had been found in Finnegan's possession at the time of his arrest.

New York yawned. It was the same old story, rumored confessions, startling new evidence, sudden arrests in the night. Finnegan was just another Kukick, another Morse, another Padley. The whole tired tale was bound to be a hoax, which is, of course, precisely what it was. Finnegan was in custody all right, but for the attemped rape of another girl on an entirely different Sunday. On the twenty-fifth of July he had driven his employer's family to church both morning and afternoon and he could prove it. There was no confession, no gang, no ring. He wouldn't have known Mary C. Rogers if he had tripped over her. Furthermore, his lawyer protested, the poor, martyred coachman wasn't even guilty of the charge that had actually been brought against him. Why, on the very night his accuser claimed she was fighting him off in a New York hotel, honest Jim Finnegan had, in fact, been in Albany escorting his white-haired old mother to sabbath services.

The authorities backed off. They were "satisfied" of Finnegan's innocence in the Rogers matter. New Yorkers looked up from their newspapers, nodded and smiled. They knew it all the time. They went back to reading about John C. Colt.

The Jersey affair dropped out of the headlines for a week. Then, at the notorious thicket, and on the shaded path beside the Sybil's Cave, the second act of the Hoboken tragedy was played.

Six

On Thursday, October 7, 1841, Daniel Payne went to Hoboken to die.

He costumed himself well for the little melodrama he was about to stage, in a brown frock coat, a black valentia vest polka dotted with white, fashionably cut black trousers and black boots. On his head he set the black hat with the black crepe band of mourning his sister-in-law had sewn on for him at the time of Mary's death. Probably he took a moment to survey his appointments in the mirror of his Ann Street bedroom. Then he sashayed forth to commence one of the most collosal binges in the history of the grape.

Sometime between drinks he journeyed to an apothecary in Park Row and purchased a small phial containing laudanum, a lethal poison. It was in his pocket when he accidentally ran into his brother John shortly after noon. Brother John was worried. It was a bit early in the day to be quite so drunk, even for Daniel. Secretly John Payne suspected his brother was losing his mind.

By three P.M. Daniel was on the ferry for Hoboken. At about four o'clock he staggered into Nick Moore's House. Mrs. Loss was away for a few days and the bar was being tended by her youngest son Ossian. Payne ordered a brandy

75

and water, and asked if the boy knew the thicket where Mary Rogers was murdered. Ossian did. He wondered if the stranger would like a guided tour of that notorious shrubbery. The boy was used to conducting curious customers to the murder site. It was fun to be important, to relate over and over the details of his great adventure for the fine ladies and gentlemen who came to drink at his mother's mahogany. And it was usually good for a small coin from the grateful tourist. But this tourist wanted no guided tours. He did want another brandy and water, on the cuff, and Ossian refused. Even a twelve-year-old child knows when a strange drunk asks for credit, it's time to close the bar.

Payne climbed the hill and sank down on one of the large rocks near the thicket's entrance. He removed some papers from his pocket and began to read them. One was the record he had carefully kept of each of the interrogations he had undergone with the authorities since August. As he perused these notes, his mind must have retraced the nightmare of the past ten weeks. The ill-conceived search for the missing girl; the ill-advised silence he had kept after her body was discovered; the sickening ordeal of identifying her corpse in the Dead House, of having to look at the thing she had become. Each detail must have come back to him: the distasteful confrontations with Crommelin, the eternal sessions with the magistrates, the snide insinuations and direct attacks on him by the newspapers, his own desperate attempts to defend himself.

The second paper contained, it would be whispered, an account of the murder. Two weeks earlier the ghost of Mary had come to him in a dream and described completely her final, horrible night. Awaking in terror, Payne had reached for a pen and transcribed every particular of the vision. Now he reread the account slowly and then took a third sheet from his coat. This one was blank. With the stub of a pencil, Daniel Payne began to write.

(At approximately five-thirty, two gentlemen were laboring up Weehawken Hill near Nick Moore's House. They noticed a well dressed young man in a brown frock coat seated on a stone near the infamous thicket and writing on a piece of paper. They began speaking of the monstrous crime and one of them said "that the murderer of Mary Rogers ought to be brought and hung on this spot." Whether Daniel Payne heard this remark or not, neither gentleman could afterwards be sure.)

With the stub of a pencil, Daniel Payne began to write. "To the World—Here I am on the very spot. May God forgive me for my misspent life." He folded the note and replaced it and the other papers in his pocket. He removed his hat. He took out the small phial of poison, opened it, and swallowed its contents. Then, with a gesture worthy of a Shakespearian tragic hero, he smashed the bottle against a rock and ran down the hill toward the river.

—————◆ ◉•◉ ◆—————

The usual Thursday night crowd was hanging around the bar in Hoboken's Phoenix Hotel. At ten o'clock a stranger entered and asked for a brandy and water. He seemed very drunk and had a strange look in his eye. He was agitated because he had lost his hat and someone in the crowd gave him one. The bartender didn't like his looks. Sort of fellow that never has money to pay. But the stranger paid for his drink and instead of asking for lodging, requested directions to Vauxhall Gardens, another inn nearby, and got them. At the door he paused. "I suppose you know me," he said. They did not. "I'm the man that was promised to Mary Rogers. I'm a man of a great deal of trouble." Daniel Payne rushed out into the darkness.

He never reached Vauxhall Gardens. He was lying in the stinkweeds near the center of the village with his head in a ditch at five the next morning when James McShane saw him and prodded him with his boot. "My dear man, are you a Frenchman?" asked McShane. Apparently that would have made a difference. Payne mumbled that he was not. "Are you American?" The barely audible answer was that he was "not

77

of any country." McShane was becoming annoyed. He kicked at the fallen man again and said, "My dear man, if you don't get shelter you'll not live fifteen minutes." Payne said he would be thankful for a glass of water. McShane and another helped him to the stoop of a tavern owned by Charles Rietty, but no attempt was made to bring him water. At last the cork cutter managed to get to his feet and stumble across the road to another tavern run by a Mr. Scudder. He rapped at the door and again asked for water.

Scudder's reply was that Payne should go back to the saloon where he'd spent his money and get his water there. After a few minutes, however, the kindly innkeeper reappeared with a glass of water and some advice: to move away from his establishment and keep moving. For Daniel Payne there was no room at the inn.

The dying man stood on the porch at Scudder's for half an hour trying to regain his strength. The drinks had worn off, but the poison was beginning to take its full effect. He groped his way a short distance to Scudder's icehouse and rested there for forty-five minutes before moving on. Slowly, painfully, he struggled through the final half mile of his life, fighting to reach the spot he had marked out as his place of death, the shaded walk near the Sybil's Cave, where ten weeks earlier the dripping corpse of a young girl had slowly blackened in the summer heat. That last half mile required ten hours of agonizing effort. On a bench near the river bank the almost lifeless form collapsed. He could hear the bubbling waters of the Sybil's spring, the elixir of life flowing out of the heart of paradise. He felt for the papers crumpled in his pocket. "Here I am on the very spot. May God forgive me. . . ." The head of Daniel Payne rolled gradually, uncontrollably to the edge of the bench and dropped off. It hung there, a few inches above the cold ground.

One thing about Gilbert Merritt, he was a man who didn't make the same mistakes twice. If these people were going to insist on wandering over from their side of the river and dying in his jurisdiction, he, at least, would not leave himself open to the same charges of negligence and incompetence, the same personal broadsides he had endured from the press on the last occasion. No hurried inquest and hasty burial this time. The body, found on Friday afternoon, had been dead only a few hours, and in the cold weather with a little ice, it would keep very nicely until Saturday morning. That would give Merritt plenty of time to round up witnesses, locate the friends and relatives of the deceased, obtain a positive identification, inform the authorities in New York, and notify the newspapers. Two doctors to examine the body, all interested parties present, everything according to Hoyle.

The inquest convened in a private room of the Perry Hotel opposite the ferry house at eleven A.M., October 9. Nominally, Justice Merritt presided, although most of the questioning was done by the mayor and coroner from New York. Throughout the proceedings, deceased lay in the room on a table, a grisly and silent witness to the infinite precision and care with which officials of that time could investigate sudden or violent death.

The first witness was not sworn in until he had given most of his testimony. He was Dr. Samuel Griswold of New York, and at five o'clock, the afternoon of the eighth, he had been walking up the path to the Elysian Fields with a friend, a Dr. Clements, when he had noticed a man stretched out on a bench near the river. The knees were down and the head was dangling off the bench. He had rushed up and loosened the collar, but his medical experience told him the man was dying. Deceased had not spoken. (At this point Griswold's evidence was interrupted by the arrival of two men who claimed to have found deceased's hat and other personal affects, including the pieces of a broken phial, near Nick Moore's House on Weehawken Hill. They were silenced and the testimony resumed.) The doctor had noted that the eyes were half opened and the man was groaning. He and Clements had moved Payne to the path, and Griswold, certain that

79

Payne had not long to live, left him with Clements and ran to call some friends who had walked ahead. (At this point Justice Merritt realized the witness had not yet been sworn. The oversight was remedied and Griswold again took up his testimony.) By the time he returned, Payne was dead. During the interim Dr. Clements had smelled the deceased's breath. It smelled "sour." The witness was excused.

Edward Hopkins and James Lawrence were examined. They were cork cutters from Williamsburg who had once known Payne and who, after reading of his death in the morning papers, had decided to come to Hoboken "out of curiosity." They had gone to the Loss' tavern, inquired for the thicket, and there found the dead man's hat, his handkerchief, and the little broken bottle labeled laudanum. The hat was identified by Payne's brother John. He deposed that Daniel had been "much affected" by the death of Mary Rogers, that his drinking had increased, that recently John had begun fearing for his sanity. Witnesses were called to account for Payne's movements in the forty-eight hours before his death. Alfred Crommelin arrived, identified the body, and stated that "there was no coolness between us." As usual Crommelin was having difficulty remembering that he was under oath.

The widow Loss took the stand. She thought she had seen Payne a year earlier hunting in the Jersey woods, but she was positive he was not the man who had brought Mary Rogers to her inn. That man had been "younger, thinner and not so tall."

The medical evidence was given by both Samuel Griswold and Dr. Cook who had jointly examined the corpse. The former had found the stomach, lungs, and heart "perfectly healthy," but Cook thought the heart "somewhat wasted, which might account for his melancholy." He also believed he might have detected the smell of laudanum in the brain, though that "might have been imagination." Griswold noticed no such odor in either the brain or the stomach. Apparently, except for nosing around the cadaver, no attempt was made to analyze the contents of the stomach. Deceased's last food "appeared" to have been potatoes.

The brain was congested but of the cause, whether alcohol or laudanum or the lowered position of the head at the time of death, neither man could be certain. There was no extravasation of blood which destroyed the possibility of apoplexy. Cook's opinion "as a medical man," concurred in by Griswold, was that Payne's "manner of passing the previous twenty-four hours of his life must have tended to his death," and that he "probably" fell on the bench "in a state of stupefaction" and the fall, coupled with his "peculiar position," "probably" caused his death.

The jury was understandably confused. The postmortem was obviously a patchwork of corpse sniffing and uneducated guesses. The physicians' conclusions were based far more on evidence of the dead man's habits and activities and on the position of his body than on medical findings. No effort was made to analyze the stomach contents or the contents of the phial. No effort was made to search the area of the thicket where Payne's effects had accidentally been discovered, or any other area in which the dead man had been seen. Though the bottle's label declared the name of the Park Row druggist who had sold it, the authorities made no attempt to contact or question him. Scarcely a note had been taken of the testimony, except by reporters from the *Herald*, *Sunday Mercury*, and *Tattler*, and in the opinion of the last, Merritt and his cohorts seemed "to be utterly ignorant of the rules of evidence, or of the manner of putting a question to a witness." The jury debated for thirty minutes before announcing the verdict: "found dead with congestion of the brain, supposed to be brought about by exposure and irregularity of living, incident to aberration of mind."

Payne's papers, with the exception of the "suicide note," had not been introduced at the hearing and were still in Merritt's possession. Speculation about them ran wild in the news-hungry press. They were letters from Mary to

81

Payne, from Payne to Mary, from Payne to Phoebe Rogers. The most intriguing rumor held that Payne had confessed to the murder and implicated at least three others. The *Tattler* scoffed at this theory as "apocryphal." "Except in melodramas, villains are not in the habit of leaving tell-tale bits of paper about, or committing themselves with pen and ink." At length Merritt announced that there was nothing among the papers likely to shed light on the Rogers affair and the press adopted this opinion. The whole issue was quickly lost in a quarrel over whether or not the *Tattler*'s police reporter was plagiarizing accounts of the investigation from the *Tribune*.

With Daniel Payne were buried the answers to several interesting questions. Why had he failed to meet Mary's omnibus that stormy night? Why had he neglected to attend her inquest or her funeral, and consented to remain silent about her death? What had the ghost of his fiancée communicated to his diseased mind? Had she suggested the painfully contrived melodrama by which he had staged his own demise? If so, the restless spirit had only begun her vengeance. Two more victims awaited her ministrations.

Seven

Nearly one year after Mary Rogers floated up to the Hoboken shore, the celebrated Parisian detective, C. Auguste Dupin, entered the case. Having recently achieved fame by his masterful solution of the horrible murders in the Rue Morgue, Dupin was far too important a man to come to New York for his investigation. The entire affair must be moved to Paris.

Mary Rogers became Marie Rogêt in Edgar Allan Poe's fictionalized account of the crime. Payne was now St. Eustache; Crommelin was Bauvais; the Hudson was the Seine; Hoboken, the Barrière de Roulé, and little Nassau Street sagged under the title of Rue Pavée Sainte-Andrée. "The Mystery of Marie Rogêt" was serialized in Snowden's *Ladies' Companion* in November and December, 1842, and February, 1843. In its opening paragraphs its author announced that any similarities between the fates of the Beautiful Seegar Girl and his little grisette were purely a matter of "scarcely intelligible coincidences," which of course fooled no one, and privately Poe wrote to a prospective publisher that he had "indicated the assassin." ". . . I, in fact, enter into a very rigorous analysis of the *real* tragedy in New-York," Poe asserted. "*No point* is omitted. I examine, each by each, the opinions and arguments of our press on the subject, and show (I think satisfactorily) that this subject has never yet been *approached*. The press has been entirely on a wrong scent."

At the time of Mary's death, Poe was editing *Graham's Magazine* in Philadelphia and all his information about the mystery had to be gleaned from the newspapers. He later identified his sources as the New York *Mercury*, the *Brother Jonathan*, the *Express*, the *Herald*, the *Journal of Commerce*, the *Commercial Advertiser*, the *Courier and Inquirer*, the *Standard*, the *Post*, and the Philadelphia *Saturday Evening Post*, a weekly which had reprinted Bennett's articles on the thicket, the Loss testimony, and the theories of a gang slaying. Whether he actually read all of these journals is doubtful. That he missed, or ignored, some of their issues is obvious. He seems, for example, unaware that the *Saturday Evening Post's* accounts had originated in the *Herald*, and though familiar with *Brother Jonathan's* arguments on the identification of the body, he seems not to have seen their interviews with Mrs. Loss and Adam Wall.

Precisely when Poe determined to test Dupin's powers on an actual murder is impossible to say. In the most recent study of Poe's relationship to the Rogers case, John Walsh has suggested he may have written the story on a dare, possibly from a young lawyer and poet, Henry B. Hirst. The detective had been born in an earlier tale, "The Murders in the Rue Morgue," in which virtually all the major conventions of the modern detective story genre first appeared. There were the locked and bolted room, the wrongly accused suspect, the dull-witted police inspector, and the brilliant but eccentric protagonist whose adventures were chronicled by his ever baffled, ever amazed, and somewhat stupid roommate. Possibly Poe originally intended, as he claimed, to limit Dupin's career to his single triumph, but in the spring of 1842, once again unemployed and driven by what he perennially called "pecuniary difficulties," the author rummaged through his press clippings and sat down to solve the mystery of Mary Rogers.

It should be said at the outset that Poe's efforts to disprove the theories of the newspapers were infinitely more successful than his attempts to advance a "solution" of his own. He sailed into the *Tattler*'s assertion that the corpse could not be Mary since she had been missing but three days, while bodies would "require from six to ten days for decomposition to take place to bring them to the top of the water." In a long and labored dissertation, Poe argued that no hard and fast rule did or could exist for measuring the length of time necessary for a cadaver to surface. (William Kurtz Wimsatt, in the most learned investigation of Poe's sources for "Marie Rogêt," cites three authorities who corroborate Poe's position, one of whom agrees "almost point for point.")

Poe was equally convincing in his defense of Crommelin's identification of the dead girl. That gentlemen, "not being an idiot," could not have based his conviction simply upon the fact of hair on the arm. "He must," reasoned the author, "have spoken of some *peculiarity* in this hair." Furthermore, the similarities of form and attire between the corpse and Mary, while not individually conclusive, were so numerous as to rule out the possibility of coincidence, and were collectively positive proof that the corpse was the missing Mary. "Each successive [similarity] is multiple evidence— proof not *added* to proof, but *multiplied* by hundreds or thousands."

Poe, while demolishing the thesis which, in fact, had never been seriously regarded by anyone but the journal that proposed it, chose, perhaps deliberately, to misread the nature of the *Tattler*'s remarks on Crommelin as insinuations of his guilt. This is not true. Over and over the newspaper insisted that it had "every confidence in Mr. Crommelin's integrity"; that "his labors in this case we conceive to have been directed with the most sincere motives, and self-denying perseverance." When Poe describes Crommelin as "a *busy-body*,

85

with much of romance and little of wit," he is echoing the worst charge the *Tattler* implies against Mary's erstwhile swain. And when Poe states flatly that "the evidence fully rebuts the assertion of [the *Tattler*] touching the matter of *apathy* on the part of the mother and other relatives," he is failing to notice the facts of Mary's burial revealed in Crommelin's open letter as published in the *Tattler* of August 30, and reprinted in the *Brother Jonathan* of September 4. Whether or not this omission is conscious is not apparent, nor is it clear why Poe, though he had read Payne's deposition, ignores its obvious evidence that the "apathy" was manifested in the family's half-hearted search, and in Daniel Payne's refusal to go to Hoboken, fully twelve hours before Alfred Crommelin set foot in the Rogers house and began throwing his weight around.

A portion of the press had found it peculiar that so notorious a figure as the Beautiful Seegar Girl had passed through the streets unrecognized. Poe argues that "at nine on Sunday, the populace are chiefly within doors preparing for church. . . . Between ten and eleven the streets are thronged, . . ." The point is dubious, and not applicable to the real case since Mary, according to her fiancé, did not go out until ten. Poe also erred in his dates for the crime. This must be a case of poetic license, since he could not fail to have known the correct dates, but his reasons for not using them remain obscure.

The author was at his best in seeking to prove that the clothing found in the thicket had been planted long after the crime. Methodically he refuted every bit of evidence offered in the *Herald* article. Bennett had cited the presence of mildew to show that the items had lain a long time in the open. Poe answered that the mildew could appear within twenty-four hours. Bennett stated that the grass had "grown around and over" some of the things. Poe replied that there was only the word of the Loss boys for that, and in any case, "grass will grow, especially in warm and damp weather . . . as much as two or three inches in a single day." If the clothes had been there, within view of the road, for a month undiscovered, it was "little less than miraculous." The arrangement of the apparel was "highly artificial," as though placed by "a not-over-acute person wishing to dispose the articles *naturally*. But it is by no means a *really* natural arrangement. I should have looked to see the things *all* lying on the ground and trampled under foot."

Even more suspicious were the two rectangular slips torn from the dress and found hanging on the thorns. Poe pounced on the *Herald*'s phrase: "They looked like strips torn off." This was because, reasoned Poe, that's exactly what they were. One piece, a part of the hem, must be ripped both vertically and horizontally to become separated from the frock. This would require the simultaneous action of two thorns, one tearing with such great force as to rend the doubled fabric of the hem. The second strip had been torn on all four sides from the interior of the garment, necessitating the simultaneous action of four different thorns. "These . . . are things," observed Poe, "which one may well be pardoned for disbelieving." He omitted comment on one even stranger circumstance. The *Herald* had reported that "one piece of the dress was so doubled as to have a thorn three times through it." It is impossible to imagine how this might happen accidentally in the course of a struggle. On the contrary, it strongly suggests the work of someone planting the cloth, having difficulty in securing it to the bush.

Next Poe launched a frontal assault on the *Herald*'s conviction that the murder was the work of a gang of ruffians, and he did a remarkable thing. Having very effectively raised serious suspicions that the clothing had been planted, he now says: "I *admit* the thicket as the scene of the outrage," and follows this amazing deduction with this statement: ". . . You will immediately perceive that the arguments urged *against* the thicket as the scene, are applicable, in chief part, only against it as the scene of an outrage committed by *more than a single individual*." This is patently false. It is Poe's privilege, as a writer of fiction, to alter or juggle the events

87

of his story as he pleases, but when he plays so fast and loose with his facts and the logic of his reasoning from them, it does little for his claim, published as a note to the second printing of his tale, that he had actually solved the crime.

The bulk of his attempt to refute the gang theory is severely weakened by the fact that his arguments are based on an assumption of the thicket as the scene. Briefly they are as follows: that signs of a violent struggle would not result from what must be a very short conflict between several strong men and a single girl; that the telltale clothing would not be abandoned by a group of men, but only, possibly, by one panic-stricken assassin; that the strips of the frock wound about the waist and neck and apparently used as handles to tote the corpse to the water would be needed only if a lone man had carried the body; that, unless for the same reason, the fence rails would not be down nor would the girl be dragged along the ground as the tracks indicated; that, since a huge reward and a full pardon had been offered, some member of the gang would certainly have come forward; and that mere evidence that such gangs had been in the area on Sunday was hardly conclusive. On the last point Poe erred in ascribing the report of one particular bunch of cutthroats to Mrs. Loss. The resulting, false implication that she had deliberately tried to cast suspicion on a gang would become extremely useful to Poe in his revision of the tale after her death.

We now come to the end of any contributions Poe can be supposed to have made toward unraveling this tangled puzzle. Many have noted that his "solution" of the murder is preposterous, but few have realized just how preposterous it is. A number of obscure items in the press caught the author's eye. He seized on and misquoted a paragraph in the August 3 *Herald*: ". . . this young girl was missing from Anderson's store, three years ago, for two weeks. It is asserted that she was then seduced by an officer of the U.S. Navy and kept at Hoboken for two weeks. His name is well known on board his ship. . . ." It should be noted: (1) that the article's wording is obviously hesitant, (2) that the officer was never mentioned again by the *Herald* or any other sheet, (3) that at the time of Mary's first disappearance there was no rumor of a naval officer, (4) that the police, who arrested over a dozen suspects, at no time issued a warrant for any naval officers. They did arrest a seaman, Kukick, who was quickly cleared, and Dr. Cook did note in his testimony that Mary's bonnet had been tied "in a slip knot, not a lady's knot. In a sailor's knot . . ." From these points alone Poe concocted the image of his prime suspect.

In accepting the thicket as the scene, Poe also accepted fully the depositions of both Frederica Loss and Adam Wall, and identified his "naval officer" with their "swarthy man." And he plucked the following item out of the papers, or more probably invented it, since the most painstaking researchers have never been able to discover its source:

> On Monday, one of the bargemen connected with the revenue service saw an empty boat floating down the [Hudson]. Sails were lying in the bottom of the boat. The bargeman towed it under the barge office. The next morning it was taken from thence without the knowledge of any of the officers. The rudder is now at the barge office.

After surveying the above and other articles collected by the fictional detective, Dupin, Poe's narrator comments, ". . . They not only seemed to me irrelevant, but I could perceive no mode in which any one of them could be brought to bear upon the matter in hand." He didn't know the half of it.

Poe jumps to some pretty fancy conclusions. He contends that Mary did go AWOL with a naval officer "who is first known to have led the unfortunate into crime." He declares that the girl planned an elopement on the day of her death with the same officer, and left her home with that purpose. ". . . It is mere folly," says Dupin, "to say that between the first and second disappearance of [Mary], there is no *supposable* connection." This is a fair statement. "Let us admit," the detective continues, "the first elopement to have resulted in a quarrel between the lovers, and the return home of the betrayed." It's possible. "We are now prepared to view a second elopement (if we *know* that an elopement has again taken place) as indicating a renewal of the betrayer's advances, rather than as the result of a new proposal by a second individual. . . ." This is clearly illogical but M. Dupin plunges forward. "The chances are ten thousand to one, that he who had once eloped with [Mary], would again propose an elopement, rather than that she, to whom proposals of elopement had been made by one individual, should have them made to her by another." No bookie in his right mind would have faded Dupin at those odds.

The author supports this idea by asserting that the period between Mary's disappearances is "precisely the general" period of a naval cruise. He retains this sentence in his later, revised version of the story, although he has changed the length of the period from "two or three years" to "three and a half years." (The correct time was two years and ten months.) With such reasoning as this is his solution achieved.

Quite logically Poe wonders what has become of Mary's swarthy escort. If he is innocent, why has he not come forward? If he is dead, why has he not been found? Guilty he must be, this naval officer who sought shelter from the sabbath shower with Mary in the thicket (the *Herald*'s assumption), and murdered her when she resisted his advances. As the author reconstructs the crime, his source is largely the final lines of the *Herald*'s September 24 article. The killer crouches by the corpse until midnight. Then he drags his victim to the river and lifts her into the boat in which they had earlier crossed from New York, neglecting a weight to fasten to the body. He rows away from the bank and drops the silent form into the murky water. Too frightened to return for the articles in the thicket, he races toward the city, debarks, and casts the boat adrift. Poe continues:

> In the morning, the wretch is stricken with unutterable horror at finding that the boat has been picked up and detained at a locality where he is in the daily habit of frequenting— at a locality, perhaps, which his duty compels him to frequent. The next night, *without daring to ask for the rudder*, he removes it. Now *where* is that rudderless boat?

Poe asks his readers to believe in a murderer, who had been seen with his victim in the immediate area of the thicket where he killed, yet did not dare, for almost a month, to return to that isolated spot and retrieve the damaging evidence which he knew to be there. Yet this murderer risked his neck to pilfer a boat which could hardly have been used to connect him in any imaginable way with the crime. The idea is not the most absurd of Poe's theories. He goes to tedious lengths to prove that Mary's lie to Payne on Sunday morning was designed to buy time in which to effect the elopement. Yet he calmly asserts that this precious time was spent, not in fleeing, but in strolling around Weehawken Hill. He compiles a mountain of facts to indicate that the clothing was planted, and then casually accepts the thicket as the murder site. In short, and in fact, his entire "solution" is a glut of misstatements, misrepresentations, contradictions, and nonsense.

This point is emphasized because our concern is not simply with Poe or his tale, but with the murder itself. And the fact is that almost every scholar who has attempted to discover the facts of this confusing case has used this little story as the starting point for his investigations, or has passively accepted some of Poe's most misleading assertions as true, even while acknowledging that Poe had "contributed little or nothing toward solving the mystery." Even so recent and so careful a scholar as William K. Wimsatt can write: "Whether or not Poe reasoned to a solution, his story, the

91

circumstances of its composition, and what was later said of it by Poe and others, may constitute the soundest means left to us for reaching an opinion about the fate of Mary Rogers." This simply is not so. Any hope of achieving an understanding of the Rogers affair lies in penetrating the dense fog of error, rumor, and miscalculation that enshrouds the facts. Of necessity the first casualty must be the celebrated French detective, C. Auguste Dupin.

Eight

With the suicide of Daniel Payne, interest lagged in the Mary Rogers mystery. For a few weeks the papers were busy printing, or inventing, rumors of new evidence, new witnesses, new suspects. A gang was implicated; a confession had been made; arrests were imminent; the police were confident; but nothing happened. None of these rumors involved the dead cork cutter. The story of his written confession had been exploded and his alibi held as well in death as it had in life. The investigation bogged down in a maze of cold trails. Other stories crowded the case out of the press. For over a year the mystery seemed every bit as dead as its tragic heroine. Then, in late October of 1842, a gun exploded in Weehawken, a woman fell mortally wounded, and once again Mary Rogers was in the headlines.

The gun was in the hands of one of Frederica Loss' sons. It discharged while he was cleaning it and the slug lodged in his mother's knee. The wound was to prove fatal. For fifteen days the widow lay dying, nursed by her sons and neighbors, attended by a doctor named Gautier whom she much preferred to Dr. Cook for reasons that can hardly be wondered at. During almost all of that time she was delirious. She raved, sometimes in English, often in her native German, usually crying out against her relatives who she thought had treated her badly. Many times, however, Mrs. Loss screamed against a woman whom she imagined to be always present, hovering close to the deathbed, though no one else could see her. She seemed to feel this shadowy figure was an evil spirit sent to haunt her last hours of agony. "Take her away!" she cried. "Hussy! Devil! Shoo away! Take her away!" Was this strange shape the soul of Mary Rogers? Perhaps, but the dying widow never spoke her name. On the ninth of November she breathed her last.

While Mrs. Loss was yet alive, her sons had been heard to say by several people that now a "great secret" would be revealed. What was this secret? Did it concern the murder of Mary Rogers? Gilbert Merritt thought he knew. On the fourteenth he went to his friend, Justice Stephen H. Lutkins of Jersey City, and dictated the following affidavit:

> STATE OF NEW JERSEY, HUDSON COUNTY—Personally appeared before a Justice of the Peace of said county, Gilbert Merritt, of said county, in the State of New Jersey, who being sworn by me, deposeth and saith:
> —That in the month of July, 1841, he (this deponent) as a magistrate, held an inquest on the body of Mary C. Rogers at Hoboken, in said county of Hudson, who this deponent believes was murdered; and this deponent further saith, that from information he has obtained, and facts in his possession, he verily believes that the murder of the said Mary C. Rogers was perpetrated in a house in Weehawken, called "the Nick Moore House," then kept by one Frederica Loss, alias Kellenbarack, (now deceased) and her three sons, to wit—Oscar Kellenbarack, Charles Kellenbarack, and Ossian Kellenbarack, all three of whom this deponent has reason to believe are worthless and profligate characters; and this deponent further saith, that he has just reason to believe that the said sons and their mother kept one of the most depraved and debauched houses in New Jersey, and that all of them had a knowledge of, were accessory to, and became participators in the murder of said Mary C. Rogers, and the concealment of her body.

94

Immediately the two older sons were arrested on a warrant issued by Judge Lutkins and imprisoned in Jersey City. The charge was murder and the news electrified New Yorkers. But the stir caused by the arrests was minor in comparison with the impact of the story that broke in the *New York Tribune* three days later. Horace Greeley had waited a long time, but he finally had his scoop. He had beaten the *Tattler*, the *Sun* and the hated *Herald* to the story that on her deathbed the widow Loss had confessed to complicity in the Rogers murder.

Before she died, the *Tribune* announced in an article headlined "The Mary Rogers Mystery Explained," Mrs. Loss had sent for Justice Merritt and made a statement. Arrangements had been made for Mary to undergo an abortion in an upper room at Nick Moore's House. On the fatal Sunday, she had arrived at the tavern "in company with a young physician, who undertook to procure for her a premature delivery. While in the hands of the physician she died and a consultation was then held as to the disposal of her body." It was finally decided that the eldest son, Oscar, was to carry the corpse to the river and throw it in at the place where it was found. They redressed the dead girl, except for the items which were later found at the thicket. Those effects were at first tied up in a bundle and sunk in a pond on the land of James King, a neighbor whose property lay between Mrs. Loss' land and the Hudson. This was done without the knowledge of King. Later, however, it was feared that the clothing was not safe from discovery there, and it was fished up and placed in the thicket. The name of the abortionist was not yet known. The paper felt sure that no doubt could be entertained of the truth of the confession. It explained "many things connected with this affair which before were wrapped in mystery—especially the apathy of the mother of Miss Rogers upon the discovery of her body. . . ."

It was a wonderful headline, a spectacular story. Unfortunately there wasn't a single shred of truth in it. Within twenty-four hours Gilbert Merritt had read the item, penned

95

his denial, and rushed it off to the newspapers. The statement relative to a confession said to have been made before him was "entirely incorrect." ". . . no such examination took place nor could it, from the deranged state of Mrs. Loss' mind." The justice had, in fact, tried to elicit some statement from the dying woman and he had failed. The *Herald* was triumphant. Again and again it demanded to know the identity of the source of the false story. The *Tribune* mumbled something about getting the account from two magistrates of New York. Then, wisely, it reprinted Merritt's denial and kept silent.

What is perhaps the most amazing aspect of this journalistic blunder is the fact that almost all of the commentators who have written about the Mary Rogers affair since it occurred have credited the phony confession and based their "solutions" to the crime on its erroneous claims.

Even without the fact of Merritt's denial, the confession story was patently ridiculous. The *Tribune* asked credence for the following: When Mary died under the knife her killers redressed the body completely except for a single petticoat, a handkerchief marked with her initials, and a scarf; these items, along with gloves and her parasol, were hidden at the bottom of a pond; later, out of a fear that the clothing might be found, they fished it up and scattered it in the woods near the road where it was far more likely to be discovered and then actually pretended to discover it themselves; and finally, with incredible stupidity, they invented a tale for the police that placed Mary at their tavern where she had actually died, although up to that time they had not been under the slightest suspicion. If Mrs. Loss and her sons had participated in the girl's death, they must rank among the most irrational murderers in history. Why had they only partially clothed the body, when the remaining items might easily have been placed on or secured to the corpse as the bonnet had been? If death had occurred accidentally during an abortion, why was it necessary to knot the strip of lace so tightly about the throat that it was concealed in the flesh? Why had they not simply burned the clothing in the first place, as (it would later be revealed) one of Mrs. Loss' sisters had urged her to do after it was found? The tale was completely absurd.

The two sons of Mrs. Loss were still behind bars in Jersey City. A hearing was arranged for Saturday, the nineteenth, before Judge Lutkins. Present were the mayor and district attorney of Jersey City, the county clerk, and three lawyers representing the prisoners. Gilbert Merritt observed but did not take part in the examination, the bulk of which was conducted by Mayor Morris of New York. Reporters from the *New York Herald* and the *Jersey City Advertiser* recorded the proceedings.

Nancy Ludlow was sworn. The Ludlow house lay above the Loss saloon at the base of Weehawken Hill near the river. She was the widow's closest neighbor and had nursed her through her last fifteen days. Most of that time Mrs. Loss had been out of her mind. She raved in German, which Nancy did not understand, but in English she talked about a female whom she imagined to be bending over her bed. Nancy remembered the day of the murder quite clearly. After the storm she had seen a young woman and a gentleman descending the hill followed by four other men, and watched them until they reached the road that led back to Hoboken. She would "ever think that was *her* coming down from the mountain."

A few days later she had gone down to Nick Moore's House and discussed the murder with the proprietress. Mrs. Loss had mentioned hearing screams that night and fearing that her boy had been gored, but she made no connection at that time between the screams and the murder, and she did not say anything about Mary's having stopped at her bar. After the clothes had been taken to the police, the two women had again spoken. The widow now regretted not having burned the items as her sister wanted her to do. It would have "saved her trouble." Nancy asked why she had held the things so long before turning them in. The answer:

97

"She supposed something might turn up to make them more useful than if she had handed them over at once."

Nancy's husband, James Sr., testified that on the day of the widow's death the eldest boy had told him that "the secret would now come out," and that the secret was his mother's special cure for rheumatism. "This was at one time during the same conversation." He was home during the whole day when Mary was killed but heard no screams. His son, James Jr., took the stand to swear that he knew absolutely nothing about the entire affair. He was excused.

Henry Fredericks, Ludlow's son-in-law, had also heard Oscar talk about a great secret but not that it was a rheumatism cure. The boy had said loose characters visited his mother's house. He had looked through a keyhole and "seen them have dealings together." Nice place, the little widow's friendly tavern. Other witnesses spoke of the great secret. One had passed the thicket twice on the murder night but noticed nothing unusual.

The three boys were brought in separately, and as each took the oath, he was informed by Lutkins that he was to be examined solely as a witness in the Rogers case, that he might reveal anything he knew with perfect safety to himself even if his evidence was self-incriminating. With this extraordinary guaranty, Charles Kellenbarack, the middle son, nine days short of eighteen years, was sworn and seated.

But the boy either knew nothing more or simply wasn't talking. Yes, he had found the clothes and given them to Dr. Cook. Yes, his mother had a recipe for rheumatism. She had many different cures, "lots of them of all kinds." Yes, he had spoken to Henry Fredericks about a secret. He meant that when his mother passed on she would learn "the big secret, all about the dead people, what became of them after they were dead."

Perhaps the boys had failed to get their story straight among themselves. Twelve-year-old Ossian, who followed his brother to the stand, deposed that "the secret talked about was to tell Dr. Gautier how to cure the rheumatism." Oscar, the eldest, agreed. Yes, he had been driving away an ox on the murder night when his mother feared he was injured. Yes, he had heard that some people believed the clothes had been brought across the river and planted. No, he knew nothing else that would help the investigation. Oscar stepped down.

T. B. Gautier had been the Loss' family physician for fifteen years. For the last fifteen days, it now developed, he had also been playing amateur detective. Learning the rumor of the boys' great secret, he decided to pretend that he knew something about it, to tell what he called a "white lie" to the oldest son and attempt to catch the lad off guard. He discussed this scheme with Dr. Cook who approved. Accordingly, Gautier "feigned the story to [Oscar] that his mother had a secret, and that she promised to tell it to me, but could not because she became delirious; and that I wanted those boys, if they knew anything about the secret, to tell me what it was. Oscar said he did not know of anything excepting it might be something about a change of life. 'No,' said I, 'I rather think it was something about Mary C. Rogers'; he said it could not be, as his mother had already told all she knew about it; this was just after his mother's death." Subsequently the doctor had visited Oscar in jail and learned the information in question was a rheumatism panacea.

Gautier testified as to the character of the widow. "Everything was very correct, moral and good. She was an accomplished woman . . . I never saw anything derogatory to her character." Like the other witnesses, the physician had never heard Mrs. Loss speak the name of Mary Rogers while delirious. He had even tried an experiment which convinced him that the dying woman was entirely innocent. He would periodically shout Mary's name near the deathbed, and watch carefully to detect any reaction from the widow. He could not.

It makes an interesting tableau, this final scene in Mrs. Loss' bedroom: the neighbor woman padding busily around the deathbed; her family trooping through the house; the

sons skulking at the door; the dying widow shrilly screaming in German at an evil spirit lurking in the room; the
kindly old G.P. bending gently over his patient and howling
the name of a dead girl in her ear.

The doctor was dismissed. The Kellenbarack boys were
set at liberty. And that, for all practical purposes, was that.
Though the *Herald* proclaimed that there was "something
more of deep and overwhelming interest yet in the wind,"
and "the magistrates are on the scent, and these investigations
will not end here," and though others were interrogated and
the press continued for a time to find space for the newest
rumors, the simple fact was that the authorities had run into
a blank wall. The investigation sputtered and then gradually
ground to a complete halt.

The *Jersey City Advertiser* was puzzled by one aspect of
the boys' hearing: ". . . and what seems wholly unaccountable
to our mind, Mr. Merritt, who was present during the whole
examination, and whose affidavit was the foundation of all
the proceedings, was not placed on the stand nor asked a
single question." He had stated in his affidavit that facts and
information were in his possession which convinced him
that Mrs. Loss and her three sons had perpetrated the murder, yet he never testified. Why not? What was this information?

Part of the answer lies in the phrasing of the original affidavit which charged the widow and her sons "had a knowledge of, were accessory to, and became participators in" the
murder. The wording clearly indicates that Merritt believed
they had not actually committed the crime, but that it, or
the situation which resulted in it, had occurred with their
knowledge, and they had become accessories after the fact,
presumably by aiding in the disposing of the body.

But what situation in Nick Moore's House might have
resulted in Mary's death? The evidence suggests one of two
possible solutions, a tryst or an abortion. Merritt had stated
that the tavern was "one of the most depraved and debauched
houses in New Jersey." Oscar had learned the facts of life

through keyholes. There are important hints to Merritt's theories in the nature of the questions put to the boys at the hearing. They were asked whether their mother ever took in lodgers, whether "sick" people ever stayed there to receive "attendance," whether Mrs. Loss had ever acted as a midwife, whether they had ever heard of fifty dollars being "offered by anyone for any purpose," whether there was a place in the house where one could "go behind the chimney." Every question was answered in the negative. But they form a pattern from which Merritt's convictions may be implied.

The Justice seems to have been certain that abortions were performed at Nick Moore's House, probably by doctors assisted by Mrs. Loss, and possibly also that rooms were available for meetings between "lovers." It is likely, however, that he thought Mary a victim of a botched operation, done by the "swarthy" man whom Adam Wall had described, for which she had agreed to pay fifty dollars, and which had been performed, perhaps, in a secret room concealed behind the chimney. Charles Kellenbarack had been specifically asked and had denied that anyone had come to his mother's establishment on Sunday for "assistance."

Merritt's theory, in other words, was substantially the one which the *Tribune* had reported as a confession made by Mrs. Loss. The magistrate reasoned that the clothing had been placed in the thicket to divert suspicion from the actual murder site, and that the widow had concocted a false story to suggest the possibility of rape by a gang of toughs, an idea already being insisted on by several newspapers, particularly the *Herald*. The physical appearance of the body would be similar to that of a victim of an unsuccessful abortion. Even the fact that Mary's hands had been tied argued for this version of the crime, since this measure was always taken in those painful days before the general use of anesthetics.

But there had been no deathbed confession. Merritt again repeated this fact for a *Herald* reporter following the hearing. There was no confession and there was no evidence whatsoever. Had there been, the three boys would certainly have been confronted with it. But there were only rumors, rumors of illicit operations and of fifty dollars and a secret room which must have been searched for without success. There was no witness except Adam Wall whose testimony, as the *Tattler* correctly observed, was far too shaky to be of any consequence, and it is significant that Wall was not asked to appear at the hearing.

It must have been extremely frustrating for Merritt, who had lived with the case from the beginning, and for Morris, who had struggled to solve it for almost as long. They were so very close to the truth and they couldn't prove a thing. The mysterious physician had vanished; the midwife was dead; from the surviving accomplices they got only stubborn denials and stony silence. The Kellenbaracks were young, but they were not stupid, and they were not poor. No less than three attorneys represented them at their examination. Several interrogations and a week in jail had not broken them down. The officials were desperate. Merritt had sworn out an affidavit and a hearing must be held, but without concrete evidence, obviously the Justice could not take the stand. There was only one road left open to them. They must forego any hope of prosecuting the boys, who had after all only been accessories after the fact, offer the Kellenbaracks immunity, and pray that with the threat of a trial removed the suspects would at last admit the truth.

They took their best shot and they failed. The investigation was stopped because the authorities were convinced they had solved the murder and equally convinced they could never prove it. Merritt continued to insist bitterly on the truth of his theory, but in vain. His hands were tied as tightly and as surely as Mary's had been.

If Merritt was correct, was it possible that the shooting of Frederica Loss was not an accident but a deliberate murder to silence the gregarious woman whose constant chattering to the neighbors, refusal to burn the clothing, and involvement with the police had begun to seriously threaten her sons? And what was the "great secret" that one of the boys had so foolishly mentioned to Henry Fredericks? No one then or now could honestly believe it had anything to do with the afterlife or a cure for rheumatism. There were open contradictions in the testimony on this point. James Ludlow Sr. swore that, on the morning of the widow's death, Oscar had told him that "the secret would now come out," and that it concerned a rheumatism cure. "This was at one time during the same conversation." Yet later in the day, after his mother had died, Oscar denied any knowledge of a secret to Doctor Gautier, and on the stand he claimed that he had not learned of it until still later from his brother Ossian. It remains a possibility that the youths might have cracked under inter-rogation had they not been forewarned by the bumbling attempts at amateur sleuthing of both Gautier and Dr. Cook who took it upon himself to quiz Charles after the inquest on Mrs. Loss.

Were the Kellenbaracks afraid their mother would make a confession before her mind became crazed? Would that confession have concerned the finding of the clothing, the story she had told police, the murder itself? Had the persistant Gilbert Merritt actually hit on the truth of Mary Cecilia Rogers' fate? Clearly Merritt was convinced that he had and probably said as much to at least one local reporter, for the *Newark Daily Advertiser* felt confident in stating: "The case of Mary Rogers remains, it seems, legally unexplained. . . . But we understand the investigation will be pursued, as it is believed that the recent statement of the manner of her death is probably true." But Merritt had no evidence. He would never have any evidence.

———————◆—◆•◆—◆———————

It is necessary here to turn our attention back to Edgar Allan Poe, for John Walsh, in his little book, *Poe The Detective,* has raised an important question concerning the original, serialized publication of "The Mystery of Marie Rogêt," which had gone unnoticed by earlier scholars: the mysterious delay by one month of the appearance, in Snowden's *Ladies' Companion*, of the tale's third and final installment. The first segment had already appeared and the second, in which Poe mentioned the naval officer, was within twenty-four hours of the newsstands when the story of Mrs. Loss' death and the arrest of her sons broke in New York. The bind in which both Poe and Snowden now found themselves is, as Walsh points out, obvious. The January issue of the magazine, with its ten and one-half columns of Poe's carefully reasoned "solution" was probably already set up in type. It was to be printed in early December and go on sale by the fifteenth of the month. And now, in the middle of November, arrests had been made and from Hoboken the authorities were making such confident noises that it certainly seemed extremely likely that the Rogers case would be solved long before December 15, leaving Poe and his claims of ratiocinative powers the laughingstock of the literary world. For the creator of C. Auguste Dupin, still unemployed and once again in a bout with the bottle, the prospect must have been terrifying.

Noting that "the five-week period in Poe's life between November 19 and December 25, 1842, has always been a blank," Walsh assumes that time to have been spent in New York and New Jersey in a desperate attempt to learn what new evidence had been unearthed and to revise the story accordingly, and he cites two events from a Poe biography to support his conjecture. The first is a meeting between one Gabriel Harrison and the author in New York which Harrison later dated as early 1843, but which "could well have been late 1842." The second, if Walsh's guesses are correct, is far more interesting for the picture it presents of Poe during this crisis. An old flame of Poe's salad days in Baltimore, identified by some biographers as Mary Devereaux, was married and settled in Jersey City when she received a surprise visit from her former beau. Her recollections of this episode were recorded years later in an article titled "Poe's Mary," published in an 1889 *Harper's Monthly* and narrated largely in her own words, though the actual author was a kinsman of hers named Augustus Van Cleef. Mrs. Devereaux now placed the visit in the spring of 1842, but Walsh justifiably doubts her memory on this point.

Poe was off on one of his binges (Mary calls it a "spree"), and he had no end of trouble locating her home. After inquiring at her husband's business in New York, he lost her address and rode back and forth on the ferry for some time, asking everyone on board where she lived until he found a deckhand who knew. "Mr. Poe," Mary records, "said he was determined to find me, if he 'had to go to hell' to do it. When my husband returned home he was told on the boat that a crazy man had been looking for his wife!"

Mary was out when Poe finally reached her house, but he made himself at home and admitted her when she returned. "He said to me: 'So you have married that cursed—[referring to her husband's business]. Do you love him truly? Did you marry him for love?' I answered 'That's nobody's business; that is between my husband and myself.' He then said: 'You don't love him. You do love me. You know you do.'"

Having gotten that off his chest, if Mary's account is accurate, Poe then accepted a cup of tea and amused himself by flailing at some radishes in a dish with a table knife. A few days later Mary was again visited, this time by Poe's mother-in-law who reported that he had been missing for days and his wife was "almost crazy with anxiety." A search was organized and Poe was at length discovered "in the woods on the outskirts of Jersey City, wandering about like a crazy man." He suffered himself to be taken back to Philadelphia.

Supposing all this to be reasonably true, supposing Walsh's thesis to be correct, it is evident that during his "spree" Poe was seldom if ever in any condition to make careful, artful revisions in "The Mystery of Marie Rogêt." It is possible, as Walsh suggests, that Poe's initial aim in going to New York was to beg Snowden to postpone publication of the third installment, but that decision, and the decision to print it in the February issue, were probably Snowden's own, the latter being made only after it became obvious that the authorities were without a clue and the Hoboken investigation had completely bogged down. Walsh, himself, can find only two probable changes in the tale as it finally appeared, a slight hedging on the thicket as the murder site, and the appending of two final "repetitious, obtuse and badly written" paragraphs insisting that any similarities between the fiction and the fact were purely coincidental.

By mid-January the *Ladies' Companion* was on the stands and Poe was back in Philadelphia. But he had not heard the last of Mary Rogers. And we have not heard the last of him.

Nine

Mary Rogers had been dead for nearly three years when, in April of 1844, with his sickly wife on his arm, five dollars in his pocket, and a hole in the seat of his breeches, Edgar Allan Poe arrived in the city of New York. He wrote cheerfully to his mother-in-law Maria Clemm in Philadelphia:

> *I feel in excellent spirits and haven't drank* [sic] *a drop —so that I hope soon to get out of trouble. The very instant I scrape together enough money I will send it on. You can't imagine how much we both do miss you. Sissy had a hearty cry last night, because you and Catterina weren't here. We are resolved to get 2 rooms the first moment we can.*

"Sissy" was Poe's wife Virginia, and Catterina was the family cat. The Poes were lodged in a single room in Greenwich Street, and as the letter indicated, the first problem was to find sufficient funds to finance a larger flat and train fare to New York for "Muddy," Mrs. Clemm. In his extremity, Poe thought of "The Great Moon Hoax."

In August, 1835, a reporter named Richard Adams Locke had launched one of journalism's most successful practical jokes in the pages of the *New York Sun*. Sir John Frederick

William Herschel, the most renowned astronomer of the day, had established an observatory in South Africa. The *Sun* announced that "by means of an immense telescope of an entirely new principle," Herschel had discovered life on the moon. For weeks New York was astounded by wondrous descriptions of the vegetation and animal life, and of creatures like human beings with simian features and bat-like wings. These were "scientifically denominated" *vespertiliohomo*, man-bat, and the astronomer had observed that "they are doubtless innocent and happy creatures, notwithstanding some of their amusements would but ill comport with our terrestrial notions of decorum." All of this nonsense was supposedly reprinted from the *Edinburgh Journal of Science*, a publication defunct for several years. A healthy portion of the press and the public was completely deceived, and when the joke was finally exposed, the *Sun's* circulation had doubled.

Poe, at that time editor of the Richmond *Southern Literary Messenger*, had been inspired by a treatise of Herschel's to compose a story on a similar theme, and the first installment of "Hans Pfaall" had already been published when Locke's articles forced him to abandon the project. At first Poe was certain that his idea had been stolen, but, later, though sneering at Locke's scientific inaccuracies and proclaiming that *he*, at least, had never been fooled for a moment, Poe admitted that the charge of literary larceny was unfounded. "Hans Pfaall" had been intended as humor rather than hoax, but Locke's incredible success convinced Poe of the virtues of the latter genre. "From the epoch of the hoax," he wrote, "the *Sun* shone with unmitigated splendor. Its success firmly established the 'penny system' throughout the country, and [through the *Sun*] consequently we are indebted to the genius of Mr. Locke for one of the most important steps ever yet taken in the pathway of human progress." This outspoken admiration for the journalistic hoax may provide a clue for understanding Poe's initial intention in writing "The Mystery of Marie Rogêt."

Now Poe was in New York and less than five dollars stood between him and starvation. While "Sissy" mended the hole in his pants, he sat down and invented "The Great Balloon Hoax." Moses Beach, who recalled Locke's accomplishment as clearly as did Poe, bought the story and it appeared in the *Sun* on April 13. The headline blared: "ASTOUNDING INTELLIGENCE BY PRIVATE EXPRESS FROM CHARLESTON, VIA NORFOLK!" Eight men had just completed a crossing of the Atlantic Ocean in only three days with a steering balloon invented by Mr. Monck Mason. The balloon had started from North Wales and set down on Sullivan's Island near the Carolina coast, perhaps on the very spot where William Legrand first encountered his "gold bug." Though Locke's joke had endured for weeks, Poe's lasted only one day, but it bought him a two-room apartment and paid "Muddy's" passage to Manhattan. Several of the newspapers had been suckered into reprinting the tale, and this gave Poe far more satisfaction than his sudden solvency, as one of his biographers, Hervey Allen, reports:

> To have taken in many, justified him in that contempt for the mob which several of his other essays and stories exhibit to a marked degree, while it pandered to his own self-esteem. It was incense to that legend of the mob's inferiority, which the very weakness of his nature demanded. To keep the air clouded with this fragrant smoke was necessary, so that he, and the world he gazed upon, might appear through the haze other than they actually were. Lastly, it tickled his own curious sense of humor, so closely involved with his essential vanity.

Poe was now within five years of his death. Of this time, Hervey Allen writes: "One of the accompanying phenomena of this later period . . . a psychic phenomena . . . was a growing and accelerated tendency to an exaltation of the ego. By 1848 . . . this tendency had already passed the last admitted borders of sanity." He had begun to use opium, a drug which greatly intensified this tendency. Baudelaire,

109

Poe's greatest admirer, has described the ultimate ecstasy of the opium dream: ". . . the drugged man . . . projects himself out of himself, as if the will of an intoxicated man had an efficacious virtue, and cries, with a cry that might strike down the scattered angels from the ways of the sky: '*Je suis un Dieu!*' "

"*Je suis un Dieu!*" I am a God! Sometime during the spring of 1845, Edgar Allan Poe uttered that cry.

The events leading up to his revision of the original "The Mystery of Marie Rogêt" must be explained. As already noted the flurry of excitement in Hoboken surrounding the Kellenbarack hearing forced a month's postponement of the final installment of the story in Snowden's magazine and seems likely to have brought Poe to New York in a panic. Three points should here be made:

(1) The only hard, biographical evidence that Poe was in New York is somewhat flimsy, but it is highly suggestive, and one of the conclusions it suggests is that the author scarcely drew a sober breath during his visit. We are forced to doubt (a) Poe's ability to investigate effectively any new developments in the case, and (b) his capacity, even if he learned of these new developments, to incorporate them with any skill into his final installment.

(2) These last two statements may be supported by several facts:
(A) The confusion surrounding Merritt's new "evidence" of a fatal abortion was incredibly great for the public, the press, and the magistrates, themselves. Merritt's information was obviously nothing of which he dared give evidence in open court and the hearing was a shambles. The affair was further clouded by the Justice's angry denial of the *Tribune*'s "con-

fession" story and that newspaper's subsequent refusal to name its sources, yet these events were mitigated by strongly worded reports in both the *Tribune* and the *Newark Daily Advertiser* that Merritt's convictions were correct and the investigation would be continued. Is it possible that Poe, in his apparent condition, could have made sense of this mess when all the forces of the press could not unravel it and when, in fact, Merritt's strange behavior has not been successfully explained to this day? (B) That Poe could not have is demonstrated by an examination of the only "revision" which could conceivably have been made. While the two final paragraphs contain a labored insistence that the solution of Marie Rogêt's death could not "for a moment be supposed" to suggest a similar answer to the Rogers affair, since it had to be considered "that the most trifling variation in the facts of the two cases might give rise to the most important miscalculations . . . ," *they do not at any point even hint at the possibility of a fatal abortion.* All such innuendos exist solely in the later version of the tale.

(3) This is the most important fact of all, and it has totally escaped all researchers including Walsh, who is the only one to have offered the theory that Poe had an opportunity to alter his conclusions after Merritt's new evidence came to light. Had Poe been aware of the fatal abortion thesis in November or December of 1842, *he could easily have rewritten his last installment to fully accommodate that thesis,* and firmly, if falsely, established his later claim to have solved the mystery.

111

A close reading of the three sections of the serial proves this conclusively. What "facts" had the first two installments established? That reports of the family's apathy were false. That Beauvais (Crommelin) and St. Eustache (Payne) were innocent. That the corpse was unquestionably Mary. That the cause of death could not have been drowning. That the murder was not committed by a gang. That Mary's first disappearance was an elopement with a naval officer which ended in a quarrel and her return. That her second disappearance was to meet the same officer. The reader is invited to examine these points. Which of them militates against the final solution of a fatal abortion? Not a single one.

True, certain phrases exist in these installments which could embarrass the abortion theory, but they are few and might easily have been combatted by a writer of Poe's talents. He states that one newspaper had made "insinuations" that "Marie, with the connivance of her friends, had absented herself from the city for reasons involving a charge against her chastity. . . ." He goes on to cast doubt on other conclusions of that journal, but not on this specific theory which might have proven very useful had he urged the abortion idea later. He has suggested that the second disappearance was an elopement (and therefore not an abortion) yet he does not stress the point and, in fact, almost immediately denies it:

> You will say however, that in the second instance there was no elopement as imagined. Certainly not—but are we prepared to say there was not the frustrated design?

Poe has thus denied that the naval officer had any expectation of eloping with Mary, implied that the idea existed entirely in her own mind, and furthermore he has, in the lines immediately preceding these, opened the possibility of a seduction *prior* to the second disappearance:

> Had the lover been interrupted in his first villany by the necessity of departure to sea, and had he seized the first

moment of his return to renew the basic designs not yet altogether accomplished?

Obviously, by sheer accident, Poe has provided himself with ideas which might easily be molded into the conclusion of a fatal abortion. The officer has seduced her. Unknown to him, she has become pregnant. Without his consent, she intends to elope with him. When he learns of the pregnancy, his response is to arrange for an abortion which proves fatal.

Accepting Wall's testimony, Poe stated that "she *did* meet with some companion, and proceed with him across the river. . . ." Popular opinion in late 1842 identifies this "companion" with a swarthy abortionist, and Poe could easily have done so in his last installment.

Although he has said, " 'We may imagine her thinking thus—I am to meet a certain person for the purpose of elopement . . .' " this has also been mitigated, almost at once:

> Such thoughts as these we may imagine to have passed through the mind of Marie, but the point is one upon which I consider it not necessary to insist. I have reasoned thus, merely to call attention, as I said a minute ago, to the culpable remissness of the police.

Poe is now free of any commitment to the concept that Mary ever intended anything but to meet a swarthy abortionist who would operate in Hoboken to relieve her of the naval officer's child.

Two facts are undeniable. Had Poe known of the fatal abortion, there was nothing in the already published parts of his tale which made it impossible to reach that solution in his final installment. As a matter of fact he had been incredibly fortunate, since the parts of the story which had already appeared not only contained nothing to contradict the abortion concept, but also included several arguments which could be made to support it and give credence to his claim that he had hit on the truth long before the authorities did.

In moving on to consider the last third of the fiction, keep in mind that its author had at least seven weeks following the

Kellenbarack hearing to alter it in whole or in part. It opens with the *single most effective and convincing argument made by Poe from the evidence at his command*, the argument that the clothing found in the thicket was planted after the murder. It is obvious how amazingly valuable this argument would have been, had Poe chosen to conclude that Mary died during an operation at Mrs. Loss' tavern, yet he failed utterly to take advantage of it.

> You will not have apprehended me rightly, however, if you suppose it my design to *deny* this thicket as the scene of the outrage. But, in fact, [Poe adds incredibly] this is a point of minor importance. We are not engaged in an attempt to discover the scene, but to produce the perpetrators of the murder. What I have adduced, notwithstanding the minuteness with which I have adduced it, has been with the view ... chiefly, to bring you, by the most natural route, to a further contemplation of the doubt whether this assassination has, or has not been the work of *a gang*.

The most damning evidence Poe has *against* the thicket as the murder scene, and therefore *in support of* the abortion theory, he has just kicked unceremoniously into the ash can. And he's not through yet!

> You will here bear in mind that I *admit* the thicket as the scene of the outrage; and you will immediately perceive the arguments urged against the thicket as the scene, are applicable, in chief part, only against it as the scene of an outrage committed by *more than a single individual*.

One conclusion is inescapable, and of three others the reader has his choice. First, and obviously, the contradictions concerning the thicket existing in the original version have not been tampered with before its publication. Second, either Poe was ignorant of Merritt's abortion theory, or he chose not to accept it, or he was never sober enough to incorporate it in a rewrite of the final installment of "The Mystery of Marie Rogêt."

All that was in 1842. Now, in 1845, once again back in New York, Poe learned the "truth" of the Mary Rogers mystery.

In the months after the balloon hoax he made constant rounds of the newspapers, subsisting largely on hack work. Forced to look for steady employment, he accepted a position as assistant editor on the *Evening Mirror* whose offices were only a short walk from the old Rogers boardinghouse. Many evenings were killed in the cellar of an Ann Street tavern in the company of fellow journalists. By now the rumors of the fate of Mary Rogers had circulated for so long that they were accepted as gospel. Either at the *Mirror* or the tavern Poe heard these rumors.

Everybody knew what had happened. The girl had sold a due bill for fifty dollars and bought herself an abortion at the widow Loss' hole. When the operation failed, the physician took the train to Philadelphia and the Kellenbarack boy dumped the body in the river. The clothing was held back and then planted to divert suspicion to the thicket and to take advantage of the *Herald*'s widely accepted gang theory, but, when no one found the items, the boys became impatient and pretended to discover the stuff themselves. When the old lady talked too much, one of her sons put a bullet in her. Merritt knew the truth, but with the mother dead, the boys couldn't be cracked and the investigation had to be abandoned.

———◆—●◆●—◆———

Poe could not have originally intended "The Mystery of Marie Rogêt" as anything but a hoax. Under the superficial pretext of a precisely parallel crime in Paris, a pretext designed to be seen through easily, he pretended to solve the real murder, a flimflam not intended to be penetrated. Any close examination of the first version renders it evident that its author did not take it seriously. Quite consciously he altered the real facts at will to accommodate his fictional detective. The skill with which he eased smoothly past the contradictions concerning the thicket argues for intentional design. You can hear him laughing behind his labored amazement at the "coincidences" of similarity between the murders of Mary Rogers and Marie Rogêt. From obscure news items and a chance remark by Richard Cook, he had conjured up a wholly fictitious assassin, as he must to avoid a libel suit; yet his tale retained enough of the facts of the actual event to make his solution at least vaguely plausible. If he wrote publishers that he had "indicated the assassin," what of it? He was trying to sell the piece. The original "Mystery of Marie Rogêt" bears every mark of a piece of fiction written by a man who knew he was writing a piece of fiction.

But now, three years later, Poe learned the "truth" of the murder. And hadn't he been right all the time? Mary *had* been betrayed by a lover. It must have been the same naval officer with whom she had earlier "eloped." The officer, the swarthy man, and the abortionist flowed together in his mind. There was a confession. "Madame Deluc" (Mrs. Loss) had admitted the crime on her deathbed. And there was a boat, a rowboat. For God's sake, there *must* have been a boat!

Through a free association of ideas which might have baffled even the eminent C. Auguste Dupin, but which seemed perfectly logical to Dupin's creator, Edgar Allan Poe became convinced that he had actually solved the murder of the Beautiful Seegar Girl.

Before the story was republished in the summer of 1845, as part of a collection of his tales, Poe revised it to accommodate the popular concept of the girl's death. His changes can most easily be seen by citing selected passages from the piece. The words appearing in SMALL CAPITALS were deleted from the revision, while those in CAPITALS were added:

> That she *did* meet with some companion, and proceed with him across the river, reaching the Barrière du Roule [Hoboken] at so late an hour as three o'clock in the afternoon, is known. But in consenting so to accompany this individual, (FOR WHATEVER PURPOSE, TO HER MOTHER

KNOWN OR UNKNOWN), she must have thought of her expressed intention when leaving home, . . .

We may imagine her thinking thus—I am to meet a certain person for the purpose of elopement, OR FOR CERTAIN OTHER PURPOSES KNOWN ONLY TO MYSELF.

But as it is my design *never* to return—OR NOT FOR SOME WEEKS, OR NOT UNTIL CERTAIN CON-CEALMENTS ARE EFFECTED— the gaining of time is the only point about which I need give myself any concern.

Notwithstanding the acclamation with which the discovery of this thicket was received by the press, and the unanimity with which it was supposed to indicate the precise scene of the outrage, it must be admitted that there was some very good reason for doubt. That it *was* the scene, I MAY OR I MAY NOT believe—but there was excellent reason for doubt.

. . . You will not have apprehended me rightly, however, if you suppose it is my design to *deny* this thicket as the scene of the outrage. THERE MIGHT HAVE BEEN A WRONG HERE, OR, MORE POSSIBLY, AN ACCI-DENT AT MADAME DELUC'S.

You will here bear in mind that I ADMIT THE THICKET AS THE SCENE OF THE OUTRAGE; AND YOU WILL IMMEDIATELY PER-CEIVE THAT the arguments urged against the thicket . . .

We will resume this question by mere allusion to the re-volting details of the surgeon examined at the inquest. It is only necessary to say that his published *inferences*, in regard to the number of the ruffians, have been properly ridiculed as unjust and totally baseless, by all the reputable anatomists of Paris. Not that the matter *might not* have been as inferred, but that there was no ground for the inference—WAS THERE NOT MUCH FOR ANOTHER?

The solitary murderer, having borne the corpse for some dis-tance (WHETHER FROM THE THICKET OR ELSE-WHERE), by means of the bandage hitched around its middle . . .

. . . that is to say, arising, as we have imagined, after quit-ting the thicket (IF THE THICKET IT WAS), and on the road between the thicket and the river.

But the gang which has drawn upon itself the pointed animadversion, although the somewhat tardy AND VERY
SUSPICIOUS evidence of Madame Deluc . . .

The horrors of this dark deed are known only to *one*,
OR TWO, living beings, and to God. AND WHO THAT ONE?

We have attained the idea, EITHER OF A FATAL ACCI-
DENT UNDER THE ROOF OF MADAME DELUC,
OR of a murder perpetrated, in the thicket at the Barrière
du Roule, by a lover, or at least by an intimate and secret
associate of the deceased.

WE ARE NOT FORCED TO SUPPOSE A PREMEDITATED DESIGN OF
MURDER OR OF VIOLATION. BUT THERE WAS THE FRIENDLY SHEL-
TER OF THE THICKET, AND THE APPROACH OF RAIN—THERE
WAS OPPORTUNITY AND STRONG TEMPTATION— AND THEN A
SUDDEN AND VIOLENT WRONG, TO BE CONCEALED ONLY BY ONE
OF DARKER DYE.

"And what means are ours of attaining the truth? We shall
find these means multiplying and gathering distinctness as
we proceed.—PROVIDED THAT OUR PREPARATORY ANALYSIS OF
THE SUBJECT HAS NOT GREATLY DIVERGED FROM THE PRINCIPLES
OF TRUTH."

Let us endeavor to ascertain, by repeated questionings of
Madame Deluc and her boys, as well as of the omnibus-
driver, Valence [Adam Wall], something more of the
personal appearances and bearing of the "man of dark complexion." Queries, skilfully directed, will not fail to elicit,
from some of these parties, information on this particular
point (OR UPON OTHERS) . . .

. . . AN INDIVIDUAL ASSASSIN WAS CONVICTED, UPON HIS OWN
CONFESSION, OF THE MURDER OF MARIE ROGET. . . .

In addition to these alterations, Poe provided the tale with
notes, the first of which proclaimed not merely that the story
had been a genuine attempt to solve the real mystery, but that
the attempt had been successful:

A young girl, Mary Cecilia Rogers, was murdered in the
vicinity of New York; and although her death occasioned
an intense and long-enduring excitement, the mystery at-

tending it had remained unsolved at the period when the present paper was written and published (November, 1842). Herein, under pretense of relating the fate of a Parisian grisette, the author has followed, in minute detail, the essential, while merely paralleling the inessential, facts of the real murder of Mary Rogers. *Thus all argument founded upon the fiction is applicable to the truth; and the investigation of the truth was the object.*

"The Mystery of Marie Rogêt" was composed at a distance from the scene of the atrocity, and with no other means of investigation than the newspapers afforded. Thus much escaped the writer of which he could have availed himself had he been upon the spot and visited the localities. It may not be improper to record, nevertheless, that *the confessions of two persons (one of them the Madame Deluc of the narrative), made at different periods, long subsequent to the publication, confirmed, in full, not only the general conclusion, but absolutely all the chief hypothetical details by which that conclusion was attained.*

(Italics here are my own.)

This time Poe is out in the open. No coquettish demurs that parallels cannot be drawn while he snickers behind his hand at the "mob's inferiority." "Absolutely all" his story's allegations have been proven, in spite of the handicaps under which it was composed.

Je suis un Dieu!

It is clear that the initial version of the story contains no hint whatsoever of either an abortion or Mrs. Loss' guilt. All such statements occur only in the revision. John Walsh considers Poe's changes "ingenious," made with "care and skill," but as a matter of fact they are nothing of the sort. It is true, as Walsh points out, that "for nearly a century," until noticed by William Wimsatt, the revisions went unobserved and Poe's claims as a detective were, to the extent that they were noticed, not strenuously challenged. This was not, one suspects, because of his "ingenious" manipulation of his tale, but because of the incurably romantic compulsion of his critics to believe those claims. Wimsatt, who first noticed Poe's sleight of hand, still felt forced to say: "Whether or not

Poe reasoned to a solution, his story, the circumstances of its composition, and what was later said of it by Poe and others, may constitute the soundest means left to us for reaching an opinion about the fate of Mary Rogers." And Walsh, while condemning Wimsatt as an example of "the extent to which scholarship can blind itself to the clear implication of fact," is unconsciously trapped in the same snare when, although admitting (in fact insisting) that Poe did not solve the murder, he still praises the author for the "greatest hoax" of his career. Walsh fails to understand that Poe intended only his original story as a hoax. He took his revised version, and his claims for it, quite seriously.

The revision is slipshod. It consists entirely of insertions suggesting the possibility of an "accident" at Nick Moore's House, and deletions of references to a single murderer. The excellent arguments against the thicket as the murder scene are retained, but again Poe fails to take advantage of them. Instead he simply adds the abortion rumors as a second, alternate possibility. His original "solution" remains intact. The story thus presents no single "general conclusion" as Poe claims, but two possible conclusions, one still strenuously argued, the other vaguely implied. The identity of the swarthy man is now hopelessly confused in the author's mind. Rumor connects him with the abortionist, and so does Poe in the early portions of his tale, but he has clearly blended with the naval officer by the end of the story. Poe attaches a note asserting that "all argument founded upon the fiction is applicable to the truth . . . ," yet he retains in the text, the statement which contradicts this claim. Little or none of the consummate sophistic skill of the original version is evident in the revision.

In its reincarnated form, "The Mystery of Marie Rogêt" is no longer fiction written by a man who knew he was writing fiction. It is the work of an author who had come to believe that his fiction was real. Its value for those who would understand the fate of the real Mary Rogers is less than nothing. Hervey Allen has noted that Poe must "keep the air clouded . . . so that he, and the world he gazed upon, might appear through the haze other than they actually were." The dense smog of Poe's ego has kept the Rogers case socked in for over a century.

———————◆—■·●·■—◆———————

There still remains the question of those two mysterious confessions alleged by Poe's note. It is a fact that Gilbert Merritt's denial of Mrs. Loss' deathbed statement was more widely printed than the original false report, therefore Poe's claim on this point must be considered a deliberate lie. He had perhaps reached the stage where he could easily ignore or discount any evidence which did not support his delusion.

But what do we make of the second confession, and of Poe's later mention of it in a private letter to George W. Eveleth dated January 4, 1848?

> *Nothing was omitted in "Marie Rogêt" but what I omitted myself—all that is mystification. The story was originally published in Snowden's "Lady's Companion." The "naval officer" who committed the murder (or rather the accidental death arising from an attempt at abortion) confessed it; and the whole matter is now well understood—but, for the sake of relatives, his is a topic on which I must not speak further.*

How seriously can this statement be taken? This is the only known reference to the confession of a naval officer. It was written in response to a direct inquiry from Eveleth. Eveleth, himself, was a young medical student from Maine whose correspondence with Poe is crammed with admiration for the author and his work. Could Poe have avoided the question? Could he have admitted the truth to his young idolator? Could he any longer discern the truth? This letter is composed in 1848, the year when according to Hervey Allen, Poe had become insane. The statement is evasive and is sandwiched in between a savage attack on Margaret Fuller and an outright lie concerning the sale of "The Gold Bug." Poe's phrasing suggests that he has now completely identified the officer with the abortionist. Could such a confession have been made? If it was, how should Poe know of it, except by the newspaper grapevine? If it was common gossip, how could it avoid appearing in the columns of some sensation hungry journal in those days when competition for circulation was fierce and the slimmest rumor was printed as truth? Was it possible that a naval officer could be so well connected that he could admit a brutal and thoroughly publicized murder to authorities who had been flailed in the press for failing to solve the slaying, and yet escape prosecution? The reader is invited to decide.

Poe's first biographer, John H. Ingram, in recording the Eveleth letter, notes: "The naval officer implicated was named Spencer." William Wimsatt, after assuring himself that no corroborating evidence exists either in Ingram's annotated copy of his book or in his collected papers, ransacked the Navy Department files and uncovered only two naval officers named Spencer, one of whom had been in Ohio in 1841. The other, however, was residing in New York "waiting orders" when Mary was murdered. For several years he had complained of poor health and constantly asked to be excused from duty, but suddenly in December of 1841 he requested a command. All very suspicious. Certainly this officer, Captain William A. Spencer, was well connected. His father was Judge Ambrose Spencer, a power in New York politics, and his brother was J. C. Spencer, Secretary of War from 1841 to 1843. Certainly too, Poe might be concerned for "the sake of relatives," since they had been drenched in scandal in December, 1842, when the Secretary's son, Philip, swung from a yardarm aboard the brig *Somers* for attempted mutiny in a sordid affair which would later inspire Herman Melville's *Billy Budd*.

All this may at first appear quite convincing, but it is, in fact, meaningless. Absolutely no evidence exists to connect William Spencer with Mary Rogers. If he lived in New

York, so did 300,000 other people. If he suddenly asked for duty, a thousand reasons may be imagined. The affairs of his relations can have no bearing on the case. It is incredible that a confession by Spencer could be known by Poe yet never even hinted at in the newspapers. That the Spencer family, powerful as they were, was not held sacred by the press is proven by the indignant howl raised against them by several journals in 1843 when they pressed for the court-martial of Commander Alexander Mackenzie, the officer who had sentenced Philip Spencer to hang. Their very prominence in politics would make the Spencers more, not less, liable to public attack by a rabidly partisan press, and the slightest whisper of a confession of murder, especially the murder of the Beautiful Seegar Girl, made by a member of so important a clan, would have provided a field day for fire-breathing editors who published the slander first and fought the lawsuits later. Men like Ben Day and James Gordon Bennett made their livings by shooting at the great and near great. The impossibility of keeping such a confession secret is demonstrated by the constant failure of the authorities to conceal the proceedings of their investigation from reporters, a failure which forced them to pathetic pleas for press silence, always unheeded. And a confession, if made, must be made to the authorities. If known only to the family, it would certainly be unknown to Poe. And why would no steps be taken to prosecute? In those years of deep political bitterness arising from the sudden death of Harrison and the succession of Tyler, and an equally bitter war raging between Whig power in Albany and Democratic power in New York, it is impossible that the opportunity should not be seized to embarrass a potent state politician and an important member of Tyler's cabinet. When a similar opportunity presented itself in the *Somers* affair, it was taken quickly enough. And the widespread notoriety which attached itself to the Spencer name at that time may very well, as Wimsatt infers, have suggested the name to Poe who suggested it to Mrs. Helen Whitman who suggested it to Eveleth who suggested it to Ingram. In fact, Poe was more than likely thinking, if he was thinking about anything at all, of *Philip* Spencer, who did not become a midshipman until four months after Mary's death. It is improbable that he ever heard of William Spencer, the one member of the clan who was not at all prominent.

Other points can be raised. The "naval officer" is clearly completely the invention of Poe's imagination. The sole reference to such a man in the press, the *Herald*'s item, specifically asserts that, "his name is well known on board his ship," and it is a fact that William Spencer was not stationed on any ship. The swarthy man supposedly seen by witnesses in Hoboken was described as a youth, but Spencer was forty-eight in 1841. The bare possibility exists that Poe, and perhaps Ingram as well, was influenced by the story of Ellen Jewett and her seaman boyfriend Sumner, whose name, after all, was not so much different from Spencer or *Somers*. Poe, at least, must have been familiar with that often printed tale. Look at it any way you will: there isn't a single shred of evidence to support Ingram's isolated and casual remark. It is only one more of the strange myths that have risen to confuse the tangled mystery of Mary Rogers.

Ten

In the months and years that have followed the death of Mary Rogers, the dominant theory of her fate has always been that she arranged for an abortion and died while under the knife. Gilbert Merritt believed it, and the examination of the Kellenbarack boys was obviously conducted in an attempt to prove it. The rumors were accepted as fact by 1844, when Poe, now in New York, was painstakingly revising "The Mystery of Marie Rogêt," and Poe, in the letter written to Eveleth on January 4, 1848, stated positively that her demise was an "accidental death arising from an attempt at abortion. . . ." William Kurtz Wimsatt accepts this explanation, as does John Walsh, though Wimsatt balks at making a definite commitment to it. To complete the picture, an occultist named Andrew Jackson Davis, who had met Poe, published a detailed account of Mary's death while she was undergoing an abortion in New York. Came to him in a vision, no doubt.

The idea of a bungled abortion seems to date almost from the discovery of the corpse. As early as the thirteenth of August, the *New York Evening Express* thought it necessary to deny the rumor. On the thirtieth, the *Tattler*, while insisting that the body was not Mary's and sneering at Dr. Cook's evidence of multiple rape, suggested that the condition of the cadaver might be attributed to an illegal operation:

> ... We do not now believe that the person when alive had been subjected to any other violence than that of some of the demoniac professions of the Restell School. The marks upon the body all prove as much, and more in such a case as any other. The hands would be tied, and the victim would be gagged to prevent outcry. The resistance of the unhappy wretch would be as violent in one case, as in the other [rape], and while we believe that the victim found was one whom it was thought better to throw into the river than to smuggle out in a merchandise box ... we cannot forbear the expression of public regret and indignation that the case was not properly investigated by the Coroner's jury.

This was the first time that the name of Madame Restell, the most notorious abortionist in New York, was mentioned in connection with the Rogers affair, but it was to be far from the last. Madame Restell, alias Mrs. Ann Lohman, known to the newspapers as Madame Killer, operated her home for unwed mothers in a mansion on Greenwich Street, just a fast walk from Mary Rogers' door. It was called "The House Built on Baby Skulls," and its owner had been heard to suggest that the best way to relieve the problem of surplus population was to arrange that "all the children of the working people after the third be disposed of by painless extinction." This charming lady had practiced her peculiar form of birth control on the girl friends of some of the city's most prominent figures, and it was widely whispered, and doubtless true, that she owed her amazing immunity to the law to the ever watchful protection afforded her by her highly placed and grateful clients.

The law would never quite catch up with the Queen Mother of abortionists. By her death in 1876, she was to amass a fortune in excess of one million dollars. In the summer of 1841, she was already thoroughly established and operating quite nicely in the black. Like any successful business entrepreneur, Madame Restell had opened a few branch stores in the suburbs, one of which was said to be managed in Hoboken by a Madame Costello. Not as lucky as her more powerful employer, Costello was arrested and convicted in 1845, and this event, coupled with the advent in the same year of still another New York daily, the *National Police Gazette*, desperately seeking a sensational story to get its circulation going, initiated a resurrection of the never ending saga of the Beautiful Seegar Girl.

The *Police Gazette*, like many fledgling sheets, saw it must create news rather than simply report it. As the *New York Daily Mirror* was to do eighty years later with the Hall-Mills case, the *Gazette* found it expedient to dredge up an old corpse. The journal labored for nine months and brought forth a scandal.

Late in 1845, the editors gingerly tested public reaction with an item accusing either Restell or Costello, or both, of Mary Rogers' death. The results must have been good for, on February 21, 1846, they let fly with a torrid editorial:

> Females are daily, nay, hourly, missing from our midst who never return. Where do they go? What becomes of them? Does funeral bell ever peal a note for their passage? Does funeral train ever leave her door? Do friends ever gather round the melancholy grave? No! An obscure hole in the earth; a consignment to the savage skill of the dissecting knife, or a splash in the cold wave, with the scream of the night blast for a requiem, is the only death service bestowed upon her victims. Witness this, ye shore of Hudson! Witness this, Hoboken beach!

This article, accompanied by an artist's sketch of a grim faced Restell attended by a winged griffin gnawing on the corpse of a naked infant, was a shameless patchwork of unsupported and savage allegations. The only "facts" cited were incorrect. The *Gazette* mistook the place where the body had been found, and based its insinuations on the rumored sighting of Mary in the vicinity of Restell's house on her last day, a story which had been proven false in the first week of the investigation. In all probability this single piece, inflammatory as it was, would not have been sufficient to provoke the public outcry that followed, had it not been for the affair of Mary Applegate.

Miss Applegate was a Philadelphia seamstress who had been seduced by Augustus Edwards, a Reading Railroad official whose wife would not have understood. Edwards determined that the girl should enroll for a semester at Madame Restell's finishing school, and there she was delivered of a living child. She saw the infant only once. Then Madame Killer took the child, saying it would be given to a nurse, but when the young mother prepared to leave, Restell denied any knowledge of an infant. Miss Applegate was more interested in her progeny than her reputation. She blew the whistle on Madame Killer and made a full statement to the authorities.

In her affidavit the girl described life in the Greenwich Street house. For the patients under Restell's tender care there was no such thing as a private room and hardly a chance of a private bed. Miss Applegate had encountered an Albany widow recuperating from a bout with a bank president and a Philadelphia lady whose vacation was prepaid by a Congressman. Another of the inmates was a New York debutante. She had been committed by her own mother who preferred anything to a scandal.

The story created a sensation. For Restell it must have been a novel experience. None of her customers had ever called a cop before. She weathered the storm like the trooper she was, eventually silencing the outraged seamstress with a baby represented, at least, as the bonafide infant, but not before the New York press had whipped the population into a frenzy. A mob gathered in Greenwich Street which for several hours threatened to raze the infamous House Built on Baby Skulls. "Haul her out!" the crowd screamed. "Hanging is too good for the monster! Where is Mary Applegate's child? Where's the thousand children murdered in this house? Who murdered Mary Rogers?"

The police surrounded the area. Restell was smuggled out

a back door, a few arrests were made, and eventually the riot was quashed. The *Gazette* continued to rage at the lady for a few issues, but they were only stirring ashes. Within a week the ghost of Mary Rogers was once again forgotten. For Madame Killer it was business as usual.

There is an intriguing postscript to this chapter of the Rogers mystery. For years there was a standing tradition at the *Police Gazette* that Edgar Allan Poe had served on the paper's staff at some point between 1846 and his death three years later. This rumor remains unproven. It is a fact, however, that Poe was in New York in late 1845 and early 1846, and that he was, as usual, broke. *The Broadway Journal,* of which he had been editor and, for a time, publisher, had collapsed in early January. *The Tales of Edgar A. Poe,* including the revised "The Mystery of Marie Rogêt," out since the preceding summer, was not selling well. Its author was once again pressed into holding off his creditors with what little he could borrow or earn from anonymous freelancing for the newspapers. Quite possibly he contributed to the *Police Gazette.* Certainly it is true that any rebirth of the Mary Rogers furor could only help to stimulate the sagging sales of a book containing a story which purported to be the solution of that mysterious affair. It is a vague possibility, and nothing more, that Poe himself was the author of the *Gazette* articles which disturbed the happy home life of Madame Restell and rekindled the flames of the mystery of Mary Rogers.

One other cryptic footnote remains. The fragment of a letter survives, written by Poe at around the time that a mob was laying siege to the Restell house:

I am exceedingly anxious. If you would be so kind as to look me up, I will consider it a great favor. You understand the whole story is purely fiction.—

Your opinion is of great consideration.—

Yr Ob. St
Edgar A. Poe

To whom was this letter addressed? Why was Poe "exceedingly anxious"? Was the "story" referred to "The Mystery of Marie Rogêt?" Did the communication have anything to do with the *Gazette*'s attempt to tie Restell to the Rogers case? Can these questions ever be answered? In all probability "nevermore."

———————◆•◦•◆———————

There is also an interesting postscript to the life of Madame Restell alias Mrs. Ann Lohman. Her husband, "Doctor" Lohman, was a prosperous quack who used the profits from his patent medicines to purchase real estate fronting on Fifth Avenue, between fifty-second and fifty-third streets. On this property he erected the last of his wife's "hospitals" by mortgaging the land on which it stood with the Mutual Life Insurance Company for $27,000. During one of their numerous separations, his spouse acquired the mortgage without his knowledge, and soon afterward she loaned him $147,000 in cash to build flats on an adjacent lot. Her two mortgages then totaled $174,000 on property valued at $600,000. Obviously Lohman was now worth more dead than alive. Shortly, the "doctor" executed a will in his wife's favor, which also included title to a valuable Chambers Street shop. Only her husband's life stood between Mrs. Lohman and a successful career as a real estate tycoon. Oddly enough, it was just a few weeks later that he took to his bed and died. The *Gazette* reported his last hours:

> The "doctor" did not seem particularly ill when he took to his bed. While he had not been feeling right for some time, no grave apprehension was felt concerning his condition. Lohman raised himself in bed and said to a young man who had been visiting him every day: "Hand me the medicine-bottle from the bureau, will you?" The visitor looked around and seeing no bottle, replied: "What bottle? There is none here." "Why, it was there a few minutes ago," the invalid exclaimed. "Who could have taken it?" In

a fit of angry impatience he rang the service bell. His wife appeared in answer to the summons, holding a medicine-bottle in her hand, and looking, so the eye-witness stated, strangely excited. "What the devil did you take my medicine for?" Lohman asked impetuously. "Well, I thought the bottle was getting empty," she replied, "and I had better replenish it." He was by no means reconciled with the explanation: "It was more than half full when I had it before and didn't need renewing." "Well, I thought it did," was the reply, and with that she deposited the bottle, which was now nearly full, on the bureau. That very night Lohman died.

Restell was a widow for an extremely short time. There were questions raised about her husband's will. There were whispers that Lohman's relatives in Prussia would have some claim on his estate. There was talk of exhuming his body. One quiet evening all problems were solved. Ann Lohman stepped into her palatial bathtub and ducked her head under the water. Unlike Mary Rogers, Madame Killer never surfaced.

Eleven

The final scenes of the Rogers affair were triggered by a questionable will, an old man's delusions, and a family feud, and were played out in three New York courtrooms. John Anderson had prospered. The canny tobacconist parlayed a small snuff shop into several million dollars in real estate and railroads, and when he breathed his last in Paris in November, 1881, his numerous relatives clustered like vultures to battle over his considerable fortune. Anderson had spawned two sons and four daughters by two wives. Five married but only two, John Charles Anderson and Mrs. Laura V. Appleton, both childless, survived him, along with his second spouse Katherine. There were eight grandchildren, five of them offspring of daughter Fannie and George Bernard, another two by daughter Amanda and the family black sheep, Carolan Bryant. The only orphaned grandchild was Mary Maud Carr, the daughter of Mary and Walter Carr, fourteen years old at the time of the old man's death.

John Charles had been his father's business partner for many years, and to him went the lion's share of the estate. The others chafed, but it was not until late in 1885 that the will was tested by the courts in an action brought by little Mary Maud. She was suing for twenty percent ownership in twelve valuable Fifth Avenue lots which, her lawyers claimed, had been Anderson's property at his demise, and which were now in the hands of two gentlemen named John D. Phyfe and James Campbell. The defendants asserted that Anderson had given them a deed of conveyance for the land, his wife Kate joining in this action. They further stated that the will, dated October 23, 1879, and a codicil, dated September 29, 1881, both duly witnessed, had been admitted to probate in March, 1882, and the probate was still in force.

The plaintiff charged that her grandfather "was not of sound mind and memory or capable of making a will," and had been under the "undue influence" of John Charles who had bribed Laura Appleton, Kate Anderson and "others" not to interfere in the probate proceedings. She herself had been deceived into leaving the city while the probate hearings were under way.

The whole thing was an ugly little mess. The central problem for Mary Maud's attorneys was to prove that old Anderson had been insane when the will was signed. For this they relied heavily on two witnesses. Former State Senator Abner C. Matoon had been a crony of Anderson's for several years, though the friendship had faltered a bit in 1865 when the senator, by his own admission a model of virtue and honor, had refused his pal's thousand-dollar bribe to vote against a certain railroad bill. The episode had culminated in a shouting match on the floor of the State Senate and Anderson's unceremonious exit from the chamber, escorted none too gently by the sergeant-at-arms. The second witness was Anderson's one-time business partner and long-time confidant, Felix McCloskey, who bore an acknowledged grudge against John Charles for allegedly forcing him out of the firm.

Abner Matoon was celebrating his seventy-second birthday when he took the stand on October 15, 1885. It was true, he testified, that John Anderson believed in spiritualism, and it was true that he thought his Tarrytown house to be haunted. The ghost of Garibaldi, for instance, hung around the place pretty regularly. Anderson had known that gentleman while alive, had given financial support to his campaign to unify Italy, and when Garibaldi refused a pension from the Italian government, had paid him an annual stipend of $2,500 until his death.

The spirit of the Beautiful Seegar Girl was another frequent guest. Matoon quoted Anderson: "I have had a good deal of trouble about Mary Rogers, but everything is settled now. I take great pleasure in communicating with her face to face." Anderson, said the senator, "spoke about Mary Rogers two or three times, and about her appearing to him. . . . He did not go into any particulars and I did not press him. Several times after when he started the subject, I turned the conversation off."

Question: Did he not state she was dead?

Answer: He spoke of her as having been spirited away or maltreated; that she had disappeared mysteriously. His appearance was sad when he spoke and he appeared excited and wild.

Question: In what way did he say she had appeared to him?

Answer: That she had appeared to him face to face and had talked to him. I told him I didn't take stock in spirits; he said I didn't understand the subject as he did. . . . I think it was in 1876 or 1877 that he first spoke of the spirit of Mary Rogers. He said he was having a good deal of trouble with Mary Rogers. I said: "There comes your spiritualism again."

Mary, it seems, had given her old employer some excellent advice on business matters. He had deep faith in the spirit world and, when discussing it, could become greatly agitated, running around the room and swinging his arms:

Question: What did he talk about principally at such times?

Answer: Mary Rogers. That always excited him.

Felix McCloskey followed Matoon into the box. There could be no doubt, he thought, that John Anderson was deranged. Once, while the witness was an overnight guest, the tobacconist had wakened him and asked to remain with him until dawn as "things were after him." On another occasion Anderson had entered McCloskey's home and threatened to kill him unless he handed over $10,000. Getting the money, he raced into the street and was later unearthed at a "house of ill repute." On still another occasion, he had run out of his house partially undressed.

Anderson feared plots against him. He was convinced his son was dipping into the company till. He suspected two old friends of conspiring to kill him and once offered McCloskey $100,000 to "prevent it." He believed his wife and John Charles had designs on his life, and kept an eye on the cook so she could not put pins in the roast beef. He would often confront a total stranger on the street, stare for several moments, and say something like, "I knew that man thirty years ago and he would slug anyone for a dollar." Yes, Mc-Closkey had heard Anderson speak about spiritualism. He talked of Garibaldi, and of his dead son, little Willie, whose ghost haunted the Tarrytown house. "It was a pleasant thing" to have Willie with him. No, he had never mentioned Mary's spirit "as far as I know."

Question: Did he ever speak to you of Mary Rogers?

Answer: He asked me once what I thought about the case and I told him that some of his friends, and myself included, considered that he had something to do with her disappearance. Mr. Anderson assured me that he had nothing whatever to do with it.

On October 20 the plaintiff called a "medical expert," Dr. Theodore Dimond, to testify that spiritualism was a delusion of a diseased mind and those who believed they communicated with ghosts were clearly insane. The good doctor got a rough going over on cross-examination:

Question: Do you remember that Luther thought he
            was haunted by ghosts and threw an ink-
            stand at them?

Answer: I do. I think Luther had an insane delu-
            sion at that time. I always thought so.

Question: Do you not know that Mahomet be-
            lieved that he had control over demons?
            What do you think of him?

Answer: He might be an imposter or a fool.

Question: You believe in the Bible. Do you believe
            that Saul talked with Samuel?

The witness was visibly suffering when the court sustained
an objection that this was "going a little too far into ancient
history."

In spite of the evidence of her grandfather's strange habits,
Mary Maud lost. The judge ruled that no testimony had been
produced to show that Anderson ever allowed his spiritual
fancies to interfere with his sound, and renowned, business
sense. The plaintiff appealed and round two of the bizarre
suit was fought in May and June of 1887. Matoon and
McCloskey were back with substantially the same stories, but
this time the defendants had a small army of witnesses to
Anderson's sanity warming up in the bullpen. One of them,
Andrew Wheeler, a Democratic journalist whose newspaper
Anderson had backed, is typical.

Wheeler had once asked Anderson if his house was haunted.
The answer: "Yes, by people who want money." The two
men had also discussed the Rogers case: "Anderson talked
about it sensibly enough and said Poe used to drop into the
tobacco shop to get the points." Did Wheeler know anything about a story that Anderson paid Poe $5,000 to write
the story so as to divert suspicion from the tobacconist?
Wheeler did not.

Nine others swore that John Anderson was the most ra-
tional man each had ever met, and two men asserted they
would not believe Abner Matoon if he were under oath,

which of course he was. All this made no impression on the jury who found for the plaintiff. Mary Maud, by this time Mrs. Watkins, had finally won her point. For four years the turbulent affairs of John Anderson's loved ones and heirs remained peaceful, though it is doubtful that the happy clan gathered round the hearth at Christmas. Then, in December, 1891, another county was heard from.

Anderson had been spinning in his grave almost twenty years to the day when his only surviving daughter, Laura Appleton, marched into New York Supreme Court for an action in ejectment to regain twenty percent ownership in the city's Hotel Plaza. The hotel's site had been bequeathed by her father to John Charles, and sold by him to a construction firm which, financed by a loan secured by a mortgage with the New York Life Insurance Company, had erected the Plaza. The mortgage had subsequently been foreclosed and the insurance firm had leased the property to a Frederick A. Hammond who now found himself a codefendant with his landlords. Mrs. Appleton claimed her intestate share of the property, charging that her father's will was invalid because he was not of sound mind.

It was the same old story with the same old cast. Felix McCloskey did another encore and Abner Matoon, now deep in his dotage, made an appearance. But this time the script was different.

Much of the testimony dealt with Mary's important role in making the tobacco shop a success. "The young sports around New York at that time used to go there," one witness said. "New York was not so big as it is now. They used to drop into Anderson's and they called her 'Mary.' She brought customers."

It was now revealed that John Anderson had been one of those arrested on suspicion in the frenzied early days of the investigation. Though he was quickly released for lack of evidence, and his arrest was kept out of the press, several people including James Gordon Bennett were aware of it, and it had severely damaged his political prospects and forced him to decline a later Tammany bid to run for mayor. (One wonders at the feelings of young, politically ambitious Anderson, attending Bennett's committee of "outraged citizens," and matching the editor's generous fifty-dollar contribution.) Abner Matoon repeated his conversations concerning Mary's ghost: "He said he had had many, *very* many, unhappy nights and days in regard to her."

But the star of the show was unquestionably Felix McCloskey. Once he and Anderson had walked past the old Rogers house. The tobacconist called it the "damned house" which was "the cause of driving him out of politics and belittling him in New York and which had kept him from advancing." McCloskey admitted that Anderson had told him "an abortion had been committed on the girl—the year before her murder took place, or a year and a half—something of that kind—and that he got into some trouble about it—and outside of *that* there was no grounds on earth for anybody to suppose he had anything to do with the murder."

At a different point in his testimony McCloskey quoted Anderson: "I want people to believe that I had no hand in her taking off—" The witness added, "He assured me that he *hadn't* anything *directly, himself,* to do with it."

Mrs. Appleton's attorneys insisted that they did not mean to suggest in any way that John Anderson was actually implicated in the murder, but only that the shock of his arrest had made "an impression which he was in after years never able to shake off and which, when his faculties began to fail and old age to creep upon him, lent a controlling force which undermined his intellectual powers." With this last statement the defendants appear to have agreed, for Laura Appleton obtained a very substantial out-of-court settlement.

———————◆—◆•◆—◆———————

And there you have it. Every known fact, every bit of testimony, every ironic twist and turn of the mystery lies before us. And somewhere within this maze of trickery and deceit, contradictory evidence, obsessive guilt, and crazed delusion, somewhere lies the answer to the central and overwhelming question.

Twelve

Who murdered Mary Rogers? From among the many theories advanced during the investigation, five possibilities are worthy of consideration:

(1) Daniel Payne

(2) the body found in the river was not Mary

(3) a gang of ruffians

(4) a "swarthy man" who escorted her to Hoboken

(5) an abortionist

Despite his strange behavior and the eerie nature of his dramatic suicide, Daniel Payne has never been seriously suspected of his fiancée's death. His alibi accounts for his every movement on Sunday and it is airtight. Every investigator from Poe to the present has denied Payne's guilt.

There can be no question about the fact that the corpse was Mary Rogers. Alfred Crommelin's identification by itself might be considered insufficient, although it was corroborated by Archibald Padley at the inquest and Payne at the Death House, but when it is supported by the positive identification of the clothing by Phoebe Rogers, Mrs. Hayes, and a close friend of the dead girl, it forms an unanswerable argument. Phoebe even recognized a tear in the frock which she had mended the day before her daughter's disappearance.

The thesis that Mary was assaulted and killed by a gang is completely implausible. In support of this idea only one fact can be cited: there were gangs present in the area. Against this theory looms a mountain of evidence, beginning with the appearance of the body. The fact that the girl was redressed and the consummate neatness of this operation argue against a gang. Even the bonnet had been carefully tied about the neck. The strip of muslin used as a gag was torn out of the petticoat evenly and with great care. A gang would have had no need to transport the corpse by means of a handle wrapped round the waist. Had Mary been attacked by several men it seems likely that her body would have borne the marks of many hands, yet the bruises on the left side of the face and the thumb and finger imprints on the throat obviously point to a single, right-handed assailant. Even if Mary were raped by more than one man, it is evident that she was subdued first, and disposed of afterwards, by one individual alone.

As for the contention of multiple rape, this is based solely on Doctor Cook's statement and that statement itself is baseless. As a physician Cook was a quack and a fraud. There is not a single shred of evidence to indicate that he undertook any internal examination of the body. His testimony and his conclusions were founded entirely on external appearances and, of all his contentions, only his proofs against the possibility of drowning are acceptable to a modern medical mind. In no way could the doctor have supported his view that Mary had been ravished "by more than two or three persons."

The gang thesis, first advanced by the press as part of a campaign for police reform and later retreated from by even its loudest adherent, the *Herald*, thus falls to pieces. Every known fact points to a lone murderer attacking and killing suddenly and violently, and then arranging and disposing of the body at leisure.

Only the testimony of two witnesses, Adam Wall and Frederica Loss, serves to establish the existence of the "tall swarthy man," and the stage driver's statement, founded on the vague recollection of a passing remark made by a stranger, may be discounted at once. For the widow's story four possible explanations come to mind: (1) She was telling the truth. (2) She had participated in a fatal abortion and was seeking to divert official suspicion from her tavern. (3) She had allowed her imagination to convince her that Mary had patronized her establishment on the murder day. (4) She deliberately concocted the story to publicize the Nick Moore's House and draw business.

It is impossible to believe she was telling the truth. Since by her own admission, she had never seen Mary before, of what possible value is her "identification"? Since, according to her statement to *Brother Jonathan*, Mary left her tavern in company with at least five other couples, why did not one of these people ever come forward? And why, when a few days following the murder she spoke to Nancy Ludlow about her son and the bull, did she make no mention of Mary's visit to Nick Moore's House? There is no evidence that the possibility of this visit occurred to her at all until after the finding of the apparel.

As for the second theory, that of a fatal abortion, it has been the most widely touted of all "solutions." Merritt was convinced of its truth. Poe came to accept it, and John Walsh proclaims, "It is morally certain that Mary's death occurred on an abortion table. . . ." *And yet the concept of a fatal abortion is the most completely absurd of all the theories ever advanced.* Even if we are to assume an abortion at the tavern; even if we are to assume that some clothing was kept back by the killers and later used to establish the thicket as the murder site: Why would the widow have chosen a place so close to her own house? Why would she draw official attention to Weehawken when the police were

143

still debating whether Mary had been killed in Hoboken or New York? Why would she allow her boys to pretend to uncover the articles, knowing that they would be closely questioned and that one of them was a mere twelve years old? Why would she invent a tale which placed her victim at her saloon on the day of the crime? Why would she immediately inform her sister and a neighbor of the false discoveries in the thicket, yet wait a full week before approaching the authorities? The answer to each and all of these questions is quite simple: She would not.

Obviously Mrs. Loss' behavior becomes incomprehensible if observed from the viewpoint that Mary died under her knife. Serious doubts must be cast over the fatal abortion theory. But any close examination of Richard Cook's evidence on the appearance of the body totally demolishes this thesis. Several facts may be cited in proof of this:

(1) The marks on the corpse in the area of the abdomen and elsewhere were sufficient to convince Cook that the girl had been the victim of violent rape before her death.

(2) Violent rape or attempted rape may well leave external bruises on the body of the victim.

(3) Abortion or attempted abortion never leaves external marks or excoriations on the body.

(4) The second examination of the corpse, conducted at the Dead House, confirmed Cook's contention of rape.

The most damning evidence against the fatal abortion theory is the abrasions found on the dead girl's face, throat, and back. These must have been inflicted before her death, for it is a fact that when an individual has been dead longer than one or two minutes, no amount of mistreatment of the body will cause discoloration of the skin. If Mary did undergo a fatal abortion, it was not until she had been

144

severely beaten and choked while her arching back was pressed against a hard surface. This is hardly the usual procedure of preparing a patient for surgery, even illegal surgery. Every fact of the condition of the body renders the abortion thesis ridiculous while it supports the implication that Mary was assaulted.

We have rejected the existence of a "swarthy" man, the idea of murder by a gang, and Justice Merritt's fatal abortion theory, and established the fact that the widow Loss lied in her statements to the police and the press; but whether she lied deliberately or unconsciously is a question we must, for the moment, leave hanging. The central question also remains: Who murdered Mary Rogers? Before seeking a solution we need first deal with the issue of the girl's strange "disappearance" in 1838.

For this episode five explanations may be offered:

(1) She underwent an abortion.

(2) She was seduced.

(3) The whole thing was a publicity stunt.

(4) She actually wrote the suicide note.

(5) She was the victim of a practical joke.

The first may be tossed out at once. No evidence exists to support it except John Anderson's statement to Felix McCloskey that "an abortion had been committed on the girl—the year before her murder took place, or a year and a half—something of that kind—and that he got into some trouble about it. . . ." As we shall see shortly, Anderson had excellent reasons for lying on this point.

For the second the corroboration is, if possible, even flimsier. It was not even hinted at in the press of 1838, and the sole mention of it in 1841 is the *Herald*'s discredited "naval officer" yarn. Only the fact that Poe seized on this story has kept the seduction theory alive, and it is a tribute to that gentleman's guile, not simply that the elusive naval officer is still accepted in some quarters, but that any connection is ever seen by anyone between the "disappearance" and the murder.

All of which brings us to the third, the fourth and the fifth, and the reader, having paid his money, is invited to take his choice. The third is possible, although Mary's widely reported agitation over the publicity she *did* get militates against it. The fourth, which oddly enough has never been suggested, is exactly the sort of empty but highly dramatic gesture to be expected from a romantic young girl who has just been jilted. It is clear from the accounts in four different papers that Mrs. Hayes actually did go to the police and that some sort of note did exist. It is unlikely that Phoebe Rogers would not recognize her daughter's handwriting.

Walsh leans toward the idea of a practical joke, a cruel hoax practiced on the girl by one of the reporters who hung around Anderson's shop. Several papers did print this version at the time and later, with the joker sometimes identified as a reporter, sometimes as one of Mary's girl friends, in fact the "Hoax theory" got such a wide play in the press that suspicions cannot help but rise that it was itself a hoax. Mary must have had many friends among the fourth estate willing to spread a false report which might cover for her adolescent foolishness and spare her further embarrassment. As Walsh himself notes, she was involved with at least one newspaperman named Canter or Carter on the staff of the *Journal of Commerce*, one of the papers which carried the story of a practical joke. In addition, if the suicide note was real, it would be the most satisfactory explanation of Mary's anguish over the notoriety and her stubborn reluctance to go back to the tobacco shop. But the point is not worth belaboring, since nothing exists to connect the affair with the subsequent homicide.

———————————◆—●•●—◆—————————

In putting together the pieces of this tangled mystery, we must deal with four apparently insoluble paradoxes:

(1) The problem of the presence of rigor mortis in the body of a girl who has been dead for three days.

(2) The problem of an abortion. The medical evidence indicates unquestionably that Mary Rogers was savagely beaten and strangled to death, and was quite probably the victim of rape or attempted rape. Her death was not the result of a bungled abortion. And yet Gilbert Merritt and Robert Morris were convinced that a fatal abortion had been performed in Nick Moore's House. May we blithely assume that they had absolutely no basis for this conviction and dismiss them as blithering idiots? It is not going to be that easy.

(3) The inexplicable actions of Frederica Loss. If she had a guilty secret to hide concerning the murder, why should she deliberately attract the attention of the authorities? If she had no guilty secret, why was Merritt so positive she did that he put himself on public record in accusing her of complicity in the crime?

(4) The problem of the thicket. The items found within it were positively identified as Mary's. Is it possible they could lie undetected for over a month? If they were planted, by whom, and for what purpose?

Each of these paradoxes individually seems impossible to unravel. Taken together, they form a pattern of events into which all the smaller pieces of the mystery fall until the murderer stands revealed.

Rigor mortis is a progressive stiffening of the muscles as a result of the coagulation of the muscle protein which usually occurs four to six hours after death. The effects of rigor mortis do not last for more than fifteen to seventeen hours. *And these effects were still present in the corpse of Mary Rogers when it was examined by Richard Cook.*

Because of Cook's obvious medical incompetence and the absurdity of most of his conclusions, investigators have tended to ignore his testimony as irrelevant. His conclusions are irrelevant but his observations are not. He deposed that

Mary's arms were bent over her chest so tightly and stiffly that force was needed to straighten them. The right hand was clenched, while the left was partially open but rigid. The body had been in the river, and cold water retards the symptoms of rigor mortis; but the water, in that July heat wave, could not possibly have been below sixty-five degrees, too warm to have any appreciable influence. The presence of rigor mortis in the body on Wednesday afternoon proves medically, scientifically, conclusively, that *Mary Rogers could not have been murdered earlier than Tuesday afternoon.*

There can be no question about this. Every investigator from Merritt to the most modern has assumed that Mary was killed on Sunday. Every one of them has been dead wrong.

———————◆━◆◆◆◆———————

Mary Rogers disappeared on Sunday morning, two and one-half days before her death. A question now confronts us which has confronted no other investigators of the case. Where did she spend those two and one-half days?

Sort out the clues. Twice on the Friday and Saturday before her disappearance, Mary tried unsuccessfully to contact Alfred Crommelin. The reason, as her mother swore to the police, was to sell him a due bill for $52. Obviously she was in urgent need of $52. Just as obviously she did not get it from Crommelin.

During their hearing in Jersey City the Kellenbarack boys were asked whether they had ever heard of fifty dollars being "offered by anyone for any purpose."

In October, 1885, Felix McCloskey testified that John Anderson "asked me once what I thought about the case and I told him that some of his friends, and myself included, considered that he had something to do with her disappearance. Mr. Anderson assured me that he had nothing whatever to do with it."

In December, 1891, McCloskey testified that Anderson had told him "an abortion had been committed on the girl—the

148

year before her murder took place, or a year and a half—
something of that kind—and that he got into some trouble
about it—and outside of *that* there was no grounds on earth
for anybody to suppose he had anything to do with the
murder." At a different point in his testimony McCloskey
quoted Anderson: "I want people to believe that I had no
hand in her taking off—." The witness added, "He assured
me that he *hadn't* anything *directly, himself,* to do with it."

On November 14, 1841, in a sworn affidavit, Gilbert Merritt stated: ". . . This deponent further saith, that from information he has obtained, and facts in his possession, he verily
believes that the murder of the said Mary C. Rogers was
perpetrated in a house in Weehawken, called 'the Nick Moore
House,' then kept by one Frederica Loss . . . and her sons
. . . all three of whom this deponent has reason to believe
are worthless and profligate characters; and . . . that the said
sons and their mother kept one of the most depraved and
debauched houses in New Jersey, and that all of them had
a knowledge of, were accessory to, and became participators
in the murder of said Mary C. Rogers and the concealment
of her body."

Four days later the *Tribune* reported the "confession"
allegedly made by Mrs. Loss to Merritt acknowledging a
fatal abortion and accusing her eldest son of disposing of the
body. When Merritt denied the confession story and the
Herald began to jeer, the *Tribune,* two days after the Kellenbarack boys' hearing, retracted the item but protested:

> We gave the facts as they were told to us by
> two magistrates of this City, and as we under-
> stood them on the authority of a statement made
> by Mr. Merritt himself to Mayor Morris. We
> said nothing about any "examination" of Mrs.
> Loss and erred in stating that the *confession* was
> made to Mr. Merritt. That it was made to *some-
> one* we have little doubt; and we firmly believe
> that the statement we give embraces the true ex-
> planation of the manner of this unfortunate wom-
> an's death.

These are the major pieces of the abortion puzzle and from them the picture begins to emerge. In late July, Mary Rogers was pregnant with an unwanted child. She had arranged, or someone else had arranged, an abortion to be performed at Nick Moore's House either by Frederica Loss, or, as Merritt suspected, by a physician. The price was fifty dollars. This sum Mary tried desperately to raise by selling a due bill to Crommelin, but he turned a deaf ear.

Mary Rogers had only two friends close enough and wealthy enough to give her fifty dollars, and it probably would have amounted to charity since the I.O.U. of an ex-boarder who had skipped town was more than likely uncollectable. She went to John Anderson and he gave her the money.

Such a small thing, yet the fatal act of Anderson's life. Like everyone else he believed Mary died under the knife and spent the rest of his life blaming himself for her death. Not only guilt, but fear gripped him when her corpse was washed up in Hoboken, and he realized the depth of the scandal in which he floundered, a fear doubled by his arrest and tripled by Bennett's knowledge of it. A young man rapidly increasing his fortunes, politically on the make, and presumably happily married, Anderson panicked. He had bought the abortion; who would believe he had not fathered the child?

Though he escaped public exposure his political ambitions were in ruins and his guilt pursued him for many years. Small wonder he found it necessary to insist he had had nothing directly to do with her "taking off." Small wonder he imagined himself haunted by her ghost. Despite Anderson's wealth and success, one only needs to glance at the testimony of McCloskey and Matoon to read the sad and tragic life of that conscience-stricken and paranoic man.

———————◆━◉◉━◆———————

And now Mary had the money. The best cover story she could come up with was a visit to Mrs. Downing's. She took her leave of Payne and vanished into a mystery which has enshrouded her from that moment to this. Now it seems easily explained. She crossed the river unobserved, reached Nick Moore's House, and *underwent a successful abortion.*

There is no reason to believe the operation was not performed on Sunday. Mary would have been anxious to be absent from home for as short a time as possible. Possibly as early as Sunday evening the physician, if there was one, was on his way home, and Mary was recuperating in an upper room of the tavern while Frederica Loss puffed up the hill to Ludlow's to see if her son had been gored.

And here, on Sunday evening in the upper room of that Weehawken saloon, the trail ended, and the troubles began for Merritt and Morris and every investigator in their wake. They could trace Mary to Nick Moore's House, and beyond that they could not trace her, nor did they try, for not one of them has ever understood that on Sunday evening Mary Rogers still had one and a half days to live.

Like his Parisian counterpart, The Perfect G— of Poe's invention, Gilbert Merritt fixed his mind on an a priori solution to the crime and gathered those facts to him which would support it, while ignoring those which would not. He obviously knew what nasty little sideline Mrs. Loss engaged in when not tending bar, and he had heard or learned something concerning Mary Rogers in the days when the widow lingered and raved on her deathbed, all of which led him to swear out his affidavit; yet the evidence was not sufficiently substantial to permit him to take the stand at the Kellenbaracks' hearing. Whatever he knew, or thought he knew, he had passed on to Morris, and it had leaked to Greeley at the *Tribune* through "two magistrates," one of whom undoubtedly was Merritt's brother Henry, a magistrate of the Lower Police Court in New York. Both the warrant for the Kellenbaracks and their Jersey City hearing were desperate moves as evinced by the fact that each boy was publicly promised immunity from prosecution if he would talk. Merritt leaped to a conclusion. He did not land on his feet. What portion of the anatomy he did land on, and how Mary Rogers passed her last day and a half of life, must await a discussion of our third paradox: the problem of Frederica Loss.

———◆—◦●◆—◆———

We need to keep in mind that we are not simply dealing with a bouncy little German barmaid. *Brother Jonathan* described Mrs. Loss as "intelligent" and "very clever" and her known accomplishments bear this out. In addition to the tavern, she owned three large lots in Weehawken, a shrewd investment; for the Hoboken Land and Improvement Company, which had already acquired the considerable properties, ferries, and docks held by the estate of Colonel John Stevens, was gobbling up land all along the Jersey shore at apparently very good prices. The profits from her inn alone were undoubtedly not sufficient to finance her real estate ventures but Mrs. Loss was an accomplished abortionist and, at fifty dollars per operation, a rich one. She left her heirs well off. The Kellenbarracks could afford three lawyers to defend them from Jersey justice. The point here is that Frederica Loss was not a stupid woman and yet, if a fatal abortion had been performed, her subsequent actions would be exceedingly stupid ones. In the light of what we now know, we can see that they were not stupid, but calculated and daring.

On Sunday Mrs. Loss operated on a young girl whose name was either unknown to her or given as something other than Mary Rogers. Until Tuesday this girl remained in her care. Then she was called for or perhaps left alone to return home. It was a cash transaction. The widow never saw her again.

On Wednesday a corpse was sighted in the Hudson, and by the following weekend the whole Jersey shore buzzed over the girl who had been murdered on *Sunday, July 25*, in *Hoboken*. Frederica buzzed excitedly with the rest. She could not possibly have made any connection in her mind

152

between the murdered Miss Rogers and the young lady who had been resting in her upper room, alive and well, at the very hour when, the papers said, Miss Rogers was being killed.

And then her sons found the clothing in the thicket.

And Frederica Loss knew the truth.

She recognized the strips of the dress, quite probably for the reason she later gave, that it was similar to a garment one of her sisters had worn on her last visit before her death.

She consulted with another sister and the advice she received was short and sound: burn the clothes. If she had taken it, the Rogers case would be forgotten and "The Mystery of Marie Rogêt" would never have been written. But Mrs. Loss delayed. She thought something might turn up to make the clothing useful to her.

Weehawken had not shared in the tourist boom the Rogers notoriety brought to the Jersey shore. In all likelihood a good deal of the widow's regular trade had been siphoned off by Hoboken taverns. Her irritation at this doubled after she realized that the girl had gotten herself throttled practically on the doorstep of Nick Moore's House. The business possibilities of such a revelation occurred to her at once. As her sister must have argued, to contact the authorities would be a damn fool risk. After all, as things stood she was in the clear. What if they discovered that the Rogers girl was still alive on Sunday night? What if they discovered what had really happened?

But the lure of all that trade and traffic across her mahogany was too much for the greedy widow.

Frederica Loss was a skillful liar. She knew, as well as did Edgar Allan Poe himself, that the successful hoax must be built on a firm foundation of true, easily verifiable fact. She concocted her story around the actual events of that Sunday. There had been several young couples in the bar, and possibly one particular girl had specified lemonade. The episode of the bull had really happened, and her sons had actually found the clothing. The precision with which her

153

testimony details the position and condition of the apparel indicates long hours of questioning her boys. She wanted to take full advantage of every genuine fact she could muster. On this foundation of truth, she erected the most melodramatic tale of agonized suffering and stifled screaming she could devise, carefully arranging her story to suggest strongly the idea of a gang rape and murder, the theory prevalent in the press in early September. It was a masterful hoax, one which fooled even the master of hoaxes, Poe, and it is the single most important chunk of flimflam in this vast webwork of misunderstanding and deceit.

Business at the tavern thrived, but the risk was far greater than the widow supposed. Horrified, she found herself and her sons under suspicion not of abortion, but of murder. The marked discrepancies between her original story reported in the *Herald* and her subsequent interview in *Brother Jonathan* are now explained. In the latter she is hesitant, and equivocating. She can't be sure how many young people were actually of Mary's party, or whether Mary was even escorted by one specific boy. All the various screams and cries of the earlier version have been reduced to one scream, and although she twice passed within ten feet of the center of the thicket, "she heard no screams or struggles, and saw nothing unusual."

You will observe she has now cut down as near to the bare bone of truth as she dares. But she must stand by her hoax in growing terror, while Merritt doggedly tightens the noose around her and her sons. For Mrs. Loss the only alternative to being suspected of murder is being convicted of abortion. It is hardly surprising that she confided her regret at not burning the clothing because it would have "saved her trouble." It is hardly surprising that, lying on her deathbed while the police searched the fireplace for secret passages and her kindly physician shouted a dead name in her ear, Frederica Loss saw lingering above her head the ghost of Mary Rogers whose murder haunted so many guilty lives.

Gilbert Merritt was so certain of a fatal abortion in Nick Moore's House that many later investigators have felt themselves irresistibly compelled to accept his thesis. There is nothing equivocal in the surprisingly strong language of his affidavit in which he specifically stated that his convictions were based on "information he [had] obtained, and facts in his possession." That he did have such facts cannot be doubted. That he confided them, at least vaguely, to his brother Henry seems evident, for Henry must have been the source of the *Tribune*'s story of a confession. But the "information" was not a confession by Mrs. Loss, and the terse wording of Merritt's immediate denial indicates that relations between the brothers were probably strained for some time.

Certain conclusions are immediately reached:

(1) From the transcript of the hearing, it is clear that Merritt was positive that abortions were performed in the tavern in a room secreted behind the chimney.

(2) He was equally certain that Mary Rogers had been operated on Sunday, July 25, by a physician assisted by Mrs. Loss (since the wording of the affidavit indicates her as an accessory after the fact).

(3) He knew for a fact the exact amount paid for the operation.

All this he knew, *yet he did not take the stand against the Kellenbaracks*. Why? And what was the source of his information?

All investigators who have considered this part of the mystery have allowed themselves to be misled by the false *Tribune* report into believing that, whatever Merritt's information, he learned it at Nick Moore's House during Mrs. Loss' last days. Some have gone so far as to credit, at least in part, the confession story which the justice flatly denied.

Yet the widow was not his informant and who else at the tavern could have supplied him with such a specific fact as the amount of the fee? Only the sons, and the fact that a hearing was held proves conclusively that they did not crack.

Only one other man knew the price of the abortion, the man who paid for it. What prompted John Anderson to come forward seems clear. Terrified of scandal since his arrest, tortured by guilt over Mary's death, Anderson had hovered in the background for over a year in silence. The report of the widow's imminent death jolted him into action. He communicated what little he knew to Merritt. Anderson must have arranged for the abortion with the widow, for he knew where it was to be held and he knew of the secret room. His dealings must have been only with Mrs. Loss because he could not supply the name of a physician. Possibly she promised him a doctor in order to justify the price and then performed the operation herself. It would have been in character.

The facts indicate either that Anderson wrote anonymously to Merritt or that he contacted him personally but obtained a guarantee that his name would be kept out of the whole sordid mess. A knowledge of Anderson's character suggests the former but the point is academic. In either case Merritt would be positive he had solved the case and yet unable to testify at the hearing. All of the Justice's actions are now explained: his frantic attempts to wring a confession from the dying widow; his feverish (and apparently unsuccessful) searches for a secret room; his strongly phrased affidavit; his extraordinary promise of immunity to the Kellenbaracks; his refusal to testify; his grim committal to the theory of a fatal abortion.

Gilbert Merritt achieved part of the truth. His mistake was his conviction that Mary had died on Sunday night. It led him to the wrong solution, a solution he could not prove but to which he clung stubbornly for the rest of his life.

And another piece of the Rogers puzzle falls into place.

Who murdered Mary Rogers? We are now very close to the answer, but first it is necessary to deal with the strange mystery of the thicket and its clothing. Here we are faced with two seemingly contradictory facts: (1) Everything about the positioning of the items indicates they were planted. (2) The articles found were positively identified by Phoebe Rogers, Mrs. Hayes, and a girl friend as being part of the dead Mary's wardrobe, and Mrs. Loss immediately recognized the strips of the frock.

Poe's arguments on the first point are particularly telling. The placement of the items appears artificial. The evidence that they had lain in the thicket for a long period of time, that is, the effects of mildew, the rotting of the fabric, the presence of insects called cellar jackass: this is not at all proof that the clothes were there longer than twenty-four hours before they were found. But they were not discovered until a month after the crime and thus might have been planted a day or a week or more after the murder and have shown the same effects of long exposure to the weather. The strips supposedly torn from the frock by "thorns" are highly suspicious, one of them being ripped on all four sides from the interior of the dress and so doubled as to have a thorn three times through it. It is impossible to imagine how this phenomenon could occur accidentally during a struggle.

An additional circumstance may be offered to support the belief that the articles were planted. The account of the finding of Mary's body states that she was wearing a pair of fingerless gloves. All accounts of the discovery in the thicket agree that among the items was a pair of gloves. Only two researchers have ever noted this strange fact and both have presumed it to be an error, one dismissing it in a footnote with the statement: "The earlier report must have been mistaken or something more would have been made of this." This contention presupposes that anyone ever *noticed* the contradiction and, considering the track record of the investigators for noticing things, it is a pretty flimsy argument. Nor is it credible that Mary left her home in ninety-degree heat wearing two pairs of gloves. The source for the fact that there were gloves on the body is a story in the *Herald* by a reporter who claimed to have been an eyewitness. Either he was present or he received his information from eyewitnesses, but it is significant that every observation he made on the appearance of the corpse except the fact of gloves can be verified. He stated that her features were scarcely visible, that her bonnet was tied on her head, that her dress was badly torn, that her shoes were on her feet (a shoe was among the items given by Cook to Crommelin after the inquest), and that she wore no jewelry, an observation which would require him to pay particular attention to her hands. Further he embellishes the description by stating that "long watery fingers" were "peering out" from the gloved hands. It is impossible to believe that such a close examination of the hands could yield a mistaken report of gloves, especially as every other detail of his description is accurate.

That there were gloves in the thicket was so widely reported that it cannot be questioned, and the point is labored here because the existence of two pairs of gloves indicates two very important facts: (1) At least two of the items found in the thicket were taken from Mary's wardrobe after the murder, since she could not have carried them with her when she left her mother's house. (2) Therefore the person who planted the clothing must have been someone with access to Mary's house and her wardrobe.

As added proof of this, there is the intriguing question of the two strips from the dress. Unquestionably they were from the same frock in which the girl was murdered. Unquestionably they were placed in the thicket simultaneously with the other things, yet where did they come from? Had the killer been carrying this damning cloth around with him since the crime as a memento of the occasion? The idea is ridiculous, yet every part of the garment was in police custody *except one.* Dr. Cook had torn a strip from the skirt and included it among the items carried by Crommelin to Phoebe Rogers after the inquest. In all probability it was the strip used as a handle to carry the body, though it is not necessary to believe this. The fact is that such a strip was in existence at the Nassau Street house and was acquired at the same time as the gloves and other articles. Consider the two swatches found in the thicket, one torn on three sides from the hem, the other torn on all four sides from the interior of the skirt. The original strip had simply been ripped in half.

This point is also labored so that an even more important one may be made. For all these facts only one explanation is possible: Mary's clothing was placed in the thicket sub-sequent to her death by someone who had access to the Nassau Street house.

Why was the clothing planted? Only one explanation occurred to Merritt and to subsequent investigators: the intention was to divert attention to the thicket and away from the real murder site. Clearly this wouldn't have made sense even for Mrs. Loss and her sons who are most often accused of it, since they succeeded in drawing attention to themselves where none had before existed. But it doesn't make sense for any murderer, since it presupposes that the authorities were close to discovering the "real murder site" when in fact they could not even decide on which side of the river the crime had been committed.

A second, and ultimately inescapable conclusion exists: The killer, crazed with guilt, liquor-logged, perilously close to insanity, sought to direct the police, not away from, but *toward* the actual site of the crime.

For the man who murdered Mary Rogers was Daniel Payne.

———————◆●◆———————

First let's dispose of three obvious points. Payne has been protected for over a century by his airtight alibi for Sunday, the 25th. Since Mary was not killed until Tuesday, the 27th, the much discussed alibi is useless, and Daniel Payne was *by his own admission in sworn testimony present in Hoboken on Tuesday.* His opportunity to murder is established.

Second, we know from the evidence of Phoebe Rogers' colored servant woman that, on Saturday, the 24th, Mary and her mother had the last in a long series of arguments over her impending marriage to Payne, culminating in Phoebe's receiving her daughter's "positive promise" that the wedding would never take place. Given Payne's acknowledged intemperance and severe mental instability, as indicated by the opinions of others and by all his known actions, his response to Mary's rejection cannot fail to have been uncontrollably emotional and violent. His motive to murder is established.

Third, we know that Mary was pregnant, and the question of the identity of the father must be discussed. Certainly it was not Anderson or Mary would have gone to him directly. If he had had designs on her virtue there was plenty of opportunity while she boarded with him, and for a man so terrified of scandal, it was totally out of character, as it was for the pious and pompous Crommelin who had moved out of the boardinghouse in early June but had months earlier realized that his strong affection for Mary was not returned. The role of seducer simply doesn't suit Crommelin's personality: the self-consciously melodramatic bravado, the gallant farewell gesture to Mary of aid in time of need, the sanctimonious pose as her moral protector, the authoritarian attempt to control the family after her death. But the role of seducer fits Payne's personality like a glove.

Mary was the sort of girl men fight over. She had the love of the respectable and successful Alfred Crommelin. On August 17, 1841, the *Herald* reported that the young newspaperman, Canter, had been "severely beaten about a year ago, by three or four rivals, in consequence of visiting her." Yet, with her pick of eligible young men, in a move that amazed her mother and Crommelin, Mary chose a drunken and unstable wastrel. There was absolutely nothing about

160

Payne apparent to Crommelin and Phoebe to indicate Mary's reasons for her preference for the cork cutter. Obviously there must have been reasons which would not occur to an aged woman and a virtuous gentleman.

Mary and Payne lived in the same house, where the opportunities for secret meetings after lights-out must have been endless. There is not one shred of evidence to connect Mary intimately or otherwise with any other man in the months before her death. Sometime before the first of June, Mary decided she was "in love" with Payne, for their engagement was announced very early in that month. The circumstances are compelling.

These three points established, every known fact falls into place as the events leading up to and following the murder are reconstructed.

The decision that Mary must undergo an abortion was made on Thursday the 22nd or Friday the 23rd as indicated by the fact that Mary's first attempt to contact Crommelin was on Friday. The decision was made by Mary and Payne alone, possibly at Payne's insistence, certainly without Phoebe's knowledge. The old lady was aware that her daughter was trying to raise $50 but not of the real reason the money was needed, as will soon become evident.

By Saturday afternoon it was clear that Crommelin could not be reached and Mary turned to John Anderson for help. Many shady Broadway characters frequented the tobacco shop. If Anderson did not know how to arrange for an abortion, he knew someone who did. It remains an intriguing possibility that the contact was made with Frederica Loss through Madame Restell. Her establishment was nearby, she was known to have agents in Jersey, and both women were Prussian. The facts are not conclusive but it is an intriguing possibility.

Some explanation was necessary for Mary's disappearance, and a visit to Downing's was chosen as plausible. She would, of course, be absent longer than one day. Possibly she would not return before Tuesday. It was Payne's job to keep her mother pacified until that time. Under no circumstances were the police to be involved. There would be no repetition of 1838.

She told her mother nothing, leaving that to Payne. On Sunday morning she knocked on his door, conferred with him for a moment, and then left the house. It is significant that Payne's later affidavit concerning that Sunday contradicts itself solely in regard to his interview with Mary and his plans concerning her. He stated that she was going to Downing's, yet the Downings did not expect her and were not at home. He stated that he intended to wait for her return on the omnibus, yet the omnibusses did not run on Sundays, and at the time he promised to meet her he was actually in a bar. (Why stand out in a violent rainstorm when he knew perfectly well where she was? He could hardly have suspected that his story would undergo such careful scrutiny as it did.) He stated that when he last saw her "she appeared cheerful and lively as usual"—unlikely for a young girl who faced what Mary faced that day. As for the rest of his movements, no contradictions exist in his testimony, since every word he spoke was true and he produced an army of witnesses to prove it. "Lucky" Daniel Payne. He did not yet know he was going to commit murder. How could he have foreseen that he would have to provide an alibi for Sunday to clear himself of a murder he would not commit until Tuesday?

Payne did not inform Phoebe that Mary had "gone to Downing's" until nine o'clock Sunday evening. It is therefore not surprising that the old lady was sick with worry. All she knew was that on Saturday she had had a violent quarrel with Mary ending with her daughter's promise not to marry Payne. And now Mary was gone. At the same time that she confided in the servant concerning the quarrel, she spoke her fear that she would never see Mary alive again. This statement, which many have interpreted as a fear that the girl was murdered, is better understood as a dread that

162

Mary had committed suicide. In any case Phoebe, as yet, did not suspect the truth.

Reluctant to face Phoebe, Payne did not return to the boardinghouse for his noon meal. By three he'd regained his confidence and gone to Nassau Street, but Phoebe was not there. She had gone to her cousin, Mrs. Hayes. Payne took a nap.

At six Payne was having a drink at the Battery. Mrs. Hayes had returned to Nassau Street with Phoebe, and when Payne came in at nine, the two women at last learned that Mary was at Downing's. If Phoebe had known the truth, she would not have accepted this explanation. She would have told Mrs. Hayes, to whom she went for help and comfort, that her daughter was undergoing an abortion. That she did not is clear since Mrs. Hayes accepted Payne's explanation, checked her own home for Mary the next morning, and contacted Mrs. Downing to see if Mary was there.

Mrs. Hayes had left the boardinghouse before Payne went down to breakfast. She requested that he remain until her return, but the cork cutter, knowing what she would discover, left for work. At noon, when he came back for his "dinner," he found himself confronted with three nearly hysterical women and determined that, to calm them, he must fake a search for Mary. Of course the police must not be involved. Mrs. Hayes, with her memories of the unpleasant publicity in 1838, was probably easily convinced of that.

From Payne's own testimony of events on Monday, it is clear that, though the female relatives were seriously agitated, he, himself, was completely unruffled. His "search" on Monday was haphazard to say the least, conducted at two widely divergent parts of the city and consisting of nothing more than random questioning of strangers, a pattern repeated at Staten Island on Tuesday morning.

By noon on Tuesday, the fearful suspense must have become intolerable for the three women, particularly when we remember that a similar romantic crisis three years before had driven Mary to consider suicide. Back from Staten Island at noon, Payne knew he could not stall much longer. One of two things happened. Either he went to Jersey to discover what had delayed Mary or they had arranged a meeting in advance. On Tuesday afternoon he crossed the river to Weehawken.

From the great strain he had been under, our knowledge of his habits, the incredible violence of the crime he committed, and the fact that immediately after the murder he signed the Washington pledge of total abstinence, we may induce that he had been drinking.

He would not have shown his face at the tavern. He waited for her in the woods near an overgrown and little used path where their rendezvous would be unobserved.

And she broke their engagement.

After all he had endured for the last three days! After the lies and the deceit and the scheming! Perhaps, at first, he pleaded, but she was adamant. He became enraged, striking her repeatedly across the face until, stunned by the blows, she sank to the ground.

In view of what followed it is evident that, influenced by drink, anger, and bitter disappointment, Payne lost all control and became temporarily deranged. Seeing the thicket, he dragged her to its entrance, crawled inside, and pulled her in behind him by the heels. With cloth ripped from her petticoat, he covered her mouth and bound her wrists, but she was beginning to regain consciousness and to claw at the gag. In another moment she would be free to scream unless he stopped her. Forcing her back against the stones, Payne gripped her throat with his right hand and tightened his hold until her struggles subsided. Then he fell across her body. She was semiconscious and helpless against his fury, but as her mind slowly cleared, she renewed her efforts to loosen the gag and Payne, enraged at her continued resistance, tore off the gag and tightened it slowly around her neck.

164

With what horrible emotions did the murderer gradually return to his senses and realize the full implications of his crime? She lay before him, her body bruised by his violent hands, her fingers, in death, still reaching hopelessly for the strip of lace at her throat. A trickle of blood issued from her gaping lips. Perhaps as he bent over her, he cradled her gently in his arms, this girl he had loved and destroyed. He covered her and, taking her bonnet, he smoothed back her hair and tied the ribbons carefully in a slip knot so they would not come undone. No abortionist, no mere rapist, no gang would have ministered as tenderly to Mary's body as the grief-stricken lover. When he had finished, he ripped a strip of her skirt to the waist and arranged it as a handle. The cloth which had bound her hands he tied now around her neck loosely, also as a handle, for rigor mortis had already set in and carrying her would be difficult.

It was dark and the road was deserted. His most direct route back to his rowboat crossed two fences and, unable to lift her body over them, he took down the rails and then replaced them. Gaining the shore undetected, he lowered her into the boat and rowed to the middle of the river where, gently and noiselessly, he committed her body to the ebony waters.

For almost a week there had been a prevalence of north and northeast winds, producing a powerful current tending down the Hudson which struck Glass House Point on the New York shore and proceeded south to the area of the Sybil's Cave. In this current the corpse of Mary Rogers was carried to the spot where it was sighted on Wednesday.

And Payne? Now Mary was dead. Now faking continued searches would not suffice. He could not bring himself to go to the police, but there must be something done, some further step taken. An advertisement was placed in the *Sun*.

The small, compelling details of proof keep mounting. Payne's ad describes in minute detail every item of Mary's clothing: ". . . a white dress, black shawl, blue scarf, leghorn hat, light colored shoes and parasol light colored."

Payne's testimony was that he had seen Mary only briefly some sixty-five hours before he worded the ad. Either he had an excellent eye for women's clothes and a photographic memory, or his account was based on a much more recent observation than he admitted.

The sudden, terrible changes in Payne's demeanor frightened Phoebe Rogers. Living in the same house, he could not long have hidden them from her. On Wednesday morning he confessed that Mary had undergone an abortion. He must have, for nothing else, as will be seen, explains the strange subsequent behavior of the family. On Crommelin's arrival Payne left at once, telling Phoebe he was going to inquire at Bellevue, normal enough under the circumstances. But, knowing what he knew, the cork cutter avoided the hospital and wasted some time checking out an anonymous tip which he knew was false. He feared that he might have been seen with Mary in Jersey, a natural fear which drove him back across the river to make trembling inquiries which apparently reassured him, for he went back to his job until seven that evening.

After his first interview with Phoebe, Alfred Crommelin also ran down a false tip. But something about that first interview disturbed him. He went back to Nassau Street and wormed the truth out of the old lady. Rounding up Padley for moral support, he immediately crossed the Hudson.

Henry Mallin later testified that when he drew the corpse up on the bank the features were still discernible and identification possible; Richard Cook concurred in this but both viewed the body earlier than Crommelin. By the time the latter arrived, at least one and perhaps three hours later, the tropical heat and the action of clostridia, an omnipresent bacteria, had combined to cause a gas gangrene which blackened and destroyed the facial tissue and rendered recognition impossible. Cook's statement that Crommelin seemed to identify Mary at once is probably true. Crommelin expected the worst, but he required a careful examination of the body and its clothing to be sure.

The incomprehensible apathy of Mary's family during

the entire affair is now eminently comprehensible. Under no circumstances would they inform the police that she had arranged for an abortion. Any desire to avenge her death was vastly overshadowed by the terror of scandal. In effect they disowned the girl after her murder, refusing to pay for the funeral or permit her burial in the family plot. Aiding the authorities only when it could not be avoided, they evaded cooperation in the investigation religiously, this last largely at the insistence of Crommelin whose one central concern from the beginning was to protect Mary's memory. Observe his suspiciously emphatic testimony at the inquest on her high moral character and chastity. Observe his strict instructions to the women that they must not speak with the police but "must let the matter be for him." Observe his violent denunciation of Payne on the day following Mary's inquest and his demand that the cork cutter be removed from the city. His motives were predictably gallant; those of the family were far more selfish, but their intention was the same and they succeeded. The shameful secret was kept, and the magistrates never seriously considered the theory of a fatal abortion until over a year later when John Anderson at last communicated with Merritt.

On Wednesday evening, H. G. Luther brought the news which the family expected and Payne dreaded. Any idea of attending the inquest or viewing Mary again was unthinkable, though two weeks later the murderer would have to do so at the Dead House. The anguish of that sickening experience could only have increased the growing sense of grief and guilt which, like a demonic possession, was gaining control of his mind. Of course he could no longer board in Nassau Street, but the move to new quarters did not help. The Washington pledge he had taken he now broke, but there was no comfort left for him in the bottle. His health broke down. He drank continuously, abandoning his work. At last his diseased imagination gave external form to his guilty obsession, and he began to believe himself haunted by the ghost of the girl he had murdered.

Consider this desperate, demented soul, tormenting itself

167

in a kind of hell of which even Edgar Allan Poe could not have conceived. Concealed and imprisoned in the unspeakable secret he could not bear alone and dared not share; unable for a single moment to avert his loathing eyes from the ugly truth in his heart; longing to be punished and incapable of confession, Daniel Payne must have cursed and cursed the stupidity of the investigators. In God's name why did they not arrest him? Why did they search in New York and Hoboken when the crime had been done in Weehawken? Very well, he would help these officious idiots to the truth.

Payne returned to the Rogers house. Without the knowledge of the old lady, he took from Mary's room the kinds of articles which the girl had worn but which had not been found with the body, the articles he had had to destroy on the murder night because they could not be fastened to the corpse, the articles he had described for the *Sun*, a copy of which he perhaps now used for reference. There must be a shawl, a scarf, a parasol. The petticoat was a large garment and it was white. It must be placed prominently to attract attention. The strip of the dress was torn in half. Its pieces would be hung on thorns, though one was so stubborn that he had to fold it until the thorn penetrated it three times. The monogrammed handkerchief was a nice touch. If those fools couldn't see through this, there was no hope for them.

Only in the matter of the gloves did his memory play him false. He had forgotten the gloves in his description for the *Sun*, and he now included a pair with the rest of the apparel. In the thicket they would be found inside out as though forcibly pulled from Mary's hands. Poor Payne wasn't thinking very clearly. Of all the items of a woman's clothing likely to be removed by a rapist, gloves must rank a distant last.

What it cost him to go back to the murder scene may be imagined. When the stage had been carefully set in the thicket, he retraced his steps to the shore, taking down the fence rails again, this time leaving them on the ground. (It should be remembered that, although the Kellenbaracks found the rails down, the lessee of the property told *Brother*

Jonathan he had not noticed that fact in the month since the murder.)

The hoax concocted by Frederica Loss proved the fatal blow to Payne's hope of capture. Though her story established the thicket as the murder site, it also convinced the police that Mary had been killed on Sunday, a day for which Payne had already produced a flawless alibi. Here is the final, incredible irony at the end of this twisted trail of ironies. With sickening horror the murderer realizes that his painfully contrived scheme to implicate himself in the crime has actually resulted in completely exonerating him. Now Daniel Payne knew he had committed the perfect murder. And that knowledge destroyed what remained of his mind.

It is terrible to think that the guilt-crazed man might have quietly discussed the plans of his self-destruction with his only confidant, the ghost of his dead sweetheart. It must have seemed to him brilliantly conceived. He would take the poison at the place where he had murdered her and die where her body had been brought to the shore. An easy death could not cleanse his soul. The poison must be slow acting. For twenty-four hours he must continue to live, feeling the slow ebbing away of his life, knowing that each breath he drew might be his last.

Here I am on the very spot. May God forgive me....

On October 7, 1841, Daniel Payne crossed the Hudson for the last time. The ghost of Mary Cecilia Rogers was avenged.

Afterword

*Some random thoughts on rigor mortis, ghosts, land
swindles, abortion, and other subjects of general
interest.*

The conclusions of this book are rooted in facts which
were unknown to, ignored by, or misunderstood by earlier
investigators of the Rogers mystery. The central piece of
evidence was the presence of rigor mortis in the body on
Wednesday which led to the realization that Mary could not
have been killed before Tuesday. With this point established,
all doors swung suddenly open, all the contradictions and
deceits and guilty secrets stood revealed. I had not been able
to understand why Merritt remained so stubbornly convinced
of a fatal abortion when the medical evidence contradicted
this thesis, nor could I separate the truth from the fabrication
in Mrs. Loss' testimony, and her motives from beginning to
end appeared incomprehensible. The weird and sudden
change in the attitudes of Mary's family and Payne on
Wednesday; the former from great anxiety to apathy and
defensiveness, the latter from apparent unconcern to intense
guilt culminating in an insanely melodramatic suicide; all this
seemed impossible to explain. Also suspicious was the amaz-

ing suddenness with which Merritt accepted the abortion theory which he had not taken seriously before the widow's accident, coupled with his failure to testify at the hearing and the confusion over reports of a deathbed confession. Finally there was the baffling puzzle of the thicket and its contents. Obviously there had to be some logical pattern underlying this maze of paradoxes. The touchstone was the missing clue, the fact of rigor mortis.

This volume is intended as the final, authoritative word on the mystery of Mary Rogers. Of course it will undoubtedly prove to be nothing of the sort. It answers, I believe, the major questions outlined in the paragraph above, and the central question, the identity of the murderer, but it raises still more issues, some so tenuous that I have omitted them from the narrative, and yet so intriguing that they must be mentioned here, if only in the form of a footnote to the book.

For example, what was Poe's source for the abortion rumor? In the Appleton testimony John Anderson was quoted as saying that Poe would drop into his shop "to get the points" of the case. We know that Anderson believed that a fatal operation had been performed. Did he say as much to Poe, omitting his own part in the events of course, and was this contact between the two men the cause of later rumors that the tobacconist had bribed Poe to write a story which would divert suspicion from him?

Was there a connection between Madame Restell and Mrs. Loss, and was the abortion arranged through Restell? Restell ran a huge organization with agents in New Jersey. Her own headquarters were close to both Nassau Street and the tobacco shop. The arrangements were made quickly on Saturday, and it would have been both natural and logical for Anderson to go to her. She was notorious, but her reputation for discretion was excellent. The investigation into the murder was at times so clumsy and bungled that mere incompetence may perhaps be insufficient to explain it. Restell's influence was widely suspected of reaching high into New York officialdom. Is it possible that Madame Killer was even vaguely involved in the fate of Mary Rogers, and if so, might she have taken steps to assure the failure of the investigation, steps later nullified by the Weehawken widow's publicity stunt and Anderson's communications with Merritt?

If you are willing to swallow everything up to this point, let's make a few wild guesses. Did Anderson mention Restell to Poe? Was Poe the *Police Gazette*'s source for the article suggesting her possible guilt in Mary's death? Was he the actual author of the article? Did Restell discover this after a mob had laid siege to her house and endangered her life, and did she then contact him, perhaps threaten him? Was it to her or her representative that Poe wrote:

> *I am exceedingly anxious. If you would be so kind as to look me up, I will consider it a great favor. You understand the whole story is purely fiction.—*

It is all guesswork. It cannot be proven. But there are so many suggestive circumstances. . . .

———◆•◦•◆———

I include the following paragraph, although the evidence to support its central conjecture is so trifling as to be almost nonexistent, in the hope that some fanatic on Jerseyanna with more stamina than I have will feel himself inspired to run down the truth. Incorporated in 1838, the Hoboken Land and Improvement Company was, by 1841, easily the largest landowner in either Hoboken or Weehawken. (The two towns were not politically separated until 1859.) The Company's directors included nearly all of the richest and most influential men in the area, and they were capable of exerting tremendous political pressure. Their lands bordered on those of Frederica Loss; in fact they came close to surrounding her. Could it be that the Company had attempted to purchase her property and that for some reason the widow balked? The minutes of their directors' meetings, carefully taken with pen and ink in a beautiful hand, still exist in the care of the New Jersey Historical Society in Newark. They

173

contain no mention of the widow or Gilbert Merritt, but there are records of dealings with Richard Cook who worked closely with Merritt throughout the investigation. It is just barely possible that Merritt's zeal in pursuing Mrs. Loss before her death, and later her principal heirs, was caused, in part, by pressure from the directors to obtain convictions and thus pave the way for acquiring the widow's real estate. No tangible evidence exists for this speculation, but since the Company bears primary responsibility for turning Hoboken from a rustic "fairyland" into what it is today, it's not hard to imagine it capable of almost anything.

The curious role played in the Rogers affair by the press, and particularly by James Gordon Bennett, invites more attention than I have given it. The murder was a significant milestone in the history and evolution of New York journalism. For one thing, it was the first sensational story to be given wide coverage in *all* the city's dailies, and it proved conclusively to every editor from the muckraking Ben Day to the patrician William Cullen Bryant the circulation value of mayhem. The position of Bennett in all this is especially interesting. No less than Poe, the fiery journalist enjoyed striking the pose of detective (a trait which will not be knocked in these pages). But more than the pose or the lure of increased circulation motivated Bennett. The *Herald* was the first and loudest advocate of the gang-murder theory, a thesis based less on fact than on wishful thinking, for Bennett's chief purpose in playing up the story was to bring attention to the unchecked lawlessness on both sides of the Hudson and to call for badly needed reforms in the police force and the courts. True, this desire for reform seems to have had its source in a personal vendetta rather than a deep concern for the public welfare. The *Herald*'s first targets were Justices Lynch and Noah, both pork barrel appointees of a lame duck Whig administration, the latter an old and bitter enemy from the bloody days of the Holy Alliance. But as the case dragged on unsolved, Bennett increased and expanded his attacks, scattered his shots, and forced most of the newspapers in New York and New Jersey into the fray behind him. There is no doubt that the judiciary and police on both banks of the river were in desperate need of sweeping improvements. Several commentators on the Rogers case have expressed surprise that her death occasioned such great attention since cadavers were even then fished out of the Hudson almost daily. The answer lies in the fact that her murder coincided with Bennett's decision to go after Lynch and Noah. When the *Herald* began making Mary a cause célèbre, its rivals, having learned their lesson well in the Ellen Jewett uproar, tumbled over each other in their haste to join the battle.

Bennett had used the Jewett case to moralize on the widespread prostitution in the city, and, in fact, took the opportunity of Mary's 1838 "disappearance" to declaim against the employment of little girls in such immoral "holes" as tobacco shops. But the coverage of Mary's murder marks, to the best of my knowledge, the first time that a sensational story was used by an American newspaper as a pretext for pressing for specific governmental reform. And it is to James Gordon Bennett, the father of yellow journalism and inventor of the personal interview, that the lion's share of the credit must go.

———————◆–•◆•–◆———————

The aftermath of the Mary Rogers murder should prove a gold mine for any enterprising spiritualist. The dead girl's "ghost" appeared to at least three people, each of them intricately involved in her ultimate fate. Frederica Loss cried out against the shape of a woman which hovered over her death bed; though she never identified this ghost, it has been widely assumed to be the shade of Mary Rogers or, if you are one of the spoilsports who do not believe in the spirit world, the dying woman's mad delusion. The "ghost" also appeared to her murderer, Daniel Payne, and to the man who clearly blamed himself for her death, her friend and benefactor, John

Anderson. On the subject of spiritualism I am not well versed, but I am told that the ghosts of those who die a violent death are more likely to linger among the living. Did Mary return to exact vengeance?

A word is necessary concerning my belief in Poe's use of (not addiction to) opium. Several biographers, George E. Woodberry and Hervey Allen among them, assert Poe's use of the drug. Many others including Arthur Hobson Quinn and Edward Wagenknecht deny it. Hard evidence in favor of the theory is found in the testimony of four people who knew Poe well: William R. Wallace to whom Poe recited "The Raven" in New York in 1844; Poe's sister Rosalie whom the poet "begged for morphine" in 1846; John Sartain from whom Poe requested laudanum in 1849; and Elizabeth Herring, Poe's cousin, who recalled in 1894 that she had "had the misfortune to see him often in those sad conditions from the use of opium. . . . After recovery his penitence was genuine, but he made good resolutions only to be broken." Against the theory stands the statement of Thomas Dunn English, a physician and, by his own admission "a man of observation," who "saw no signs of" an "opium habit" in Poe, and dismissed the charge as "baseless slander." Wagenknecht considers "the most cogent testimony" against Poe's addiction is the fact that he took a less than lethal dose of laudanum in attempting suicide in Boston in 1848, implying that he could not "calculate a lethal dose," and therefore was not "familiar with the effects of the drug." This presupposes that Poe actually intended to take his life which I find problematical. The vast majority of attempted suicides are, in psychiatric jargon, merely "gestures." If Poe's attempt is seen as what it probably was, a "gesture," then his failure to take a fatal dose argues for, not against, his understanding of the drug and its effects.

Enough. As for the ghosts of Edgar Allan Poe and Mary Cecilia Rogers, I must now accord them the courtesy generally reserved for sleeping dogs.

APPENDIX I

The Cast of Characters

JOHN ANDERSON	the "seegar" merchant who employed Mary Rogers, and whose last years were haunted by her ghost.
JOHN CHARLES ANDERSON	who was suspected by his father of plotting to murder him.
MARY APPLEGATE	who paid a terrible price for her illegitimate child.
LAURA V. APPLETON	who sought to prove her father insane.
MOSES Y. BEACH	who edited the *New York Sun* in 1841.
PARK BENJAMIN	editor of the *New York Evening Signal* and leader of the "Holy Allies" against the *New York Herald*.
JAMES GORDON BENNETT	editor of the *New York Herald* who sought to prove Mary Rogers had been murdered by a street gang.
JOHN BERTRAM	who testified at Mary's inquest.

THOMAS BICKFORD	whose saloon Daniel Payne twice visited on the murder day.
EDWARD BOOKOUT	the errant apprentice who fingered his boss for the police.
JAMES M. BOULLARD	who helped to tow Mary's corpse to shore.
WILLIAM CULLEN BRYANT	editor of the *New York Evening Post*.
MR. CALLENDER	the police clerk who swore he had paid for Mary's funeral.
MARY MAUD CARR	who went to court to prove her loving grandpa was crazy.
DR. CLEMENTS	who was with Daniel Payne at his death.
MARIA "MUDDY" CLEMM	Edgar Allan Poe's mother-in-law.
DR. RICHARD F. COOK	who performed postmortems on Mary Rogers and Daniel Payne; who doubted that Payne was a suicide; who was convinced that Mary was the victim of a gang.
MADAME COSTELLO	a Hoboken abortionist suspected of Mary's murder.
ALFRED CROMMELIN	Mary's former suitor who identified her body and sought to dominate her family during the investigation.
BENJAMIN H. DAY	who founded the *New York Sun* and edited the *New York Evening Tattler* in 1841; who was certain that Mary was still alive.

178

MRS. DOWNING	Mary's cousin, whose home Mary was supposed to have visited on the "murder day."
MR. DOWNING	her husband, who may have represented the family at Mary's funeral.
GEORGE W. EVELETH	to whom Poe communicated the "solution" of the Rogers Mystery.
MR. FANSHAW	who thought he saw Mary being accosted by a gang of young punks.
JAMES FINNEGAN	a coachman rumored to be Mary's killer.
HENRY FREDERICKS	who heard the Kellenbaracks whisper of a "great secret."
DR. T. B. GAUTIER	who amused himself by shouting a dead girl's name in a dying woman's ear.
MR. GOSLIN	at whose restaurant Daniel Payne dined on the "murder day."
HORACE GREELEY	editor of the *New York Tribune* who published Mrs. Loss' "confession" of murder.
DR. SAMUEL GRISWOLD	who pronounced Daniel Payne dead.
MRS. HAYES	Mary's cousin, who comforted Phoebe Rogers during the investigation.
EDWARD B. HAYES	her son, who swore that Alfred Crommelin had forced the family's strange silence.
OFFICER HILLIKER	who tracked down Joseph Morse.
EDWARD HOPKINS	who, with James Lawrence, discovered Payne's broken phial of poison.

JOHN H. INGRAM	Poe's first biographer, who named the guilty "naval officer."
ELLEN JEWETT	the lovely "Queen of the Pave," cut down with an ax in 1836.
CHARLES KELLENBARACK	the son of Frederica Loss, who found Mary's clothing in the thicket and was later arrested for her murder.
OSCAR KELLENBARACK	charged with his brother for Mary's murder.
OSSIAN KELLENBARACK	who, with his brother Charles, discovered the clothing.
WILLIAM KUKICK	a mariner falsely accused of the murder.
JAMES LAWRENCE	who, with Edward Hopkins, discovered Payne's broken phial of poison.
RICHARD ADAMS LOCKE	author of the *Sun's* "Great Moon Hoax"; editor of the *New York New Era* in 1841, who thought Mary a suicide.
"DOCTOR" LOHMAN	a quack who trusted his wife a bit more than was wise or healthy.
FREDERICA LOSS	who swore Mary had visited her Weehawken tavern on the murder day.
JAMES LUDLOW SR.	a neighbor of Mrs. Loss, who had heard the talk of the "great secret."
NANCY LUDLOW	his wife, who was certain she had seen Mary on the "murder day."
H. G. LUTHER	who informed Daniel Payne and the family of Mary's death.

STEPHEN H. LUTKINS	the Jersey City justice who ordered the Kellenbaracks arrested.
HENRY LYNCH	a justice of the New York Criminal Court.
HENRY MALLIN	who discovered Mary's body but was not invited to testify at her inquest.
ABNER C. MATOON	to whom John Anderson described his meetings with Mary's ghost.
MR. McCADDEN	the undertaker who buried Mary.
FELIX McCLOSKEY	who thought John Anderson knew more about Mary than he would admit.
JAMES McSHANE	who found Daniel Payne asleep in the stinkweeds.
GILBERT MERRITT	Hoboken justice of the peace who conducted the inquests on Mary and Payne; who became convinced he had cracked the Rogers case.
ROBERT H. MORRIS	New York mayor who led the investigation after August 20, but refused to offer a reward.
JOSEPH W. MORSE	the engraver whose romantic escapades ended in a charge of murder.
MRS. JOSEPH W. MORSE	a lady who could forgive anything.
MORDECAI MANUEL NOAH	former editor of the *New York Evening Star* and a justice of the New York Criminal Court.
ARCHIBALD PADLEY	friend of Alfred Crommelin who confirmed the identi-

MILNE PARKER | fication of the body and was later arrested for the murder.
the shady New York judge who faced impeachment.

DANIEL PAYNE | Mary's fiancé who claimed to be the last person certain to have seen her alive, and who took his life on the site of her murder.

JOHN PAYNE | his brother, who supported his alibi and identified his body.

WILLIAM PENNINGTON | the governor of New Jersey who refused to offer a reward for Mary's killer.

EDGAR ALLAN POE | the eminent author who came to believe he had solved the Rogers murder.

ELIJAH PURDY | the New York alderman who, as acting mayor, was involved in the early investigation.

MADAME RESTELL | a lady who advocated an unorthodox method of birth control.

RICHARD ROBINSON | who was acquitted of Ellen Jewett's murder.

MARY CECILIA ROGERS | the Beautiful Seegar Girl foully murdered in Hoboken in 1841.

PHOEBE ROGERS | her aged mother, said to be too infirm to attend her daughter's funeral, and too poor to pay for it.

MR. SCUDDER | the Hoboken barkeeper who angrily and reluctantly gave a glass of water to a dying man.

182

WILLIAM SEWARD	the governor of New York who finally offered a reward for Mary's murderer.
PHILIP SPENCER	who swung from a yard-arm for mutiny.
WILLIAM A. SPENCER	his uncle, who became identified with Poe's "naval officer."
MR. SUMNER	the seaman whose love for Ellen Jewett led him to his death.
ROBERT TAYLOR	a New York justice, one of the major figures in the investigation.
MR. THOMAS	who thought he saw Mary being accosted by a gang of young punks.
ROSINA TOWNSEND	in whose "house" Ellen Jewett was murdered.
ADAM WALL	the stage driver who thought he had seen Mary with a swarthy man on the day of her death.
WILLIAM WALLER	who secured Mary's body to the shore and testified at her inquest.
JAMES WATSON WEBB	editor of the *New York Courier and Enquirer*.
JUDGE WESTON	who lobbed Ellen Jewett out into the snow.
ANDREW WHEELER	who thought John Anderson was as sane as he was.

APPENDIX II

❧❧❧

A Note on the Sources of This Volume

At the outset I must acknowledge the incalculable assistance I have received from the article entitled "Poe and the Mystery of Mary Rogers" by William Kurtz Wimsatt, Jr., of Yale University, published in March, 1941, in Vol. 56, No. 1, of the *Publication of the Modern Language Association of America*, pp. 230–248. Mr. Wimsatt's highly accurate and painstaking research of the press reports of the crime and later treatments of it has spared me months of effort, and earned both my gratitude and admiration.

Of the many accounts of the Rogers mystery three are worthy of comment:

> Edmund Pearson, "Mary Rogers and a Heroine of Fiction," *Vanity Fair*, XXXII, no. 5, pp. 59, 110 (July, 1929), and *Instigation of the Devil*. Charles Scribner's Sons, New York, 1930, pp. 177–185.

> Winthrop D. Lane, "The Mystery of Mary Rogers," *Collier's*, LXXXV, no. 10, pp. 19, 50, 52 (March 8, 1930).

> Russell Crouse, *Murder Won't Out*. Doubleday, Doran & Company, Inc., New York, 1932, pp. 52–74.

Pearson's article is brief and his research is sparse but sound; he tends somewhat reluctantly toward the abortion theory in which he is joined with what seems equal hesitation by Mr. Wimsatt. Lane's piece contains errors but is an honest attempt at factual reporting, and Crouse, while venturing no solution of the case, presents a thorough documentation of the principal events.

In preparation for this book, the author has read the following journals:

For October, 1838:
NEW YORK HERALD
NEW YORK JOURNAL OF COMMERCE
NEW YORK TIMES & COMMERCIAL INTELLIGENCER

For July 25, 1841, through December 31, 1841:
NEW YORK AMERICAN
BROTHER JONATHAN
NEW YORK COMMERCIAL ADVERTISER
NEW YORK COURIER & ENQUIRER
NEW YORK EVENING POST
NEW YORK EVENING TATTLER
NEW YORK HERALD
NEW YORK JOURNAL OF COMMERCE
NEW YORK STANDARD
NEW YORK SUN
NEW YORK TIMES & EVENING STAR
NEW YORK TRIBUNE

NEWARK DAILY ADVERTISER
JERSEY CITY ADVERTISER
PHILADELPHIA SATURDAY EVENING POST

For November through December, 1842:
The same as above.

Newspapers read in part for these periods:
NEW YORK EXPRESS
NEW YORK NEW ERA
NEW YORK NEWS
SUNDAY MERCURY

ALBANY ARGUS
BOSTON TRANSCRIPT

For October, 1885, and May through June, 1887:
NEW YORK HERALD
NEW YORK TIMES
NEW YORK TRIBUNE
NEW YORK WORLD

The material concerning Madame Restell may chiefly be found in Edward Van Every, *Sins of New York as "Exposed" by the*

Police Gazette (New York, 1930), pp. 95–104. For the testimony in the case of *Laura V. Appleton v. The New York Life Insurance Company and Frederick A. Hammond*, see two articles by Samuel Copp Worthen: "A Strange Aftermath of the Mystery of Marie Rogêt," *Proceedings of the New Jersey Historical Society*, LX, no. 123 (April, 1942), pp. 116–123; and "Poe and the Beautiful Cigar Girl," *American Literature*, XX (November, 1948), pp. 305–312. Mr. Worthen had access to the only copy of the minutes of the Appleton trial which had been preserved at the offices of the law firm of McLanahan, Merritt and Ingraham, successors of the firm which represented John Anderson's daughter. These minutes have since vanished, leaving Worthen as the only source of their content.

For the background on New York's newspapers and "The Holy War," I am primarily indebted to the following:

> Oliver Carlson, *The Man Who Made News: James Gordon Bennett*. Duell, Sloan & Pearce, Inc., New York, 1942, pp. 121–190.

> Frank M. O'Brien, *The Story of the Sun*. George H. Doran and Company, New York, 1918, pp. 64–163.

and to:

> William Harlan Hale, *Horace Greeley: Voice of the People*. Harper and Brothers, New York, 1950, pp. 63–90.

> Don C. Seitz, *The James Gordon Bennetts*. Bobbs Merrill Co., Indianapolis, 1928, pp. 38–101.

Frank O'Brien's book is also the major source for both the "Great Balloon Hoax" and the "Great Moon Hoax." Oliver Carlson (pp. 143–167) and Russell Crouse (pp. 27–51) furnish information on the Ellen Jewett murder.

For Poe biography I have relied principally on:

> Hervey Allen, *Israfel: The Life and Times of Edgar Allan Poe*. George H. Doran and Company, New York, 1934, 2 vols.

> Edward Wagenknecht, *Edgar Allan Poe: The Man Behind the Legend*. Oxford University Press, New York, 1963.

> John Ward Ostrom, ed., *The Letters of Edgar Allan Poe*. Harvard University Press, Cambridge, Mass., 1948, 2 vols.

For their assistance and courtesy I thank: The Newark Public Library • The New Jersey Historical Society, Newark • The New York Public Library • The New York Historical Society, New York City • The American Antiquarian Society, Worcester, Massachusetts • The Jersey City Public Library • The Princeton University Library • The Library of Stevens Institute of Technology, Hoboken (and particularly Dick Widdicombe.)

To attorney Paul Ross of Hackensack, New Jersey, an old friend, my appreciation for his advice on many legal aspects of the case; and for their help in evaluating the medical testimony my gratitude to Dr. Raymond Carnes of Saint Michael's Hospital, Newark; Dr. Hugo O. Gellman of Mountainside Hospital in Montclair, New Jersey, a patient gentleman; and especially to another old friend. Dr. Gordon Randolph Kelly of Rutland, Vermont.

APPENDIX III

Other Treatments of the Rogers Case

Among the many writers who have treated the Rogers case, only four, excepting Poe, have offered solutions. It is a tricky business, this criticism of authors who have posed as explicators of the mysterious murder by an author who is striking the same pose, but a complete history of the affair cannot ignore their arguments.

Writing in *Era Magazine* for November, 1904 (XIV, 450–463), Will M. Clemens proposed to prove that:

> The face of the corpse was *not* entirely destroyed, nor was the corpse frightfully disfigured.
>
> There was *no* stout cord about the waist, nor was there a heavy stone attached to the cord.
>
> There was *no* lace encircling the neck.
>
> The hands were *not* covered with light kid gloves.
>
> The exact spot of the murder was *not* the thicket in the woods.
>
> The dark-complexioned man seen with Mary Rogers *was not* the suspected young naval officer.
>
> Mary Rogers and the "tall, dark" man were at the roadhouse kept by Mrs. Loss on the afternoon of July 25. . . . They never left the house alive.
>
> Robbery was unquestionably the motive for the slaughter of Mary Rogers and the "tall, dark" man.
>
> Mrs. Loss was a mother of three worthless sons. She had lied to the coroner to save them; she had lied to the police to save them; she lied even upon her death-

bed to save those three profligate sons from a trial for murder. Could mother love do more?

Clemens supported these claims with evidence from "the yellow files of eight newspapers," and the recollections of a few Hoboken octogenarians. The newspapers are unnamed, save for the *Commercial Advertiser*, but they included issues of the *Herald*, the *Express*, the *Tribune* and the *New Era*. His solution is unique: that the Kellenbaracks robbed and murdered Mary and her escort and raped the girl on Sunday night and dumped both bodies into the Hudson on Wednesday before dawn. The theory seems first to have been suggested by his conversations with Jersey residents with whom the guilt of the boys was traditional, and he went to his research determined to verify their guilt. He was understandably confused, as several others have been, on the first two points he raises. Henry Mallin testified that severe decomposition had not taken place; Alfred Crommelin testified that it had, but the difference in the times when these men viewed the corpse easily accounts for this. Some early accounts of the finding of the body had falsely reported that the rope and rock were attached to it before it was drawn from the river, and thus presumably by the murderer, whereas this had actually been done after Mary was towed to shore. Clemens also noticed the two pairs of gloves but mistakenly interpreted this as proof that the corpse wore no gloves, rejecting the testimony of eyewitnesses, including a *Herald* reporter. He picked up the fact that Mary had promised to break her engagement but gave it no significance, and he credited the exploded rumor that the girl had been seen with a man on Sunday morning and the absurd evidence of Adam Wall.

All these are honest mistakes, but many of Clemens' "facts" are deliberate falsifications. Put simply, the gentleman was a liar and among his fabrications are the following:

> There was no lace encircling the neck. (His article indicates familiarity with Dr. Cook's testimony, yet he stuck to this assertion even though the lace did not interfere with his "solution.")
>
> Mrs. Loss testified at Mary's inquest, mentioning a gang who accompanied the girl to the tavern on Sunday, and later, after Wall had come forward, she changed her story to include his "tall, swarthy" man. (The widow did not enter the case until September,

189

never spoke of a gang, and her statement predated that of the stage driver.)

Mrs. Loss made a confession on her deathbed implicating her sons in abortion and murder in order to save them from a trial for robbery and murder. ("Could mother love do more?")

The body of a tall, swarthy man was "found floating near the foot of Barclay Street" in the Hudson, "badly decomposed" and clad in "a white shirt, silk vest, dark pantaloons, 'morocco' shoes and worsted hose," and this was the same who had been murdered in Weehawken.

On this last point, though he quoted the item, Clemens failed to identify the newspaper, but that relentless researcher William Wimsatt unearthed the original in the *Express* of August 4. A John Doe dressed in "morocco shoes, worsted hose, drab cloth pantaloons, white shirt and satin vest," was found on August 3, but he was neither tall nor swarthy and he was not in the Hudson, but "in the East River, at the foot of Catherine Street."

On behalf of Mr. Clemens, it should be said that he had contracted with *Era Magazine* for a series of articles entitled "Famous American Unsolved Murder Mysteries," and his publishers expected solutions on one ground or another, which is exactly what they got.

———————◆━◗◖━◆———————

Samuel Copp Worthen produced two essays on the minutes of the Laura Appleton trial. The first (*Proceedings of the New Jersey Historical Society*, LX, April, 1942) limited itself to an objective reporting of the pertinent testimony, but in the second (*American Literature*, XX, November, 1948) Worthen, while insisting that he would not "presume to offer at this late date any positive solution" of the crime, presumes to do precisely that. "Certain conclusions are irresistibly forced upon the mind of any unprejudiced reader of the testimony," says Worthen, and he lists the following:

> That the girl was the victim of an operation intended to bring about an abortion.
>
> That (if we are to credit such testimony) her patron, and former employer, John Anderson, admitted having been responsible for such an operation on a former occasion.

That when similar circumstances arose after she had left his employ, she appealed to him (as one of her friends and admirers best able financially to do so) to come again to her rescue.

That he gallantly responded by putting up the money and making the necessary arrangements.

That the tavern of Mrs. Loss was chosen as the scene of the projected event.

That the tall, dark man who escorted Mary to Hoboken was the abortionist employed.

That Mary died during or immediately after the operation, and that the abortionist, panic-stricken, got rid of her body.

It is wonderful the way that mythical swarthy man keeps popping up. He is a tribute to the conjuring skill, not so much of Poe as of his true inventor, Frederica Loss, and he stands as a monument to the wistful, childlike, romantic faith of Poe's critics in his claims. Once again he has become the mysterious abortionist and convinced a presumably otherwise sane and intelligent man that physicians about to perform illegal operations accompany their patients on public conveyances in broad daylight to the scenes of their crimes.

If there was one distinguishing feature of the man described by Adam Wall other than a dark complexion, it was his height; yet Mrs. Loss, in her testimony at Payne's inquest, stated that Mary's escort was "not so tall" as Payne. Since Payne was not above five foot seven, we may conclude that if Wall and the widow saw the same man, the poor little stage driver must have been a dwarf.

Worthen's only accurate assumptions concern the abortion on Sunday and Anderson's role in it. He accounts for the suicide of Payne in the same manner as every investigator who has bothered to account for it at all:

Payne left a note which read, "Here I am on the very spot. God forgive me for my misspent life."

This is a confession not of a deed but a failure to do something. No investigators in later times have regarded Payne as the guilty man. . . . The unhappy fate of the girl he had loved had of course preyed on his mind, and he may have felt remorse for what he thought a sin of omission, viz., his failure to marry her when he might have done so and thus saved her life and protected her good name. To an average, inexperienced young man, the situation must have been bewildering and distracting. The note he wrote before ending his life suggests this interpretation.

Payne could not, of course, have grieved over any "sin of omission," since the decision not to marry was Mary's, but what is really astounding is the universal reluctance of researchers to suspect Payne of the murder. When dealing with the Rogers' affair, it seems, scholars become hypnotized by Poe to such an extent that all laws of common sense are suspended or abandoned. Two facts have kept Payne from being suspected of either siring the child or of murdering his fiancée. One is the universal conviction that she was killed on Sunday. The other, flimsy but far more significant, is simply that in "The Mystery of Marie Rogêt," Poe absolved Payne of guilt.

Of John Walsh's *Poe the Detective* much has already been said. My own book was composed prior to the publication of Walsh's and I found little in his volume which had escaped my own research. Where I am indebted to Walsh that debt has been acknowledged.

In his chapter on "Marie Rogêt" in *The Fabulous Originals*, Irving Wallace, relying heavily, if not exclusively, on the secondary sources listed by Wimsatt, has "played the game" of detective by suggesting three possible solutions. He considers Alfred Crommelin the "most suspicious" of the "major suspects," declaring that Mary was his mistress at the time of her death and that he may have arranged the abortion of their child. Or Phoebe Rogers, having employed her daughter "for the pleasure of her guests," might herself have insisted on the fatal operation and then "disposed of the body with the aid of Crommelin or another."

His third alternative, and it was only a matter of time until someone suggested it, is that the killer was "one of the most illustrious names in literature," Edgar Allan Poe. Of course there is, Mr. Wallace admits, no "actual evidence" that Poe is the murderer, but then Wallace is merely "playing a game. . . ."

192

APPENDIX IV

❧❦❧

The Mystery of Marie Rogêt

Here, for the first time, is an edition of "The Mystery of Marie Rogêt" which incorporates both published versions of the story and indicates every addition and deletion of possible significance made by Poe in his 1845 revision. Annotations are included to set the tale clearly against the background of Poe's sources and the actual case, and to illuminate Poe's creative method.

✦▬•▶✦

The Mystery of Marie Rogêt[1]

A Sequel to "The Murders in the Rue Morgue"

Es giebt eine Reihe idealischer Begeben-
heiten, die der Wirklichkeit parallel lauft.
Selten fallen sie zusammen. Menschen und
zufalle modificiren gewohnlich die idealische
Begebenheit, so dass sie unvollkommen er-
scheint, und ihre Folgen gleichfalls unvollkommen sind. So bei der Reformation; statt des
Protestantismus kam das Lutherthum hervor.

There are ideal series of events which run
parallel with the real ones. They rarely coincide.
Men and circumstances generally modify the

[1] Upon the original publication of "Marie Rogêt," the
footnotes now appended were considered unnecessary, but
the lapse of several years since the tragedy upon which
the tale is based, renders it expedient to give them, and
also to say a few words in explanation of the general
design. A young girl, *Mary Cecilia Rogers*, was murdered
in the vicinity of New York; and, although her death
occasioned an intense and long-enduring excitement, the
mystery attending it had remained unsolved at the period
when the present paper was written and published (November, 1842). Herein, under pretence of relating the fate
of a Parisian *grisette*, the author has followed, in minute
detail, the essential, while merely paralleling the inessential facts of the real murder of Mary Rogers. Thus all
argument founded upon the fiction is applicable to the
truth: and the investigation of the truth was the object.
   The "Mystery of Marie Rogêt" was composed at a
distance from the scene of the atrocity, and with no other
means of investigation than the newspapers afforded. Thus
much escaped the writer of which he could have availed
himself had he been upon the spot, and visited the local-

ideal train of events, so that it seems imperfect, and its consequences are equally imperfect. Thus with the Reformation; instead of Protestantism came Lutheranism.—Novalis,[2] *Moral Anischten.*

There are few persons, even among the calmest thinkers, who have not occasionally been startled into a vague yet thrilling half-credence in the supernatural, by *coincidences* of so seemingly marvellous a character that, as *mere* coincidences, the intellect has been unable to receive them. Such sentiments—for the half-credences of which I speak have never the full force of *thought*—such sentiments are seldom thoroughly stifled unless by reference to the doctrine of chance, or as it is technically termed, the Calculus of Probabilities. Now this Calculus is, in its essence, purely mathematical; and thus we have the anomaly of the most rigidly exact in science applied to the shadow and spirituality of the most intangible in speculation.

The extraordinary details which I am now called upon to make public, will be found to form, as regards sequence of time, the primary branch of a series of scarcely intelligible *coincidences,* whose secondary or concluding branch will be recognized by all readers in the late murder of MARY CECILIA ROGERS, at New York.

When, in an article entitled "The Murders in the Rue Morgue,"[3] I endeavored, about a year ago, to depict

---

ities. It may not be improper to record, nevertheless, that the confessions of *two* persons, (one of them the Madame Deluc of the narrative) made, at the different periods, long subsequent to the publication, confirmed, in full, not only the general conclusion, but absolutely *all* the chief hypothetical details by which that conclusion was attained. [Poe's note. This, and all subsequent notes by Poe were appended only to the 1845 revision of the story.]

[2] The *nom de plume* of Von Hardenburg. [Poe's note.]

[3] In this story Poe literally invented the genre of detective fiction and virtually all of its most durable conventions including the locked room, the wrongly suspected man, and the surprise solution.

some very remarkable features in the mental character of my friend, the Chevalier C. Auguste Dupin, it did not occur to me that I should ever resume the subject.[4] This depicting of character constituted my design; and this design was thoroughly fulfilled in the wild train of circumstances brought to instance Dupin's idiosyncrasy. I might have adduced other examples, but I should have proven no more. Late events, however, in their surprising development, have startled me into some further details, which will carry with them the air of extorted confession. Hearing what I have lately heard, it would be strange should I remain silent in regard to what I both heard and saw so long ago.

Upon the winding up of the tragedy involved in the deaths of Madame L'Espanaye and her daughter, the Chevalier dismissed the affair at once from his attention, and relapsed into his old habits of moody reverie. Prone, at all times, to abstraction, I readily fell in with his humor; and continuing to occupy our chambers in the Faubourg Saint Germain, we gave the Future to the winds, and slumbered tranquilly in the Present, weaving the dull world around us into dreams.

But these dreams were not altogether uninterrupted. It may readily be supposed that the part played by my friend, in the drama at the Rue Morgue, had not failed of its impression upon the fancies of the Parisian police. With its emissaries, the name of Dupin had grown into a household word. The simple character of those inductions by which he had disentangled the mystery never having been explained even to the Prefect, or to any other individual than myself, of course it is not surprising that the affair was regarded as little less than miraculous, or that the Chevalier's analytical abilities acquired for him the credit of intuition. His frankness would have led him to disabuse every inquirer of such prejudice; but his indolent

[4] In Dupin, Poe established the archetypal hero of detective fiction, the brilliant, eccentric recluse whose investigations are chronicled by an admiring and ever baffled friend.

humor forbade all farther agitation of a topic whose interest to himself had long ceased. It thus happened that he found himself the cynosure of the political eyes; and the cases were not few in which attempt was made to engage his services at the Prefecture. One of the most remarkable instances was[5] that of the murder of a young girl named Marie Rogêt.

This event occurred about two years after the atrocity in the Rue Morgue. Marie, whose Christian and family name will at once arrest attention from their resemblance to those of the unfortunate "cigar-girl,"[6] was the only daughter of the widow Estelle Rogêt.[7] The father had died during the child's infancy, and from the period of his death, until within eighteen months before the assassination which forms the subject of our narrative, the mother and daughter had dwelt together in the Rue Pavée Sainte-Andrée;[8] Madame there keeping a *pension*,[9] assisted by Marie. Affairs went on thus until the latter had attained her twenty-second year,[10] when her great beauty attracted the notice of a perfumer, who occupied one of the shops in the basement of the Palais Royal, and whose custom lay chiefly among the desperate adventurers infesting the neighborhood.[11] Monsieur Le Blanc[12] was not unaware of the advantages to be derived from

[5] The original reads: "The only instance, nevertheless, in which such attempt proved successful, was the instance to which I have already alluded. . . ." Poe published a third Dupin story, "The Purloined Letter," in 1845.

[6] "seegar-girl" in the original.

[7] Phoebe Rogers.

[8] Nassau Street. [Poe's note.]

[9] boardinghouse.

[10] Mary was sixteen when she went to work for Anderson. Poe reverses the chronology of her occupations.

[11] Anderson's clientele were somewhat shady but hardly "desperate adventurers."

[12] Anderson. [Poe's note.]

the attendance of the fair Marie in his perfumery; and his liberal proposals were accepted eagerly by the girl, although with somewhat more of hesitation by Madame.

The anticipations of the shopkeeper were realized, and his rooms soon became notorious through the charms of the sprightly *grisette*. She had been in his employ about a year, when her admirers were thrown into confusion by her sudden disappearance from the shop. Monsieur Le Blanc was unable to account for her absence, and Madame Rogêt was distracted with anxiety and terror. The public papers immediately took up the theme, and the police were upon the point of making serious investigations, when, one fine morning, after the lapse of a week, Marie, in good health, but with a somewhat saddened air, made her re-appearance at her usual counter in the perfumery. All inquiry, except that of a private character, was of course immediately hushed. Monsieur Le Blanc professed total ignorance, as before. Marie, with Madame, replied to all questions, that the last week had been spent at the house of a relation in the country.[13] Thus the affair died away, and was generally forgotten; for the girl, ostensibly to relieve herself from the impertinence of curiousity, soon bade a final adieu to the perfumer, and sought the shelter of her mother's residence in the Rue Pavée Sainte-Andrée.

It was about five months[14] after this return home, that her friends were alarmed by her sudden disappearance for the second time. Three days elapsed, and nothing was heard of her. On the fourth her corpse was found floating in the Seine[15] near the shore which is opposite

---

[13] The story that Mary Rogers had been visiting relatives in Brooklyn first appeared on October 6, 1838, in the *Times*, the *Herald*, and the *Journal of Commerce*. Her alleged beau, Canter or Carter, wrote for the *Journal of Commerce*.

[14] Actually two years and nine months.

[15] The Hudson. [Poe's note.]

the Quartier of the Rue Sainte-Andrée, and at a point not very far distant from the secluded neighborhood of the Barrière du Roule.[16] The atrocity of this murder (for it was at once evident that murder had been committed), the youth and beauty of the victim, and, above all, her previous notoriety, conspired to produce intense excitement in the minds of the sensitive Parisians. I can call to mind no similar occurrence producing so general and so intense an effect. For several weeks, in the discussion of this one absorbing theme, even the momentous political topics of the day were forgotten. The Prefect made unusual exertions; and the powers of the whole Parisian police were, of course, tasked to the utmost extent.

Upon the first discovery of the corpse, it was not supposed that the murderer would be able to elude, for more than a very brief period, the inquisition which was immediately set on foot. It was not until the expiration of a week[17] that it was deemed necessary to offer a reward; and even then this reward was limited to a thousand francs.[18] In the meantime the investigation proceeded with vigor, if not always with judgment, and numerous individuals were examined to no purpose; while, owing to the continual absence of all clew to the mystery, the popular excitement greatly increased. At the end of the tenth day it was thought advisable to double the sum originally proposed;[19] and, at length, the second week having elapsed without leading to any discoveries, and the prejudice which always exists in Paris against the Police having given vent to itself in several serious *émeutes*,[20] the Prefect took it upon himself to offer the sum of twenty thousand francs "for the conviction of the assassin," or, if more than one should prove to have been implicated, "for the

[16] Weehawken. [Poe's note.]

[17] The first reward was offered on August 11, fourteeen days after Mary's body was discovered.

[18] The original amount was $300.

[19] By August 30 the reward had risen to $600.

[20] Riots. No riots occurred in New York or New Jersey.

conviction of any one of the assassins."[21] In the proclamation setting forth this reward, a full pardon was promised to any accomplice who should come forward in evidence against his fellow; and to the whole was appended, wherever it appeared, the private placard of a committee of citizens, offering ten thousand francs, in addition to the amount proposed by the Prefecture. The entire reward thus stood at no less than thirty thousand francs, which will be regarded as an extraordinary sum when we consider the humble condition of the girl, and the great frequency, in large cities, of such atrocities as the one described.

No one doubted now that the mystery of this murder would be immediately brought to light. But although, in one or two instances, arrests were made which promised elucidation, yet nothing was elicited which could implicate the parties suspected; and they were discharged forthwith. Strange as it may appear, the third week from the discovery of the body had passed, and passed without any light being thrown upon the subject, before even a rumor of the events which had so agitated the public mind reached the ears of Dupin and myself. Engaged in researches which had absorbed our whole attention, it had been nearly a month since either of us had gone abroad, or received a visitor, or more than glanced at the leading political articles in one of the daily papers. The first intelligence of the murder was brought to us by G——, in person.[22] He called upon us early in the afternoon of the thirteenth of July, 18—, and remained with us until late in the night. He had been piqued by the failure of all his endeavors to ferret out the assassins. His reputation—so he said with a peculiarly Parisian air—was at stake. Even his honor was concerned. The eyes of the public were upon him; and there was really no sacrifice which he

[21] On September 2, New York Governor William Seward offered $750, bringing the total reward to $1,350.

[22] The Prefect G——, born in "The Murders in The Rue Morgue," is the prototype of the plodding police-man, the inevitable foil of the dilettante detective.

would not be willing to make for the development of the mystery. He concluded a somewhat droll speech with a compliment upon what he was pleased to term the *tact* of Dupin, and made him a direct and certainly a liberal proposition, the precise nature of which I do not feel myself at liberty to disclose, but which has no bearing upon the proper subject of my narrative.

The compliment my friend rebutted as best he could, but the proposition he accepted at once, although its advantages were altogether provisional. This point being settled, the Prefect broke forth at once into explanations of his own views, interspersing them with long comments upon the evidence; of which latter we were not yet in possession. He discoursed much, and beyond doubt, learnedly; while I hazarded an occasional suggestion as the night wore drowsily away. Dupin, sitting steadily in his accustomed armchair, was the embodiment of respectful attention, He wore spectacles, during the whole interview; and an occasional glance beneath their green glasses, sufficed to convince me that he slept not the less soundly, because silently, throughout the seven or eight leaden-footed hours which immediately preceded the departure of the Prefect.

In the morning, I procured, at the Prefecture, a full report of all the evidence elicited, and, at the various newspaper offices, a copy of every paper in which, from first to last, had been published any decisive information in regard to this sad affair. Freed from all that was positively disproved, this mass of information stood thus:

Marie Rogêt left the residence of her mother, in the Rue Pavée Sainte-Andrée about nine o'clock in the morning of Sunday, June the twenty-second, 18—.[23]

---

[23] Mary left at ten A.M. on Sunday, July 25, 1841. Wimsatt observes "The sequence of dates which Poe uses for his story . . . running from June 22 as the day of the murder to July 13, the day when the Prefect calls on Dupin (and including June 31!) is not commensurate with the actual sequence. . . ."

In going out, she gave notice to a Monsieur des Jacques Saint-Eustache,[24] and to him only of her intention to spend the day with an aunt who resided in the Rue des Drômes.[25] The Rue des Drômes is a short and narrow but populous thoroughfare, not far from the banks of the river, and at a distance of some two miles, in the most direct course possible, from the *pension* of Madame Rogêt. St. Eustache was the accepted suitor of Marie, and lodged, as well as took his meals, at the *pension*. He was to have gone for his betrothed at dusk, and to have escorted her home. In the afternoon, however, it came on to rain heavily; and, supposing that she would remain all night at her aunt's (as she had done under similar circumstances before), he did not think it necessary to keep his promise.[26] As night drew on, Madame Rogêt (who was an infirm old lady, seventy years of age) was heard to express a fear "that she should never see Marie again"; but this observation attracted little attention at the time.[27]

On Monday it was ascertained that the girl had not been to the Rue des Drômes; and when the day elapsed without tidings of her, a tardy search was instituted at several points in the city and its environs. It was not, however, until the fourth day from the period of her disappearance that anything satisfactory was ascertained respecting her. On this day (Wednesday, the twenty-fifth of June) a Monsieur Beauvais,[28] who, with a friend, had been making inquiries for Marie near the Barrière du Roule, on the shore of the Seine

[24] Payne. [Poe's note.]

[25] Jane Street.

[26] This passage indicates Poe had read Payne's deposition, probably in the *Commercial Advertiser*, Aug. 12, p. 2, col. 3; or (condensed) in *Brother Jonathan*, Aug. 14, p. 3, col. 6.

[27] Mrs. Rogers' "fear" for her daughter was reported in the *Evening Post*, Aug. 16, p. 2, col. 2. Poe's probable source was *Brother Jonathan*, Aug. 28, p. 2, col. 8.
[28] Crommelin. [Poe's note.]

which is opposite the Rue Pavée Sainte-Andrée, was informed that a corpse had just been towed ashore by some fishermen, who had found it floating in the river. Upon seeing the body, Beauvais, after some hesitation, identified it as that of the perfumery girl. His friend recognized it more promptly.[29]

The face was suffused with dark blood, some of which issued from the mouth. No foam was seen, as in the case of the merely drowned. There was no discoloration in the cellular tissue. About the throat were bruises and impressions of fingers. The arms were bent over on the chest and were rigid. The right hand was clenched; the left partially open. On the left wrist were two circular excoriations, apparently the effect of ropes, or of a rope in more than one volution. A part of the right wrist, also, was much chafed, as well as the back throughout its extent, but more especially at the shoulder-blades. In bringing the body to the shore the fishermen had attached to it a rope, but none of the excoriations had been effected by this. The flesh of the neck was much swollen. There were no cuts apparent, or bruises which appeared the effect of blows. A piece of lace was found tied so tightly around the neck as to be hidden from sight; it was completely buried in the flesh, and was fastened by a knot which lay just under the left ear. This alone would have sufficed to produce death. The medical testimony spoke confidently of the virtuous character of the deceased. She had been subjected, it said, to brutal violence. The corpse was in such condition when found, that there could have been no difficulty in its recognition by friends.[30]

[29] There was considerable dispute over the speed and care with which Crommelin's identification was made. Poe's source for the idea that Archibald Padley recognized the corpse "more promptly" is unknown.

[30] This paragraph and the next are paraphrased from Dr. Richard Cook's testimony as reported in the *Herald*, Aug. 17, p. 1, col. 4; reprinted in *Brother Jonathan*, Aug. 21, p. 2, cols. 5–6.

The dress was much torn and otherwise disordered. In the outer garment, a slip, about a foot wide, had been torn upward from the bottom hem to the waist, but not torn off. It was wound three times around the waist, and secured by a sort of hitch in the back. The dress immediately beneath the frock was of fine muslin; and from this a slip eighteen inches wide had been torn entirely out—torn very evenly and with great care. It was found around her neck, fitting loosely, and secured with a hard knot. Over this muslin slip and the slip of lace the strings of a bonnet were attached, the bonnet being appended. The knot by which the strings of the bonnet were fastened, was not a lady's, but a slip or sailor's knot.

After the recognition of the corpse, it was not, as usual, taken to the Morgue (this formality being superfluous), but hastily interred not far from the spot at which it was brought ashore. Through the exertions of Beauvais, the matter was industriously hushed up, as far as possible; and several days had elapsed before any public emotion resulted. A weekly paper,[31] however, at length took up the theme; the corpse was disinterred, and a re-examination instituted; but nothing was elicited beyond what has been already noted. The clothes, however, were now submitted to the mother and friends of the deceased, and fully identified as those worn by the girl upon leaving home.[32]

Meantime, the excitement increased hourly. Several individuals were arrested and discharged. St. Eustache fell especially under suspicion; and he failed, at first,

[31] The New York *Mercury*. [Poe's note.]
Poe credits the *Mercury* as the first to report the murder probably on the authority of the *Evening Tattler* of August 23. Actually the "honor" belongs to the July 29 edition of the *Sun*.

[32] The exhumation, second autopsy, and identification of the clothes on August 11–12 was widely reported. Poe's source was perhaps the *Commercial Advertiser*, Aug. 12, p. 2, col. 3; Aug. 13, p. 2, col. 2.

to give an intelligible account of his whereabouts during the Sunday on which Marie left home. Subsequently, however, he submitted to Monsieur G——, affidavits accounting satisfactorily for every hour of the day in question.[33] As time passed and no discovery ensued, a thousand contradictory rumors were circulated, and journalists busied themselves in *suggestions*. Among these, the one which attracted the most notice was the idea that Marie Rogêt still lived—that the corpse found in the Seine was that of some other unfortunate.[34] It will be proper that I submit to the reader some passages which embody the suggestion alluded to. These passages are *literal* translations from *L'Etoile*,[35] a paper conducted, in general, with much ability.

"Mademoiselle Rogêt left her mother's house on Sunday morning, June the twenty-second, 18—, with the ostensible purpose of going to see her aunt, or some other connection, in the Rue des Drômes. From that hour, nobody is proved to have seen her. There is no trace or tidings of her at all. * * * There has been no person, whatever, come forward, so far, who saw her at all, on that day, after she left her mother's door. * * * Now, though we have no evidence that Marie Rogêt was in the land of the living after nine o'clock on Sunday, June the twenty-second, we have proof that, up to that hour, she was alive. On Wednesday noon, at twelve, a female body was discovered afloat on the shore of the Barrière du Roule. This was, even if we presume that Marie Rogêt was thrown into the river within three hours after she

[33] The attack on Payne was launched in the August 12 *New York Times and Evening Star*. On the 17th the same paper, having read the affidavits, announced Payne stood "exonerated from even a shadow of suspicion."

[34] This theory was first advanced by the *Evening Tattler*, Aug. 23, p. 2, cols. 1 and 2.

[35] The New York *Brother Jonathan*, edited by H. Hastings Weld, Esq. [Poe's note.]
This paper was the Sunday organ of Benjamin Day's *Evening Tattler*.

left her mother's house, only three days from the time she left her home—three days to an hour. But it is folly to suppose that the murder, if murder was committed on her body, could have been consummated soon enough to have enabled her murderers to throw the body into the river before midnight. Those who are guilty of such horrid crimes choose darkness rather than light. * * * Thus we see that if the body found in the river *was* that of Marie Rogêt, it could only have been in the water two and a half days, or three at the outside. All experience has shown that drowned bodies, or bodies thrown into the water immediately after death by violence, require from six to ten days for sufficient decomposition to take place to bring them to the top of the water. Even where a cannon is fired over a corpse, and it rises before at least five or six days' immersion, it sinks again, if let alone. Now, we ask, what was there in this case to cause a departure from the ordinary course of nature? * * * If the body had been kept in its mangled state on shore until Tuesday night, some trace would be found on shore of the murderers. It is a doubtful point, also, whether the body would be so soon afloat, even were it thrown in after having been dead two days. And, furthermore, it is exceedingly improbable that any villains who had committed such a murder as is here supposed, would have thrown the body in without weight to sink it, when such a precaution could have so easily been taken."

The editor here proceeds to argue that the body must have been in the water "not three days merely, but, at least, five times three days," because it was so far decomposed that Beauvais had great difficulty in recognizing it. This latter point, however, was fully disproved.[36] I continue the translation:

"What, then, are the facts on which M. Beauvais says that he has no doubt the body was that of Marie

[36] The point was never disproved although several papers reported falsely that it had been.

Rogêt? He ripped up the gown sleeve, and says he found marks which satisfied him of the identity. The public generally supposed those marks to have consisted of some description of scars. He rubbed the arm and found *hair* upon it—something as indefinite, we think, as can readily be imagined—as little conclusive as finding an arm in the sleeve. M. Beauvais did not return that night, but sent word to Madame Rogêt, at seven o'clock, on Wednesday evening, that an investigation was still in progress respecting her daughter. If we allow that Madame Rogêt, from her age and grief, could not go over (which is allowing a great deal), there certainly must have been some one who would have thought it worth while to go over and attend the investigation, if they thought the body was that of Marie. Nobody went over. There was nothing said or heard about the matter in the Rue Pavée Sainte-Andrée, that reached even the occupants of the same building. M. St. Eustache, the lover and intended husband of Marie, who boarded in her mother's house, deposes that he did not hear of the discovery of the body of his intended until the next morning, when M. Beauvais came into his chamber and told him of it. For an item of news like this, it strikes us it was very coolly received."[37]

In this way the journal endeavored to create the impression of an apathy on the part of the relatives of Marie, inconsistent with the supposition that these relatives believed the corpse to be hers. Its insinuations amount to this: that Marie, with the connivance of her friends, had absented herself from the city for reasons involving a charge against her chastity; and that these friends, upon the discovery of a corpse in the Seine, somewhat resembling that of the girl, had availed themselves of the opportunity to impress the public with the belief of her death. But *L'Etoile* was again over-hasty. It was distinctly proved that no

[37] These *"literal* translations from *L'Etoile"* are taken, almost verbatim, from the *Evening Tattler*, Aug. 23, p. 2, cols. 1 and 2.

apathy, such as was imagined, existed; that the old lady was exceedingly feeble, and so agitated as to be unable to attend to any duty;[38] that St. Eustache, so far from receiving the news coolly, was distracted with grief, and bore himself so frantically, that M. Beauvais prevailed upon a friend and relative to take charge of him, and prevent his attending the examination at the disinterment.[39] Moreover, although it was stated by *L'Etoile*, that the corpse was re-interred at the public expense—that an advantageous offer of private sepulture was absolutely declined by the family, and that no member of the family attended the ceremonial;—although, I say, all this was asserted by *L'Etoile* in furtherance of the impression it designed to convey—yet *all* this was satisfactorily disproved.[40] In a subsequent number of the paper, an attempt was made to throw suspicion upon Beauvais himself. The editor says:

"Now, then, a change comes over the matter. We are told that, on one occasion, while a Madame B——[41] was at Madame Rogêt's house, M. Beauvais, who was going out, told her that a *gendarme* was expected there, and that she, Madame B——, must not say anything to the *gendarme* until he returned, but let the matter be for him. * * * In the present posture of affairs, M. Beauvais appears to have the whole matter locked up in his head. A single step cannot be taken without M. Beauvais; for, go which way you will,

[38] Poe's source here was very possibly the August 19 *Tribune* which excused Phoebe's failure to attend the funeral or inquest on grounds of her "grief and age." Her daughter's death, said the *Tribune*, "drives the iron deep into her soul."

[39] Payne did attend the examination at the Dead House. Crommelin, in urging John Payne to get his brother out of New York, labeled the cork cutter a "madman."

[40] Mary was buried at public expense. According to Crommelin's letter of August 26 to the *Evening Tattler* only one unidentified man attended the funeral.

[41] Mrs. Hayes.

you run against him. * * * For some reason, he determined that nobody shall have anything to do with the proceedings but himself, and he has elbowed the male relatives out of the way, according to their representations, in a very singular manner. He seems to have been very much averse to permitting the relatives to see the body.[42]

By the following fact, some color was given to the suspicion thus thrown upon Beauvais. A visitor at his office, a few days prior to the girl's disappearance, and during the absence of its occupant, had observed a *rose* in the keyhole of the door, and the name *"Marie"* inscribed upon a slate which hung near at hand.

The general impression, so far as we were enabled to glean it from the newspapers, seemed to be, that Marie had been the victim of *a gang* of desperadoes— that by these she had been borne across the river, maltreated and murdered. *Le Commerciel,*[43] however, a print of extensive influence, was earnest in combating this popular idea. I quote a passage or two from its columns:

"We are persuaded that pursuit has hitherto been on a false scent, so far as it has been directed to the Barrière du Roule. It is impossible that a person so well known to thousands as this young woman was, should have passed three blocks without some one having seen her; and any one who saw her would have remembered it, for she interested all who knew her. It was when the streets were full of people, when she went out. * * * It is impossible that she could have gone to the Barrière du Roule, or to the Rue des Dromês, without being recognized by a dozen persons; yet no one has come forward who saw her outside her mother's door, and there is no evidence, except the testimony concerning her *expressed intentions*, that

[42] Quoted from the *Evening Tattler*, Aug. 25, p. 2, col. 2. Poe's source for all above articles from the *Tattler* was their reprint in *Brother Jonathan*, Aug. 28.

[43] New York *Journal of Commerce*. [Poe's note.]

she did go out at all. Her gown was torn, bound round her, and tied; and by that the body was carried as a bundle. If the murder had been committed at the Barrière du Roule, there would have been no necessity for any such arrangement. The fact that the body was found floating near the Barrière, is no proof as to where it was thrown into the water. * * * A piece of one of the unfortunate girl's petticoats, two feet long and one foot wide, was torn out and tied under her chin around the back of her head, probably to prevent screams. This was done by fellows who had no pocket-handkerchiefs."[44]

A day or two before the Prefect called upon us, however, some important information reached the police which seemed to overthrow, at least, the chief portion of *Le Commerciel*'s argument. Two small boys, sons of a Madame Deluc,[45] while roaming among the woods near the Barrière du Roule, chanced to penetrate a close thicket, within which were three or four large stones, forming a kind of seat with a back and footstool. On the upper stone lay a white petticoat; on the second, a silk scarf. A parasol, gloves, and a pocket-handkerchief were also here found. The handkerchief bore the name "Marie Rogêt." Fragments of dress were discovered on the brambles around. The earth was trampled, the bushes were broken, and there was every evidence of a struggle. Between the thicket and the river, the fences were found taken down, and the ground bore evidence of some heavy burthen having been dragged along it.[46]

[44] Quoted from the *Journal of Commerce* of August 23, p. 2, col. 1.

[45] Mrs. Loss.

[46] Poe's source is the *Herald*, Sept. 17, p. 2, cols. 3 and 4. He probably read not the original but its reprint in either the *Saturday Evening Post*, Sept. 25, p. 2, col. 3; or *Brother Jonathan*, Sept. 25, p. 2, col. 7. The former is more likely since Poe seems ignorant of another article in the Sept. 25 *Brother Jonathan*. (See note 49.)

A weekly paper, *Le Soleil*,[47] had the following comments upon this discovery—comments which merely echoed the sentiment of the whole Parisian press: "The things had all evidently been there at least three or four weeks; they were all mildewed down hard with the action of the rain, and stuck together from mildew. The grass had grown around and over some of them. The silk on the parasol was strong, but the threads of it were run together within. The upper part, where it had been doubled and folded, was all mildewed and rotten, and tore on its being opened. * * * The pieces of her frock torn out by the bushes were about three inches wide and six inches long. One part was the hem of the frock, and it had been mended; the other piece was part of the skirt, not the hem. They looked like strips torn off, and were on the thorn bush, about a foot from the ground. * * * There can be no doubt, therefore, that the spot of this appalling outrage has been discovered."[48]

Consequent upon this discovery, new evidence appeared. Madame Deluc testified that she keeps a roadside inn not far from the bank of the river, opposite the Barrière du Roule. The neighborhood is secluded—particularly so. It is the usual Sunday resort of blackguards from the city, who cross the river in boats. About three o'clock, in the afternoon of the Sunday in question, a young girl arrived at the inn, accompanied by a young man of dark complexion. The two remained here for some time. On their departure, they took the road to some thick woods in the vicinity. Madame Deluc's attention was called to the dress worn by the girl, on account of its resemblance to one worn by a deceased relative. A scarf was particularly noticed. Soon after the departure of the couple, a gang

[47] Philadelphia *Saturday Evening Post*, edited by C. I. Peterson, Esq. [Poe's note.]

[48] Quoted from the *Herald* of September 17, reprinted in the September 25 *Brother Jonathan* and *Saturday Evening Post*. (See note 46.)

of miscreants made their appearance, behaved boisterously, ate and drank without making payment, followed in the route of the young man and girl, returned to the inn about dusk, and recrossed the river as if in great haste.

It was soon after dark, upon this same evening, that Madame Deluc, as well as her eldest son, heard the screams of a female in the vicinity of the inn. The screams were violent but brief. Madame D. recognized not only the scarf which was found in the thicket, but the dress which was discovered upon the corpse. An omnibus driver, Valence,[49] now also testified that he saw Marie Rogêt cross a ferry on the Seine, on the Sunday in question, in company with a young man of dark complexion. He, Valence, knew Marie, and could not be mistaken in her identity. The articles found in the thicket were fully identified by the relatives of Marie.[50]

The items of evidence and information thus collected by myself, from the newspapers, at the suggestion of Dupin, embraced only one more point—but this was a point of seemingly vast consequence. It appears that, immediately[51] after the discovery of the clothes as above described, the lifeless, or nearly lifeless body of St. Eustache, Marie's betrothed, was found in the vicinity of what all now supposed the scene of the

---

[49] Adam. [Poe's note.]
The driver's real name was Adam Wall. The *Herald* identified him as Adam——. *Brother Jonathan* (Sept. 25) gave his full name. Poe's ignorance on this seemingly minor point is important because it suggests he missed the article which cast serious doubts on the Loss and Wall testimony, which appeared, so far as I can learn, only in that edition of *Brother Jonathan*.

[50] Poe's original source for this and the preceding paragraph is again the *Herald* of September 17. The *Herald's* report of a suspicious "gang of miscreants" is mistakenly attributed by Poe to Mrs. Loss herself.

[51] Forty-five days elapsed between discovery of the thicket and Payne's death.

outrage. A phial labelled "laudanum," and emptied, was found near him. His breath gave evidence of the poison. He died without speaking. Upon his person was found a letter, briefly stating his love for Marie, with his design of self-destruction.[52]

"I need scarcely tell you," said Dupin, as he finished the perusal of my notes, "that this is a far more intricate case than that of the Rue Morgue; from which it differs in one important respect. This is an *ordinary*, although an atrocious, instance of crime. There is nothing peculiarly *outré* about it. You will observe that, for this reason, the mystery has been considered easy, when, for this reason, it should have been considered difficult, of solution.[53] Thus, at first, it was thought unnecessary to offer a reward. The myrmidons of G—— were able at once to comprehend how and why such an atrocity *might have been* committed. They could picture to their imaginations a mode—many modes—and a motive—many motives;[54] and because it was not impossible that either of these numerous modes and motives *could* have been the actual one, they have taken it for granted that one of them *must*. But the ease with which these variable fancies were entertained, and the very plausibility which each assumed, should have been understood as indicative rather of the difficulties than of the facilities which each assumed, should have been understood as that it is by prominences above the plane of the ordinary, that reason feels her way, if at all, in her

[52] Payne's suicide note read: "Here I am on the very spot. May God forgive me my misspent life."

[53] Poe here restates what has become a basic premise of detective fiction: the weirder the crime, the easier its solution. In "The Murders in the Rue Morgue" Dupin had said, "It appears to me that this mystery is considered insoluble for the very reason which should cause it to be regarded as easy of solution—I mean for the *outré* character of its features . . ."

[54] In the locked-room mystery of "Rue Morgue," the police could imagine neither mode nor motive.

search for the true, and that the proper question in cases such as this, is not so much 'what has occurred?' as 'what has occurred that has never occurred before?' In the investigations at the house of Madame L'Espanaye,[55] the agents of G—— were discouraged and confounded by that very *unusualness* which, to a properly regulated intellect, would have afforded the surest[56] omen of success; while this same intellect might have been plunged in despair at the ordinary[57] character of all that met the eye in the case of the perfumery-girl, and yet told of nothing but easy triumph to the functionaries of the Prefecture.

"In the case of Madame L'Espanaye and her daughter, there was even at the beginning of our investigation, no doubt that murder had been committed. The idea of suicide was excluded at once. Here, too, we are freed, at the commencement, from all supposition of self-murder.[58] The body found at the Barrière du Roule was found under such circumstances as to leave us no room for embarrassment upon this important point. But it has been suggested that the corpse discovered is not that of the Marie Rogêt for the conviction of whose assassin, or assassins, the reward is offered, and respecting whom, solely, our agreement has been arranged with the Prefect. We both know this gentleman well. It will not do to trust him too far. If, dating our inquiries from the body found, and thence tracing a murderer, we yet discover this body to be that of some other individual than Marie; or, if starting from the living Marie, we find her, yet find her unassassinated—in either case we lose our labor; since it is Monsieur G—— with whom we have to deal. For our own purpose, therefore, if not

---

[55] See "Murders in the Rue Morgue." [Poe's note.]

[56] In the original: "sweet."

[57] In the original: "*especially* ordinary."

[58] The *New Era*, edited by Richard Adams Locke, had suggested suicide, but this theory was naturally discounted at once.

for the purpose of justice, it is indispensable that our first step should be the determination of the identity of the corpse with the Marie Rogêt who is missing.

"With the public the arguments of *L'Etoile* have had weight;[59] and that the journal itself is convinced of their importance would appear from the manner in which it commences one of its essays upon the subject —'Several of the morning papers of the day,' it says, 'speak of the *conclusive* article in Monday's *Etoile*.'[60] To me, this article appears conclusive of little beyond the zeal of its inditer. We should bear in mind that, in general, it is the object of our newspapers rather to create a sensation—to make a point—than to further the cause of truth. The latter end is only pursued when it seems coincident with the former. The print which merely falls in with ordinary opinion (however well founded this opinion may be) earns for itself no credit with the mob. The mass of the people regard as profound only him who suggests *pungent contradictions* of the general idea. In ratiocination, not less than in literature, it is the *epigram* which is the most immediately and the most universally appreciated. In both, it is of the lowest order of merit.

"What I mean to say is, that it is the mingled epigram and melodrame of the idea, that Marie Rogêt still lives, rather than any true plausibility in this idea, which have suggested it to *L'Etoile*, and secured it a favorable reception with the public. Let us examine the heads of this journal's argument; endeavoring to avoid the incoherence with which it is originally set forth.

"The first aim of the writer is to show, from the brevity of the interval between Marie's disappearance and the finding of the floating corpse, that this corpse cannot be that of Marie. The reduction of this interval to its smallest possible dimension, becomes thus, at once, an object with the reasoner. In the rash pursuit

---

[59] In the original: "I know not what effect the arguments of *L'Etoile* may have wrought upon your own understanding. With the public they have had weight."

[60] The *Evening Tattler*, Aug. 24, p. 2, col. 2.

of this object, he rushes into mere assumption at the outset. 'It is folly to suppose,' he says, 'that the murder, if murder was committed on her body, could have been consummated soon enough to have enabled her murderers to throw the body into the river before midnight.' We demand at once, and very naturally, *why?* Why is it folly to suppose that the murder was committed *within five minutes* after the girl's quitting her mother's house? Why is it folly to suppose that the murder was committed at any given period of the day? There have been assassinations at all hours. But, had the murder taken place at any moment between nine o'clock in the morning of Sunday, and a quarter before midnight, there would still have been time enough 'to throw the body into the river before midnight.' This assumption, then, amounts precisely to this—that the murder was not committed on Sunday at all—and, if we allow *L'Etoile* to assume this, we may permit it any liberties whatever.[61] The paragraph beginning 'It is folly to suppose that the murder, etc.,' however it appears as printed in *L'Etoile*, may be imagined to have existed actually *thus* in the brain of its inditer: 'It is folly to suppose that the murder, if murder was committed on the body, could have been committed soon enough to have enabled her murderers to throw the body into the river before midnight; it is folly, we say, to suppose all this, and to suppose at the same time (as we are resolved to suppose), that the body was *not* thrown in until *after* midnight'[62]—a sentence sufficiently inconsequential in itself, but not so utterly preposterous as the one printed.

"Were it my purpose," continued Dupin, "merely to

[61] It is ironic how close Poe here came to the truth without realizing it. On August 2 the *Tribune* noted: "The inquiry has been, thus far, confined to evidence relative to the commission of the crime on *Sunday evening*. Might it not . . . have been committed on Monday or Monday evening . . .?"

[62] Poe indicts the *Tattler* for its a priori reasoning. The superiority of inductive over deductive logic is another underlying premise of the detective genre.

make out a case against this passage of *L'Etoile*'s argument, I might safely leave it where it is. It is not, however, with *L'Etoile* that we have to do, but with the truth. The sentence in question has but one meaning, as it stands; and this meaning I have fairly stated: but it is material that we go behind the mere words, for an idea which these words have obviously intended, and failed to convey. It was the design of the journalist to say that at whatever period of the day or night of Sunday this murder was committed, it was improbable that the assassins would have ventured to bear the corpse to the river before midnight. And herein lies, really, the assumption of which I complain. It is assumed that the murder was committed at such a position, and under such circumstances, that *the bearing it* to the river became necessary. Now, the assassination might have taken place upon the river's brink, or on the river itself; and, thus, the throwing the corpse in the water might have been resorted to, at any period of the day or night, as the most obvious and most immediate mode of disposal. You will understand that I suggest nothing here as probable, or as coincident with my own opinion. My design, so far, has no reference to the *facts* of the case. I wish merely to caution you against the whole tone of *L'Etoile's suggestion*, by calling your attention to its *ex-parte*[63] character at the outset.

"Having prescribed thus a limit to suit its own preconceived notions; having assumed that, if this were the body of Marie, it could have been in the water but a very brief time, the journal goes on to say:

" 'All experience has shown that drowned bodies, or bodies thrown into the water immediately after death by violence, require from six to ten days for sufficient decomposition to take place to bring them to the top of the water. Even when a cannon is fired over a corpse, and it rises before at least five or six days' immersion, it sinks again if let alone.'

[63] One-sided.

"These assertions have been tacitly received by every paper in Paris, with the exception of *Le Moniteur*.[64] This latter print endeavors to combat that portion of the paragraph which has reference to 'drowned bodies' only, by citing some five or six instances in which the bodies of individuals known to be drowned were found floating after the lapse of less time than is insisted upon by *L'Etoile*.[65] But there is something excessively unphilosophical in the attempt on the part of *Le Moniteur*, to rebut the general assertion of *L'Etoile*, by a citation of particular instances militating against that assertion. Had it been possible to adduce fifty instead of five examples of bodies found floating at the end of two or three days, these fifty examples could still have been properly regarded only as exceptions to *L'Etoile*'s rule, until such time as the rule itself should be confuted. Admitting the rule (and this *Le Moniteur* does not deny, insisting merely upon its exceptions), the argument of *L'Etoile* is suffered to remain in full force; for this argument does not pretend to involve more than a question of the *probability* of the body having risen to the surface in less than three days; and this probability will be in favor of *L'Etoile*'s position until the instances so childishly adduced shall be sufficient in number to establish an antagonistical rule.[66]

"You will see at once that all argument upon this

[64] The New York *Commercial Advertiser*, edited by Colonel Stone. [Poe's note.]

Wimsatt notes that the press, far from "tacitly" receiving the *Tattler's* "assertions," attacked them vigorously, and cites: *Evening Express*, Aug. 24, p. 3, col. 2; *Courier and Enquirer*, Aug. 24, p. 2, col. 3; *Herald*, Aug. 25, p. 1, col. 5; Aug. 26, p. 2, col. 2; *Journal of Commerce*, Aug. 26, p. 2, col. 2; *Sunday Mercury*, Aug. 29, p. 2, col. 1.

[65] Poe's source is the *Commercial Advertiser*, Aug. 25, p. 2, col. 2.

[66] Conclusion of the first installment of "The Mystery of Marie Rogêt" in Snowden's *Ladies' Companion*, November, 1842, pp. 15-20.

head should be urged, if at all, against the rule itself; and for this end we must examine the *rationale* of the rule. Now the human body, in general, is neither much lighter nor much heavier than the water of the Seine; that is to say, the specific gravity of the human body, in its natural condition, is about equal to the bulk of fresh water which it displaces. The bodies of fat and fleshy persons, with small bones, and of women generally, are lighter than those of the lean and large-boned, and of men; and the specific gravity of the water of a river is somewhat influenced by the presence of the tide from the sea. But, leaving this tide out of the question, it may be said that *very* few human bodies will sink at all, even in fresh water, *of their own accord*. Almost any one, falling into a river, will be enabled to float, if he suffer the specific gravity of the water fairly to be adduced in comparison with his own—that is to say, if he suffer his whole person to be immersed, with as little exception as possible. The proper position for one who cannot swim, is the upright position of the walker on land, with the head thrown fully back, and immersed; the mouth and nostrils alone remaining above the surface. Thus circumstanced, we shall find that we float without difficulty and without exertion. It is evident, however, that the gravities of the body, and of the bulk of water displaced, are very nicely balanced, and that a trifle will cause either to preponderate. An arm, for instance, uplifted from the water, and thus deprived of its support, is an additional weight sufficient to immerse the whole head, while the accidental aid of the smallest piece of timber will enable us to elevate the head so as to look about. Now, in the struggles of one unused to swimming, the arms are invariably thrown upwards, while an attempt is made to keep the head in its usual perpendicular position. The result is the immersion of the mouth and nostrils, and the inception, during efforts to breathe while beneath the surface, of water into the lungs. Much is also received into the stomach, and the whole body becomes heavier by the difference between the weight of the air originally distending these cavities, and that of the fluid which now fills them. This difference is sufficient to cause the body to sink, as a general rule; but is insufficient in the cases of individuals with small bones and an abnormal quantity of flaccid or fatty matter. Such individuals float even after drowning.

"The corpse, being supposed at the bottom of the river, will there remain until, by some means, its specific gravity again becomes less than that of the bulk of water which it displaces. This effect is brought about by decomposition, or otherwise. The result of decomposition is the generation of gas, distending the cellular tissues and all the cavities, and giving the *puffed* appearance which is so horrible. When this distension has so far progressed that the bulk of the corpse is materially increased without a corresponding increase of *mass* or weight, its specific gravity becomes less than that of the water displaced, and it forthwith makes its appearance at the surface. But decomposition is modified by innumerable circumstances—is hastened or retarded by innumerable agencies; for example, by the heat or cold of the season, by the mineral impregnation or purity of the water, by its depth or shallowness, by its currency or stagnation, by the temperament of the body, by its infection or freedom from disease before death. Thus it is evident that we can assign no period, with anything like accuracy, at which the corpse shall rise through decomposition. Under certain conditions this result would be brought about within an hour; under others, it might not take place at all. There are chemical infusions by which the animal frame can be preserved *for ever* from corruption; the bichloride of mercury is one. But, apart from decomposition, there may be, and very usually is, a generation of gas within the stomach, from the acetous fermentation of vegetable matter (or within other cavities from other causes), sufficient to induce a distension which will bring the body to the surface. The effect produced by the firing of a cannon is that of simple vibration. This may either loosen the corpse from the soft mud or ooze in which it is imbedded, thus permitting it to rise when other agencies have already prepared it for so doing; or it may overcome the tenacity of some putrescent portions of the cellular tissue, allowing the cavities to distend under the influence of the gas.[67]

"Having thus before us the whole philosophy of this subject, we can easily test by it the assertions of *L'Etoile*. 'All experience shows,' says this paper, 'that drowned bodies, or bodies thrown into the water immediately after death by violence, require from six to ten days for sufficient decomposition to take place to bring them to the top of the water. Even when a cannon is fired over a corpse, and it rises before at least five or six days' immersion, it sinks again if let alone.'

"The whole of this paragraph must now appear a tissue of inconsequence and incoherence. All experience does *not* show that 'drowned bodies' *require* from six to ten days for sufficient decomposition to take place to bring them to the surface. Both science and experience show that the period of their rising is, and

---

[67] "Cf. George E. Male, *Elements of Juridical or Forensic Medicine* (London, 1818), p. 186; Theodric R. Beck and John B. Beck, *Elements of Medical Jurisprudence*, (Albany, 1835), II, 163. Neither of these is detailed enough to be Poe's source. But I find an almost point-for-point agreement with Poe in a later authority, Alfred S. Taylor, *Principles and Practice of Medical Jurisprudence* (Philadelphia, 1873), II, 24-27." [Wimsatt's note.]
Poe's exact source is unknown. Coincidentally, an exchange of letters on this subject appeared in the *Times and Evening Star* in early August, 1841. A naval officer, Lieutenant Ross Crawford of the schooner *Nautilus*, fell overboard and sank immediately on July 30. On August 2 a letter, signed "Veritas," asked "why persons who fall into the water do not in all cases rise to the surface." On August 5, "Veritas" is answered by "Medicus" in a long, learned discourse. The arguments parallel some of Poe's but not the wording, making it unlikely that Poe saw the article.

necessarily must be, indeterminate. If, moreover, a
body has risen to the surface through firing of cannon,
it will *not* 'sink again if let alone,' until decomposition
has so far progressed as to permit the escape of
generated gas. But I wish to call your attention to the
distinction which is made between 'drowned bodies,'
and 'bodies thrown into the water immediately after
death by violence.' Although the writer admits the
distinction, he yet includes them all in the same
category. I have shown how it is that the body of a
drowning man becomes specifically heavier than its
bulk of water, and that he would not sink at all, except
for the struggle by which he elevates his arms above
the surface, and his gasps for breath while beneath the
surface—gasps which supply by water the place of
the original air in the lungs. But these struggles and
these gasps would not occur in the body 'thrown into
the water immediately after death by violence.' Thus,
in the latter instance, *the body, as a general rule,*[68]
would not sink at all—a fact of which *L'Etoile* is
evidently ignorant. When decomposition had
proceeded to a very great extent—when the flesh had
in a great measure left the bones—then, indeed, but
not *till* then, should we lose sight of the corpse.

"And now what are we to make of the argument,
that the body found could not be that of Marie Rogêt,
because, three days only having elapsed, this body was
found floating? IF DROWNED, BEING A
WOMAN, SHE MIGHT NEVER HAVE SUNK;
OR HAVING SUNK, MIGHT HAVE REAP-
PEARED IN TWENTY-FOUR HOURS, OR LESS.
BUT[69] no one supposes her to have been drowned;
and, dying before being thrown into the river, she
might have been found floating at any period
afterward whatever.

[68] The words "as a general rule" do not appear in the
original.

[69] Poe's additions are indicated by capital letters. The deletions are indicated by SMALL CAPITALS.

" 'But,' says *L'Etoile*, 'if the body had been kept in its mangled state on shore until Tuesday night, some trace would be found on shore of the murderers.' Here it is at first difficult to perceive the intention of the reasoner. He means to anticipate what he imagines would be an objection to this theory—viz.: that the body was kept on shore two days, suffering rapid decomposition—*more* rapid than if immersed in water. He supposes that, had this been the case, it *might* have appeared at the surface on the Wednesday, and thinks that *only* under such circumstances it could so have appeared. He is accordingly in haste to show that it *was not* kept on shore; for, if so, 'some trace would be found on shore of the murderers.' I presume you smile at the *sequitur*. You cannot be made to see how the mere *duration* of the corpse on the shore could operate to multiply *traces* of the assassins. Nor can I.

" 'And furthermore it is exceedingly improbable,' continues our journal, 'that any villains who had committed such a murder as is here supposed, would have thrown the body in without weight to sink it, when such a precaution could have so easily been taken.' Observe, here, the laughable confusion of thought! No one—not even *L'Etoile*—disputes the murder committed *on the body found*. The marks of violence are too obvious. It is our reasoner's object merely to show that this body is not Marie's. He wishes to prove that *Marie* is not assassinated—not that the corpse was not. Yet his observation proves only the latter point. Here is a corpse without weight attached. Murderers, casting it in, would not have failed to attach a weight. Therefore it was not thrown in by murderers. This is all which is proved, if anything is. The question of identity is not even approached, and *L'Etoile* has been at great pains merely to gainsay now what it has admitted only a moment before. 'We are perfectly convinced,' it says, 'that the body found was that of a murdered female.'

"Nor is this the sole instance, even in this division

of his subject, where our reasoner unwittingly reasons against himself. His evident object, I have already said, is to reduce, as much as possible, the interval between Marie's disappearance and the finding of the corpse. Yet we find him *urging* the point that no person saw the girl from the moment of her leaving her mother's house. 'We have no evidence,' he says, 'that Marie Rogêt was in the land of the living after nine o'clock on Sunday, June the twenty-second.' As his argument is obviously an *ex parte* one, he should, at least, have left this matter out of sight; for had anyone been known to see Marie, say on Monday, or on Tuesday, the interval in question would have been much reduced, and, by his own ratiocination, the probability much diminished of the corpse being that of the *grisette*. It is, nevertheless, amusing to observe that *L'Etoile* insists upon its point in the full belief of its furthering its general argument.

"Re-peruse now that portion of this argument which has reference to the identification of the corpse by Beauvais. In regard to the *hair* upon the arm, *L'Etoile* has been obviously disingenuous. M. Beauvais, not being an idiot, could never have urged, in identification of the corpse, simply *hair upon its arm*. No arm is *without* hair. The *generality* of the expression of *L'Etoile* is a mere perversion of the witness' phraseology. He must have spoken of some *peculiarity* in this hair. It must have been a peculiarity of color, of quantity, of length, or of situation.

" 'Her foot,' says the journal, 'was small'—so are thousands of feet. Her garter is no proof whatever—nor is her shoe—for shoes and garters are sold in packages. The same may be said of the flowers in her hat. One thing upon which M. Beauvais strongly insists is, that the clasp on the garter found had been set back to take it in. This amounts to nothing; for most women find it proper to take a pair of garters home and fit them to the size of the limbs they are to encircle, rather than to try them in the store where they purchase.'[70] Here it is difficult to suppose the reasoner[71] in earnest. Had M. Beauvais, in his search for the body of Marie, discovered a corpse corresponding in general size and appearance to the missing girl, he would have been warranted (without reference to the question of habiliment at all) in forming an opinion that his search had been successful. If, in addition to the point of general size and contour, he had found upon the arm a peculiar hairy appearance which he had observed upon the living Marie, his opinion might have been justly strengthened; and the increase of positiveness might well have been in the ratio of the peculiarity, or unusualness, of the hairy mark. If, the feet of Marie being small, those of the corpse were also small, the increase of probability that the body was that of Marie would not be an increase in a ratio merely arithmetical,[72] but in one HIGHLY GEOMETRICAL, OR accumulative. Add to all this shoes such as she had been known to wear upon the day of her disappearance, and, although these shoes may be 'sold in packages,' you so far augment the probability as to verge upon the certain. What, of itself, would be no evidence of identity, becomes through its corroborative position, proof most sure. Give us, then, flowers in the hat corresponding to those worn by the missing girl, and we seek for nothing further. If only *one* flower, we seek for nothing further—what then if two or three, or more? Each successive one is multiple evidence—proof not *added* to proof, but *multiplied* by hundreds or thousands. Let us now discover, upon the deceased, garters such as the living used, and it is almost folly to proceed. But these garters are

[70] Quoted from the *Evening Tattler*, Aug. 23, p. 2, col. 2. This portion of the article was not cited earlier by the narrator.

[71] "Reasoner" is substituted for the original word "journal."

[72] "Arithmetical" is substituted for the original word "direct."

found to be tightened, by the setting back of a clasp, in just such a manner as her own had been tightened by Marie, shortly previous to her leaving home. It is now madness or hypocrisy to doubt. What *L'Etoile* says in respect to this abbreviation of the garters being an usual occurrence, shows nothing beyond its own pertinacity in error. The elastic nature of the clasp-garter is self-demonstration of the *unusualness* of the abbreviation. What is made to adjust itself, must of necessity require foreign adjustment but rarely. It must have been by an accident, in its strictest sense, that these garters of Marie needed the tightening described. They alone would have amply established her identity. But it is not that the corpse was found to have the garters of the missing girl, or found to have her shoes, or her bonnet, or the flowers of her bonnet, or her feet, or a peculiar mark upon the arm, or her general size and appearance—it is that the corpse had each, and *all collectively*. Could it be proved that the editor *of L'Etoile really* entertained a doubt, under the circumstances, there would be no need, in his case, of a commission *de lunatico inquirendo*. He has thought it sagacious to echo the small talk of the lawyers, who, for the most part, content themselves with echoing the rectangular precepts of the courts. I would here observe that very much of what is rejected as evidence by a court, is the best evidence to the intellect. For the court, guiding itself by the general principles of evidence—the recognized and *booked* principles—is averse from swerving at particular instances. And this steadfast adherence to principle, with rigorous disregard of the conflicting exception, is a sure mode of attaining the *maximum* of attainable truth, in any long sequence of time. The practice, *en masse*, is therefore philosophical; but it is not the less certain that it engenders vast individual error.[73]

[73] "A theory based on the qualities of an object, will prevent its being unfolded according to its objects; and

"In respect to the insinuations levelled at Beauvais, you will be willing to dismiss them in a breath.[74] You have already fathomed the true character of this good gentleman. He is a *busy-body*, with much of romance and little of wit. Anyone so constituted will readily so conduct himself, upon occasion of *real* excitement, as to render himself liable to suspicion on the part of the over-acute, or the ill-disposed. M. Beauvais (as it appears from your notes) had some personal interviews with the editor of *L'Etoile*, and offended him by venturing an opinion that the corpse, notwithstanding the theory of the editor, was, in sober fact, that of Marie. 'He persists,' says the paper, 'in asserting the corpse to be that of Marie, but cannot give a circumstance, in addition to those which we have commented upon, to make others believe.'[75] Now, without re-adverting to the fact that stronger evidence 'to make others believe,' could *never* have been adduced, it may be remarked that a man may very well be understood to believe, in a case of this kind, without the ability to advance a single reason for the belief of a second party. Nothing is more vague than impressions of individual identity. Each man recognizes his neighbor, yet there are few instances in which any one is prepared *to give a reason* for his recognition.

---

he who arranges topics in reference to their causes, will cease to value them according to their results. Thus the jurisprudence of every nation will show that, when law becomes a science and a system, it ceases to be justice. The errors into which a blind devotion to *principles* of classification has led the common law, will be seen by observing how often the legislature has been obliged to come forward to restore the equity its scheme had lost." —*Landor*, [Poe's note.]

[74] Poe implies the *Tattler* has hinted at Crommelin's guilt. This is unjust and illogical, for the *Tattler* insists the corpse is not Mary and therefore not anyone Crommelin knew.

[75] *Evening Tattler*, Aug. 24, p. 2, col. 3.

The editor of *L'Etoile* had no right to be offended at M. Beauvais' unreasoning belief.

"The suspicious circumstances which invest him, will be found to tally much better with my hypothesis of *romantic busy-bodyism*, than with the reasoner's suggestion of guilt. Once adopting the more charitable interpretation, we shall find no difficulty in comprehending the rose in the keyhole; the 'Marie' upon the slate; the 'elbowing the male relatives out of the way'; the 'aversion to permitting them to see the body'; the caution given to Madame B——, that she must hold no conversation with the *gendarme* until his (Beauvais') return; and, lastly, his apparent determination 'that nobody should have anything to do with the proceedings except himself.' It seems to me unquestionable that Beauvais was a suitor of Marie's; that she coquetted with him; and that he was ambitious of being thought to enjoy her fullest intimacy and confidence. I shall say nothing more upon this point; and, as the evidence fully rebuts the assertion of *L'Etoile*, touching the matter of *apathy* on the part of the mother and other relatives[76]—an apathy inconsistent with the supposition of their believing the corpse to be that of the perfumery-girl—we shall now proceed as if the question of *identity* were settled to our perfect satisfaction."

"And what," I here demanded, "do you think of the opinions of *Le Commerciel?*"

"That, in spirit, they are far more worthy of attention than any which have been promulgated upon the subject. The deductions from the premises are philosophical and acute; but the premises, in two instances, at least, are founded in imperfect observation. *Le Commerciel* wishes to intimate that Marie was seized by some gang of low ruffians not far from her mother's door. 'It is impossible,' it urges, 'that a person so well known to thousands as this young woman was, should have passed three blocks without someone

[76] The evidence, of course, does nothing of the sort.

having seen her.' This is the idea of a man long resident in Paris—a public man—and one whose walks to and fro in the city have been mostly limited to the vicinity of the public offices. He is aware that *he* seldom passes so far as a dozen blocks from his own *bureau*,[77] without being recognized and accosted. And, knowing the extent of his personal acquaintance with others, and of others with him, he compares his notoriety with that of the perfumery-girl, finds no great difference between them, and reaches at once the conclusion that she, in her walks, would be equally liable to recognition with himself in his. This could only be the case were her walks of the same unvarying, methodical character, and within the same *species* of limited region as are his own. He passes to and fro, at regular intervals, within a confined periphery, abounding in individuals who are led to observation of his person through interest in the kindred nature of his occupation with their own. But the walks of Marie may, in general, be supposed discursive. In this particular instance, it will be understood as most probable, that she proceeded upon a route of more than average diversity from her accustomed ones. The parallel which we imagine to have existed in the mind of *Le Commerciel* would only be sustained in the event of the two individuals traversing the whole city. In this case, granting the personal acquaintances to be equal, the chances would be also equal that an equal number of personal encounters would be made. For my own part, I should hold it not only as possible, but as very far more than probable, that Marie might have proceeded, at any given period, by any one of the many routes between her own residence and that of her aunt, without meeting a single individual whom she knew, or by whom she was known. In viewing this question in its full and proper light, we must hold steadily in mind the great disproportion between the personal acquaintances of even the most noted indi-vidual in Paris, and the entire population of Paris itself.

[77] Office.

"But whatever force there may still appear to be in the suggestion of *Le Commerciel*, will be much diminished when we take into consideration *the hour* at which the girl went abroad. 'It was when the streets were full of people,' says *Le Commerciel*, 'that she went out.' But not so. It was at nine o'clock in the morning.[78] Now at nine o'clock of every morning in the week, *with the exception of Sunday*, the streets of the city are, it is true, thronged with people. At nine on Sunday, the populace are chiefly within doors *preparing for church*. No observing person can have failed to notice the peculiarly deserted air of the town, from about eight until ten on the morning of every Sabbath. Between ten and eleven the streets are thronged, but not at so early a period as that designated.

"There is another point at which there seems a deficiency of *observation*[79] on the part of *Le Commerciel*. 'A piece,' it says, 'of one of the unfortunate girl's petticoats, two feet long, and one foot wide, was torn out and tied under her chin, and around the back of her head, probably to prevent screams. This was done by fellows who had no pocket-handkerchiefs. Whether this idea is or is not well founded, we will endeavor to see hereafter; but by 'fellows who have no pocket-handkerchiefs,' the editor intends the lowest class of ruffians. These, however, are the very description of people who will always be found to have handkerchiefs even when destitute of shirts. You must have had occasion to observe how

[78] Since Poe could not fail to know that Mary left at ten, his entire argument on this point must be considered part of his hoax. (See note 115).

[79] Another presupposition of detective fiction: truth is discoverable only through careful, objective, empirical observation. In "Murders in the Rue Morgue," Dupin has said: "The analyst makes . . . a host of observations and inferences . . ., [the value of which] lies not so much in the validity of the inference as in the quality of the observation. The necessary knowledge is that of *what* to observe."

absolutely indispensable, of late years, to the thorough blackguard, has become the pocket-handkerchief."

"And what are we to think," I asked, "of the article in *Le Soleil*?"

"That it is a vast pity its inditer was not BORN A PARROT— IN WHICH CASE HE WOULD HAVE BEEN THE MOST ILLUSTRIOUS PARROT OF HIS RACE.[80] He has merely repeated WHAT OTHERS HAVE DONE (WITHOUT ESTABLISHING ANY INCONTROVERTIBLE PROOFS) the individual items of the already published opinion; collecting them, with a laudable industry, from this paper and from that. 'The things had all *evidently* been there,' he says, 'at least, three or four weeks, and there can be *no doubt* that the spot of this appalling outrage has been discovered.' HERE, AGAIN, HE SPEAKS BUT FROM SUSPICION, AND BRINGS NOTHING TO BEAR CONCLUSIVELY UPON THE MATTER. The facts here re-stated by *Le Soleil*, are very far indeed from removing my own doubts upon this subject, and we will examine them more particularly hereafter in connection with another division of the theme.

"At present we must occupy ourselves with other investigations. You cannot fail to have remarked the extreme laxity of the examination of the corpse. To be sure, the question of identity was readily determined, or should have been; but there were other points to be ascertained. Had the body been in any respect *despoiled*? Had the deceased any articles of jewelry about her person upon leaving home? If so, had she any when found?[81] These are important questions

---

[80] The original reads: "That it is a vast pity its inditer was not more minute. It is easy to surmise and as easy to assert."

[81] Wimsatt notes that Poe apparently never read the depositions of Henry Mallin and James Boulard who found the body and testified she wore no jewelry. Thus it is probable he also missed Crommelin's deposition, reported at the same time, e.g., *Courier and Enquirer*, Aug. 13, p. 2, col. 3.

utterly untouched by the evidence; and there are others of equal moment, which have met with no attention. We must endeavor to satisfy ourselves by personal inquiry. The case of St. Eustache must be re-examined. I have no suspicion of this person; but let us proceed methodically. We will ascertain beyond a doubt the validity of the *affidavits* in regard to his whereabouts on the Sunday. Affidavits of this character are readily made matter of mystification. Should there be nothing wrong here, however, we will dismiss St. Eustache from our investigations. His suicide, however corroborative of suspicion, were there found to be deceit in the affidavits, is, without such deceit, in no respect an unaccountable circumstance, or one which need cause us to deflect from the line of ordinary analysis.

"In that[82] which I now propose, we will discard the *interior* points of this tragedy, and concentrate our attention upon its *outskirts*. Not the least usual error, in investigations such as this, is the limiting of inquiry to the immediate, with total disregard of the collateral or circumstantial events. It is the malpractice of the courts to confine evidence and discussion to the bounds of apparent relevancy. Yet experience has shown, and a true philosophy will always show, that a vast, perhaps the larger portion of truth, arises from the seemingly irrelevant. It is through the spirit of this principle, if not precisely through its letter, that modern science has resolved to *calculate upon the unforeseen*. But perhaps you do not comprehend me. The history of human knowledge has so uninterrupt-edly shown that to collateral, or incidental, or accidental events we are indebted for the most numerous and most valuable discoveries, that it has at length become necessary, in any prospective view of improvement, to make not only large, but the largest allowances for inventions that shall arise by chance, and quite out of the range of ordinary expectation. It is no longer

[82] Originally: "In the analysis . . ."

233

philosophical to base upon what has been a vision of what is to be. *Accident* is admitted as a portion of the substructure. We make chance a matter of absolute calculation. We subject the unlooked for and un-imagined to the mathematical *formulae* of the schools.

"I repeat that it is no more than fact, that the *larger* portion of all truth has sprung from the collateral; and it is but in accordance with the spirit of the principle involved in this fact, that I would divert inquiry, in the present case, from the trodden and hitherto unfruitful ground of the event itself, to the contem-porary circumstances which surround it. While you ascertain the validity of the affidavits, I will examine the newspapers more generally than you have as yet done. So far, we have only reconnoitred the field of investigation; but it will be strange indeed if a comprehensive survey, such as I propose, of the public prints, will not afford us some minute points which shall establish a *direction* for inquiry."[83]

In pursuance of Dupin's suggestion, I made scrupu-lous examination of the affair of the affidavits. The result was a firm conviction of their validity, and of the consequent innocence of St. Eustache.[84] In the meantime my friend occupied himself, with what seemed to me a minuteness altogether objectless, in a scrutiny of the various newspaper files. At the end of a week he placed before me the following extracts:

"About three years and a half ago,[85] a disturbance very similar to the present, was caused by the disappearance of this same Marie Rogêt, from the

---

[83] In this and the preceding paragraph Poe establishes his rationale for Dupin's method of investigation. (See note 97.)

[84] "For the affidavits . . . Poe could have used: e.g. *Herald*, Aug. 18, p. 1, col. 1; *Brother Jonathan*, Aug. 21, p. 2, col. 6, though of course what he adds about verifying the affidavits . . . is part of his fiction." [Wimsatt's note.]

[85] In the original version this reads: "Two or three years since . . ."

parfumerie of Monsieur Le Blanc, in the Palais Royal. At the end of a week, however, she re-appeared at her customary *comptoir*, as well as ever, with the exception of a slight paleness not altogether usual. It was given out by Monsieur Le Blanc and her mother that she had merely been on a visit to some friend in the country; and the affair was speedily hushed up. We presume that the present absence is a freak of the same nature, and that, at the expiration of a week, or perhaps of a month, we shall have her among us again."—*Evening Paper*, Monday, June 23.[86]

"An evening journal of yesterday, refers to a former mysterious disappearance of Mademoiselle Rogêt. It is well known that, during the week of her absence from Le Blanc's *parfumerie*, she was in the company of a young naval officer, much noted for his debaucheries. A quarrel, it is supposed, providentially led to her return home. We have the name of the Lothario in question, who is at present stationed in Paris, but for obvious reasons forbear to make it public."— *Le Mercure*, Tuesday Morning, June 24.[87]

[86] New York *Express*. [Poe's note.]
It is possible Poe had seen a similar article in the August 2 *Sun* which stated Mary had been in "one or two equivocal situations," and had been supposed to have fled with a man "about a year ago. . . . A cry of abduction was raised. This was hushed and a story was put forth that she had been to Brooklyn visiting friends." This paragraph, if Poe knew it, could have suggested to him the ideas of a secret boyfriend, an earlier "abduction," and an elopement ending in murder.

[87] New York *Herald*. [Poe's note.]
This paragraph, and the one Poe quotes from the *Express*, do not appear in those papers nor, so far as I can determine, anywhere else, and are apparently Poe's invention. An article in the *Commercial Advertiser*, Aug. 25, p. 2, col. 2, may have suggested the *Express* extract. The naval officer is mentioned, to the best of my knowledge, only once in the press; e.g., the *Herald*, Aug. 3, p. 2, col. 4: "This young girl was missing from Anderson's store, three years ago, for two weeks. It is asserted that she was then seduced by an officer of the U.S. Navy and kept

"An outrage of the most atrocious character was perpetrated near this city the day before yesterday. A gentleman, with his wife and daughter, engaged, about dusk, the services of six young men, who were idly rowing a boat to and fro near the banks of the Seine, to convey him across the river. Upon reaching the opposite shore, the three passengers stepped out, and had proceeded so far as to be beyond the view of the boat, when the daughter discovered that she had left in it her parasol. She returned for it, was seized by the gang, carried out into the stream, gagged, brutally treated, and finally taken to the shore at a point not far from that at which she had originally entered the boat with her parents. The villains have escaped for the time, but the police are upon their trail, and some of them will soon be taken."— *Morning Paper*, June 25.[88]

"We have received one or two communications, the object of which is to fasten the crime of the late atrocity upon Mennais; but as this gentleman has been

---

at Hoboken for two weeks. His name is well known on board his ship." In composing these two paragraphs, Poe probably had before him the *Herald* of Aug. 26 which reprinted the articles from the *Commercial Advertiser* and the *Journal of Commerce* (Aug. 26, p. 2, col. 3) stating Mary's annoyance at the publicity her "country excursion" aroused.

[88] New York *Courier and Inquirer*. [Poe's note.]
The article is not in the *Courier and Inquirer* and is doubtless Poe's invention. The original of his source is a letter published in the Aug. 9 *Evening Tattler*. On Aug. 10 the *Tribune* asserted that the girl was not Mary but "a common creature of the town." On Sept. 2 the *Tattler* announced: ". . . the young woman so badly treated on the twenty-fifth of July was a mere child of fifteen, and . . . she went to Hoboken in company with her father, mother, and a young man, a friend of the family, in a rowboat. Afterwards stepping into the boat with the young man, she was taken from it by the villains, . . . the person thus abused . . . is respectable and no girl of the town." It seems likely Poe had seen this article.

236

fully exonerated by a legal[89] inquiry, and as the
arguments of our several correspondents appear to be
more zealous than profound, we do not think it
advisable to make them public."—*Morning Paper,*
June 25.[90]

"We have received several forcibly written communications, apparently from various sources, and
which go far to render it a matter of certainty that
the unfortunate Marie Rogêt has become a victim of
one of the numerous bands of blackguards which
infest the vicinity of the city upon Sunday. Our own
opinion is decidedly in favor of this supposition. We
shall endeavor to make room for some of these
arguments hereafter."—*Evening Paper,* Tuesday,
June 31.[91]

"On Monday, one of the bargemen connected with
the revenue service saw an empty boat floating down
the Seine. Sails were lying in the bottom of the boat.
The bargeman towed it under the barge office. The
next morning it was taken from thence without the

---

[89] Mennais was one of the parties originally suspected and
arrested, but discharged through total lack of evidence.
[Poe's note.]
   "Mennais" is undoubtedly Joseph Morse who was arrested August 13 and released August 21.

[90] New York *Courier and Inquirer.* [Poe's note.]

[91] New York *Evening Post.* [Poe's note.]
   "These letters, says Poe . . . were received immediately
before the finding of the clothes (according to Poe's own
dating this is not true) and form part of the same plan to
divert attention from the real culprit. I have not been
able to find this passage in the *Post,* nor another, which
Poe quotes as from the *Courier and Inquirer,* saying that
the paper has received letters arguing the guilt of 'Mennais'—and which Poe makes part of the same plan. But it
would seem that a number of such letters were sent to
the papers." [Wimsatt's note.] Wimsatt cites such letters
in the *Herald,* Aug. 11 and Aug. 16; *Brother Jonathan,*
Aug. 21; *Journal of Commerce,* Sept. 3. The *Evening
Tattler* reports the same, Aug. 13. Nothing in the press
corresponds directly to Poe's two paragraphs which, like
the rest of Dupin's six "extracts," are Poe's own creations.

knowledge of any of the officers. The rudder is now at the barge office."—*Le Diligence*, Thursday, June 26.[92]

Upon reading these various extracts, they not only seemed to me irrelevant, but I could perceive no mode in which any one of them could be brought to bear upon the matter in hand. I waited for some explanation from Dupin.

"It is not my present design," he said, "to *dwell* upon the first and second of these extracts. I have copied them chiefly to show you the extreme remissness of the police, who, as far as I can understand from the Prefect, have not troubled themselves, in any respect, with an examination of the naval officer alluded to. Yet it is mere folly to say that between the first and second disappearance of Marie, there is no *supposable* connection. Let us admit the first elopement to have resulted in a quarrel between the lovers, and the return home of the betrayed. We are now prepared to view a second *elopement* (if we *know* that an elopement has again taken place) as indicating a renewal of the betrayer's advances, rather than as the result of new proposals by a second individual—we are prepared to regard it as a 'making up' of the old *amour*, rather than as the commencement of a new one. The chances are ten to one that he who had once eloped with Marie would again propose an elopement, rather than that she to whom proposals of elopement had been made by one individual should have them made to her by another.[93] And here let me call your

---

[92] New York *Standard*. [Poe's note.]

No such article exists in the *Standard* or any other paper. "Poe could have gotten the idea of a boat from the *Herald*, Sept. 24, p. 1, col. 3, where 'G' in the panorama of Weehawken is identified as 'the spot at the edge of the river . . . where the boat lay in which it is believed the dead body of Mary Rogers was carried into the stream.' " [Wimsatt's note.]

[93] The best that can be said of this conclusion and the arguments by which it is reached is that they are highly dubious.

attention to the fact, that the time elapsing between
the first ascertained and the second supposed elopement
is a few months more than the general period[94] of the
cruises of our *men-of-war*. Had the lover been interrupted in his first villany by the necessity of departure
to sea, and had he seized the first moment of his return
to renew the base designs not yet altogether accomplished—or not yet altogether accomplished *by him?*
Of all these things we know nothing.

"You will say, however, that, in the second instance,
there was *no* elopement as imagined. Certainly not—
but are we prepared to say that there was not the
frustrated design? Beyond St. Eustache, and perhaps
Beauvais, we find no recognized, no open, no honorable
suitors of Marie. Of none other is there anything
said. Who, then, is the secret lover, of whom the
relatives *(at least most of them)* know nothing, but
whom Marie meets upon the morning of Sunday, and
who is so deeply in her confidence, that she hesitates
not to remain with him until the shades of the evening
descend, amid the solitary groves of the Barrière du
Roule? Who is that secret lover, I ask, of whom, at
least, *most* of the relatives know nothing? And what
means the singular prophecy of Madame Rogêt on the
morning of Marie's departure?—'I fear that I shall
never see Marie again.'

"But if we cannot imagine Madame Rogêt privy to
the design of elopement, may we not at least suppose
this design entertained by the girl? Upon quitting
home, she gave it to be understood that she was about
to visit her aunt in the Rue des Drômes, and St.
Eustache was requested to call for her at dark. Now
at first glance, this fact strongly militates against my
suggestion;—but let us reflect. That she *did* meet some
companion, and proceed with him across the river,
reaching the Barrière du Roule at so late an hour as
three o'clock in the afternoon, is known. But in
consenting so to accompany this individual *(for
whatever purpose—to her mother known or*

[94] In the original: "precisely the general period . . ."

239

unknown), she must have thought of her expressed
intention when leaving home, and of the surprise and
suspicion aroused in the bosom of her affianced suitor,
St. Eustache, when, calling for her, at the hour
appointed, in the Rue des Drômes, he should find that
she had not been there, and when, moreover, upon
returning to the *pension* with this alarming intelligence, he should become aware of her continued
absence from home. She must have thought of these
things, I say. She must have foreseen the chagrin of
St. Eustache, the suspicion of all. She could not have
thought of returning to brave this suspicion; but the
suspicion becomes a point of trivial importance to her,
if we suppose her *not* intending to return.

"We may imagine her thinking thus—'I am to meet
a certain person for the purpose of elopement, OR
FOR CERTAIN OTHER PURPOSES KNOWN
ONLY TO MYSELF. It is necessary that there be no
chance of interruption—there must be sufficient time
given us to elude pursuit—I will give it to be understood that I shall visit and spend the day with my
aunt at the Rue des Drômes—I will tell St. Eustache
not to call for me until dark—in this way, my absence
from home for the longest possible period, without
causing suspicion or anxiety, will be accounted for,
and I shall gain more time than in any other manner.
If I bid St. Eustache call for me at dark, he will be
sure not to call before; but, if I wholly neglect to bid
him call, my time for escape will be diminished, since
it will be expected that I return the earlier, and my
absence will the sooner excite anxiety. Now, if it were
my design to return *at all*—if I had in contemplation
merely a stroll with the individual in question—it
would not be my policy to bid St. Eustache call; for,
calling, he will be *sure* to ascertain that I have played
him false—a fact of which I might keep him for ever
in ignorance, by leaving home without notifying him
of my intention, by returning before dark, and by
then stating that I had been to visit my aunt in the
Rue des Drômes. But, as it is my design *never* to return
—OR NOT FOR SOME WEEKS—OR NOT

UNTIL CERTAIN CONCEALMENTS ARE
EFFECTED[95]—the gaining of time is the only point
about which I need give myself any concern.'

"SUCH THOUGHTS AS THESE WE MAY IMAGINE TO HAVE
PASSED THROUGH THE MIND OF MARIE, BUT THE POINT IS
ONE UPON WHICH I CONSIDER IT NECESSARY NOW TO
INSIST. I HAVE REASONED THUS, MERELY TO CALL
ATTENTION, AS I SAID A MINUTE AGO, TO
THE CULPABLE REMISSNESS OF THE POLICE.

"You have observed, in your notes, that the most
general opinion in relation to this sad affair is, and
was from the first, that the girl had been the victim
of *a gang* of blackguards.[96] Now, the popular opinion,
under certain conditions, is not to be disregarded.
When arising of itself—when manifesting itself in a
strictly spontaneous manner—we should look upon it
as analogous with that *intuition* which is the idiosyncrasy of the individual man of genius.[97] In ninety-
nine cases from the hundred I would abide by its
decision. But it is important that we find no palpable
traces of *suggestion*. The opinion must be rigorously
the public's own; and the distinction is often
exceedingly difficult to perceive and to maintain.

[95] Note that this inserted equivocation seriously weakens
the logic of this and the preceding paragraph.

[96] This was James Gordon Bennett's theory. See the
Herald, Aug. 9, p. 2, col. 6; Aug. 11, p. 2, col. 2; Aug. 12,
p. 2, cols. 1-2; Sept. 17, p. 2, cols. 3-4; Sept. 21, p. 2, col.
3; Sept. 24, p. 1, cols. 3-4. Other papers supported the
Herald and crimes of gang violence seem to have increased. On August 26, the *Sun* reported that ten of the
"Clinton Market gang" on August 20 raped a girl "till
she foamed at the mouth, by Jesus!"

[97] An important clue to Poe's method of achieving "solutions." For all his talk of inductive reasoning, Dupin,
unlike Sherlock Holmes and his other celebrated descend-
ants, reaches many conclusions through flashes of inspired
insight during which the "intuition" (or perhaps, more
properly, the imagination) of the "man of genius" sees
all at once the relevance of "the seemingly irrelevant."
In just this manner Dupin connects his murderer with the
rudderless boat. (See note 83).

In the present instance, it appears to me that this 'public opinion,' in respect to *a gang*, has been super-induced by the collateral event which is detailed in the third of my extracts. All Paris is excited by the discovered corpse of Marie, a girl young, beautiful, and notorious. This corpse is found, bearing marks of violence, and floating in the river. But it is now made known that, at the very period, or about the very period, in which it is supposed that the girl was assassinated, an outrage similar in nature to that endured by the deceased, although less in extent, was perpetrated by a gang of young ruffians, upon the person of a second young female. Is it wonderful that the one known atrocity should influence the popular judgment in regard to the other unknown? This judgment awaited direction, and the known outrage seemed so opportunely to afford it! Marie, too, was found in the river; and upon this very river was this known outrage committed. The connection of the two events had about it so much of the palpable, that the true wonder would have been a *failure* of the populace to appreciate and to seize it. But, in fact,[98] the one atrocity, known to be so committed, is, if anything, evidence that the other, committed at a time nearly coincident, was *not* so committed. It *would* have been a miracle indeed, if, while a gang of ruffians were perpetrating, at a given locality, a most unheard-of wrong, there should have been another similar gang, in a similar locality, in the same city, under the same circumstances, with the same means and appliances, engaged in a wrong of precisely the same aspect, at precisely the same period of time! Yet in what, if not in this marvellous train of coincidence, does the accidentally *suggested* opinion of the populace call upon us to believe?[99]

[98] The original reads: "But, to the philosophical, . . ."

[99] "Poe has asserted the contrary of one of the principles of *a priori* probability. A seven thrown once has no effect on the *chance* that seven will be thrown again. One girl

242

"Before proceeding farther, let us consider the supposed scene of the assassination, in the thicket at the Barrière du Roule. This thicket, although dense, was in the close vicinity of a public road. Within were three or four large stones, forming a kind of seat with a back and footstool. On the upper stone was discovered a white petticoat; on the second, a silk scarf. A parasol, gloves, and a pocket-handkerchief, were also here found. The handkerchief bore the name, 'Marie Rogêt.' Fragments of dress were seen on the branches around. The earth was trampled, the bushes were broken, and there was every evidence of a violent struggle.

"Notwithstanding the acclamation with which the discovery of this thicket was received by the press, and the unanimity with which it was supposed to indicate the precise scene of the outrage,[100] it must be admitted that there was some very good reason for doubt. That it *was* the scene, I MAY OR I MAY NOT believe—but there was excellent reason for doubt. Had the *true* scene been, as *Le Commerciel* suggested, in the neighborhood of the Rue Pavée Saint-Andrée, the perpetrators of the crime, supposing them still resident in Paris, would naturally have been stricken with terror at the public attention thus acutely directed into the proper channel; and, in certain classes of minds, there would have arisen, at once, a sense of the necessity of some exertion to redivert this attention. And thus, the thicket of the Barrière du Roule having been already suspected, the idea of placing the articles where they were found, might have been naturally entertained.[101] There is no real evidence, although

---

seized by a gang has no effect on the *chance* that another will be seized." [Wimsatt's note.]

The second installment in Snowden's *Ladies' Companion* (Dec. 1842) ended here (pp. 93-99).

[100] The *Tattler* was an exception to this "unanimity." See *Brother Jonathan*, Sept. 25, p. 2, col. 8.

[101] The thicket was not suspected until the clothing was discovered there.

Le Soleil so supposes, that the articles discovered had been more than a very few days in the thicket; while there is much circumstantial proof that they could not have remained there, without attracting attention, during the twenty days[102] elapsing between the fatal Sunday and the afternoon upon which they were found by the boys. 'They were all *mildewed* down hard,' says *Le Soleil*, adopting the opinions of its predecessors, 'with the action of the rain, and stuck together from *mildew*. The grass had grown around and over some of them. The silk of the parasol was strong, but the threads of it were run together within. The upper part, where it had been doubled and folded, was all *mildewed* and rotten, and tore on being opened.' In respect to the grass having 'grown around and over some of them,' it is obvious that the fact could only have been ascertained from the words, and thus from the recollections, of two small boys; for these boys removed the articles and took them home before they had been seen by a third party. But grass will grow, especially in warm and damp weather (such as was that of the period of the murder), as much as two or three inches in a single day. A parasol lying upon a newly turfed ground, might, in a single week, be entirely concealed from sight by the upspringing grass. And touching that *mildew* upon which the editor of *Le Soleil* so pertinaciously insists, that he employs the word no less than three times in the brief paragraph just quoted, is he really unaware of the nature of this *mildew*? Is he to be told that it is one of the many classes of *fungus*, of which the most ordinary feature is its upspringing and decadence within twenty-four hours?

"Thus we see, at a glance, that what has been most triumphantly adduced in support of the idea that the articles had been 'for at least three or four weeks in the thicket, is most absurdly null as regards any evidence of that fact. On the other hand, it is exeed-

---

[102] Actually thirty-one days.

ingly difficult to believe that these articles could have remained in the thicket specified for a longer period than a single week—for a longer period than from one Sunday to the next. Those who know anything of the vicinity of Paris know the extreme difficulty of finding *seclusion*, unless at a great distance from its suburbs. Such a thing as an unexplored or even an unfrequently visited recess, amid its woods or groves, is not for a moment to be imagined. Let anyone who, being at heart a lover of nature, is yet chained by duty to the dust and heat of this great metropolis—let any such one attempt, even during the week-days, to slake his thirst for solitude amid the scenes of natural loveliness which immediately surround us. At every second step, he will find the growing charm dispelled by the voice and personal intrusion of some ruffian or party of carousing blackguards. He will seek privacy amid the densest foliage, all in vain. Here are the very nooks where the unwashed most abound—here are the temples most desecrate. With sickness of the heart the wanderer will flee back to the polluted Paris as to a less odious because less incongruous sink of pollution. But if the vicinity of the city is so beset during the working days of the week, how much more so on the Sabbath! It is now especially that, released from the claims of labor, or deprived of the customary opportunities of crime, the town blackguard seeks the precincts of the town, not through love of the rural, which in his heart he despises, but by way of escape from the restraints and conventionalities of society. He desires less the fresh air and the green trees, than the utter *license* of the country. Here, at the roadside inn, or beneath the foliage of the woods, he indulges, unchecked by any eye except those of his boon companions, in all the mad excess of a counterfeit hilarity—the joint offspring of liberty and of rum. I say nothing more than what must be obvious to every dispassionate observer, when I repeat that the circumstance of the articles in question having remained undiscovered, for a longer period than from one

Sunday to another, in *any* thicket in the immediate neighborhood of Paris, is to be looked upon as little less than miraculous.

"But there are not wanting other grounds for the suspicion that the articles were placed in the thicket with the view of diverting attention from the real scene of the outrage. And, first, let me direct your notice to the *date* of the discovery of the articles. Collate this with the date of the fifth extract made by myself from the newspapers. You will find that the discovery followed, almost immediately, the urgent communications sent to the evening paper.[103] These communications, although various, and apparently from various sources, tended all to the same point— viz., the directing of attention to *a gang* as the perpetrators of the outrage, and to the neighborhood of the Barrière du Roule as its scene. Now here, of course, the suspicion is not that, in consequence of these communications, or of the public attention by them directed, the articles were found by the boys; but the suspicion might and may well have been, that the articles were not *before* found by the boys, for the reason that the articles had not before been in the thicket; having been deposited there only at so late a period as at the date, or shortly prior to the date of the communications, by the guilty authors of these communications themselves.

"This thicket was a singular—an exceedingly singular one. It was unusually dense. Within its naturally walled enclosure were three extraordinary stones, *forming a seat with a back and footstool*. And this thicket, so full of a natural art, was in the immediate vicinity, *within a few rods*, of the dwelling of Madame Deluc, whose boys were in the habit of closely examining the shrubberies about them in search of the bark of the sassafras. Would it be a rash wager —a wager of one thousand to one—that a *day* never passed over the heads of these boys without finding at least one of them ensconced in the umbrageous hall,

---

[103] This does not correspond to the facts. (See note 91).

and enthroned upon its natural throne? Those who would hesitate at such a wager, have either never been boys themselves, or have forgotten the boyish nature. I repeat—it is exceedingly hard to comprehend how the articles could have remained in this thicket, undiscovered, for a longer period than one or two days; and that thus there is good ground for suspicion, in spite of the dogmatic ignorance of *Le Solieil*, that they were, at a comparatively late date, deposited where found.

"But there are still other and stronger reasons for believing them so deposited, than any which I have as yet urged. And, now, let me beg your notice to the highly artificial arrangement of the articles. On the *upper* stone lay a white petticoat; on the *second*, a silk scarf; scattered around, were a parasol, gloves, and a pocket-handkerchief bearing the name, 'Marie Rogêt.' Here is just such an arrangement as would *naturally* be made by a not-over-acute person wishing to dispose the articles *naturally*. But it is by no means a *really* natural arrangement. I should rather have looked to see the things *all* lying on the ground and trampled under foot. In the narrow limits of that bower, it would have been scarcely possible that the petticoat and scarf should have retained a position upon the stones, when subjected to the brushing to and fro of many struggling persons. 'There was evidence,' it is said, 'of a struggle; and the earth was trampled, the bushes were broken,'—but the petticoat and the scarf are found deposited as if upon shelves. 'The pieces of the frock torn out by the bushes were about three inches wide and six inches long. One part was the hem of the frock and it had been mended. They *looked like strips torn off.*' Here, inadvertently, *Le Soleil* has employed an exceedingly suspicious phrase. The pieces, as described, do indeed 'look like strips torn off'; but purposely and by hand. It is one of the rarest of accidents that a piece is 'torn off,' from any garment such as is now in question, by the agency *of a thorn*. From the very nature of such fabrics, a thorn or nail becoming entangled in them,

tears them rectangularly—divides them into two
longitudinal rents, at right angles with each other, and
meeting at an apex where the thorn enters—but it is
scarcely possible to conceive the piece 'torn off.'
I never so knew it, nor did you. To tear a piece *off*
from such fabric, two distinct forces, in different
directions, will be, in almost every case, required.
If there be two edges to the fabric—if, for example,
it be a pocket-handkerchief, and it is desired to tear
from it a slip, then, and then only, will the one force
serve the purpose. But in the present case the question
is of a dress, presenting but one edge. To tear a piece
from the interior, where no edge is presented, could
only be effected by a miracle through the agency of
thorns, and no *one* thorn could accomplish it. But,
even where an edge is presented, two thorns will be
necessary, operating, the one in two distinct directions,
and the other in one. And this in the supposition that
the edge is unhemmed. If hemmed, the matter is nearly
out of the question. We thus see the numerous and
great obstacles in the way of pieces being 'torn off'
through the simple agency of 'thorns'; yet we are
required to believe not only that one piece but that
many have been so torn. 'And one part,' too, '*was the
hem of the frock*!' Another piece was '*part of the
skirt, not the hem*,'—that is to say, was torn completely
out, through the agency of thorns, from the unedged
interior of the dress! These, I say, are things which
one may well be pardoned for disbelieving; yet, taken
collectedly, they form, perhaps, less of reasonable
ground for suspicion, than the one startling circumstance of the articles having been left in this thicket at
all, by any *murderers* who had enough precaution to
think of removing the corpse. You will not have
apprehended me rightly, however, if you suppose it
my design to *deny* this thicket as the scene of the
outrage.[104] THERE MIGHT HAVE BEEN A

[104] With this sentence Poe abruptly abandons the most
logical and accurate argument in his story. The rest of
the paragraph is, therefore, confused and contradictory.

WRONG *HERE*, OR, MORE POSSIBLY, AN
ACCIDENT AT MADAME DELUC'S. But, in fact,
this is a point of minor importance. We are not
engaged in an attempt to discover the scene, but to
produce the perpetrators of the murder. What I have
adduced, notwithstanding the minuteness with which
I have adduced it, has been with the view, first, to
show the folly of the positive and headlong assertions
of *Le Soleil*, but secondly, and chiefly, to bring you,
by the most natural route, to a further contemplation
of the doubt whether this assassination has, or has not,
been the work of *a gang*.[105]

"We will resume this question by mere allusion to
the revolting details of the surgeon examined at the
inquest. It is only necessary to say that his published
inferences, in regard to the number of the ruffians,
have been properly ridiculed as unjust and totally
baseless, by all the reputable anatomists of Paris.
Not that the matter *might not* have been as inferred,
but that there was no ground for the inference:—
WAS THERE NOT MUCH FOR ANOTHER?[106]

"Let us reflect now upon 'the traces of a struggle';
and let me ask what these traces have been supposed
to demonstrate. A gang. But do they not rather
demonstrate the absence of a gang? What *struggle*
could have taken place—what struggle so violent and

[105] Poe is in a bind. He refuses to omit his excellent evidence that the clothing was planted in the thicket, yet
he needs the thicket to discredit the *Herald's* theory of
a gang. By means of some devious sophistry he attempts
to ease past the contradiction.

[106] "At this point Poe rightly rejects Dr. Cook's testimony
that the girl was violated 'by more than two or three
persons.' . . . *Brother Jonathan*, Sept. 4, p. 2, col. 7, spoke
of [the testimony] as 'disgustingly ridiculous.' The *Herald*
had made enthusiastic use of it in the campaign against
gangs; in one article the doctor was 'confident that Mary
Rogers was brutally violated by six, or possibly eight
ruffians of that fact, he had ocular proof, but which is
unfit for publication.' (*Herald*, Aug. 16, p. 2, col. 4)"
[Wimsatt's note.]

so enduring as to have left its 'traces' in all directions—
between a weak and defenceless girl and the *gang* of
ruffians imagined? The silent grasp of a few rough
arms and all would have been over. The victim must
have been absolutely passive at their will. You will
here bear in mind that I ADMIT THE THICKET AS THE
SCENE OF THE OUTRAGE; AND YOU WILL IMMEDIATELY
PERCEIVE THAT the arguments urged against the thicket
as the scene are applicable, in chief part, only against
it as the scene of an outrage committed by *more than
a single individual*.[107] If we imagine but *one* violator,
we can conceive, and thus only conceive, the struggle
of so violent and so obstinate a nature as to have left
the 'traces' apparent.

"And again. I have already mentioned the suspicion
to be excited by the fact that the articles in question
were suffered to remain *at all* in the thicket where
discovered. It seems almost impossible that these
evidences of guilt should have been accidentally left
where found. There was sufficient presence of mind
(IT IS SUPPOSED) to remove the corpse; and yet a more
positive evidence than the corpse itself (whose features
might have been quickly obliterated by decay), is
allowed to lie conspicuously in the scene of the outrage
—I allude to the handkerchief with the *name* of the
deceased.[108] If this was accident, it was not the accident
of a gang. We can imagine it only the accident of an
individual. Let us see. An individual has committed the
murder. He is alone with the ghost of the departed.
He is appalled by what lies motionless before him.
The fury of his passion is over, and there is abundant
room in his heart for the natural awe of the deed.
His is none of that confidence which the presence of
numbers inevitably inspires. He is *alone* with the dead.
He trembles and is bewildered. Yet there is a necessity
for disposing of the corpse. He bears it to the river,

[107] Untrue. An excellent example of the sophistic tricks by
which Poe escapes his contradictions on the thicket.

[108] Mary's handkerchief was only monogrammed.

and leaves behind him the other evidences of guilt; for it is difficult, if not impossible to carry all the burden at once, and it will be easy to return for what is left. But in his toilsome journey to the water his fears redouble within him. The sounds of life encompass his path. A dozen times he hears or fancies he hears the step of an observer. Even the very lights from the city bewilder him. Yet, in time, and by long and frequent pauses of deep agony, he reaches the river's brink, and disposes of his ghastly charge—perhaps through the medium of a boat. But *now* what treasure does the world hold—what threat of vengeance could it hold out—which would have power to urge the return of that lonely murderer over that toilsome and perilous path, to the thicket and its blood-chilling recollections? He returns *not*, let the consequences be what they may. He *could* not return if he would. His sole thought is immediate escape. He turns his back *forever* upon those dreadful shrubberies, and flees as from the wrath to come.[109]

"But how with a gang? Their number would have inspired them with confidence; if, indeed, confidence is ever wanting in the breast of the arrant blackguard; and of arrant blackguards alone are the supposed *gangs* ever constituted. Their number, I say, would have prevented the bewildering and unreasoning terror which I have imagined to paralyze the single man. Could we suppose an oversight in one, or two, or three, this oversight would have been remedied by a fourth. They would have left nothing behind them;

[109] Poe's inspiration for this passage was probably the *Herald*, Sept. 24, p. 1, col. 4: ". . . [He] stayed by the dead and mangled body of his victim, in that dark thicket, with no eye but that of God upon the murderer and the murdered maid, until all was still—perhaps till near midnight. Then, tying the frock around her to form a handle, he carried her to the river, and hurled her in, and fled, too horror stricken to think of returning to the scene of the murder, to remove the articles found by the boys." By this time even Bennett was hedging on his theory of a guilty gang.

for their number would have enabled them to carry *all* at once. There would have been no need of *return*.

"Consider now the circumstance that, in the outer garment of the corpse when found, 'a slip, about a foot wide, had been torn upward from the bottom hem to the waist, wound three times round the waist, and secured by a sort of hitch in the back.' This was done with the obvious design of affording *a handle* by which to carry the body. But would any *number* of men have dreamed of resorting to such an expedient? To three or four, the limbs of the corpse would have afforded not only a sufficient, but the best possible, hold. The device is that of a single individual; and this brings us to the fact that 'between the thicket and the river the rails of the fences were found taken down, and the ground bore evident traces of some heavy burden having been dragged along it!' But would a *number* of men have put themselves to the super-fluous trouble of taking down a fence, for the purpose of dragging through it a corpse which they might have *lifted over* any fence in an instant? Would a *number* of men have so *dragged* a corpse at all as to have left evident *traces* of the dragging?

"And here we must refer to an observation of *Le Commerciel*; an observation upon which I have already, in some measure, commented. 'A piece,' says this journal, 'of one of the unfortunate girl's petticoats was torn out and tied under her chin, and around the back of her head, probably to prevent screams. This was done by fellows who had no pocket-handkerchiefs.

"I have before suggested that a genuine blackguard is never *without* a pocket-handkerchief. But it is not this fact that I now especially advert. That it was not through want of a handkerchief for the purpose imagined by *Le Commerciel*, that this bandage was employed, is rendered apparent by the handkerchief left in the thicket; and that the object was not 'to prevent screams' appears, also, from the bandage having been employed in preference to what would so much better have answered the purpose.

252

But the language of the evidence speaks of the strip
in question as 'found around the neck, fitting loosely,
and secured with a hard knot.' These words are
sufficiently vague, but differ materially from those
of *Le Commerciel*. The slip was eighteen inches wide,
and therefore, although of muslin, would form a
strong band when folded or rumpled longitudinally.
And thus rumpled it was discovered. My inference
is this. The solitary murderer, having borne the corpse,
for some distance (WHETHER FROM THE
THICKET OR ELSEWHERE), by means of the
bandage *hitched* around its middle, found the weight,
in this mode of procedure, too much for his strength.
He resolved to drag the burden—the evidence goes to
show that it *was* dragged. With this object in view,
it became necessary to attach something like a rope to
one of the extremities. It could be best attached about
the neck, where the head would prevent its slipping
off. And, now, the murderer bethought him, unquestionably, of the bandage about the loins. He
would have used this, but for its volution about the
corpse, the *hitch* which embarrassed it, and the
reflection that it had not been 'torn off' from the
garment. It was easier to tear a new slip from the
petticoat. He tore it, made it fast about the neck, and
so *dragged* his victim to the brink of the river. That
this 'bandage,' only attainable with trouble and delay,
and but imperfectly answering its purpose—that this
bandage was employed *at all*, demonstrates that the
necessity for its employment sprang from circumstances arising at a period when the handkerchief was
no longer attainable—that is to say, arising, as we have
imagined, after quitting the thicket (IF THE
THICKET IT WAS), and on the road between the
thicket and the river.

"But the evidence, you will say, of Madame
Deluc (!)[110] points especially to the presence of
a gang, in the vicinity of the thicket, at or about the

---

[110] The exclamation point is not in the original

epoch of the murder. This I grant. I doubt if there were not a *dozen* gangs, such as described by Madame Deluc, in and about the vicinity of the Barrière du Roule at *or about* the period of this tragedy. But the gang which has drawn upon itself the pointed animadversion, through the somewhat tardy AND VERY SUSPICIOUS evidence, of Madame Deluc, is the *only* gang which is represented by that honest and scrupulous old lady as having eaten her cakes and swallowed her brandy, without putting themselves to the trouble of making her payment. *Et hinc illae irae?*

"But what *is* the precise evidence of Madame Deluc? 'A gang of miscreants made their appearance, behaved boisterously, ate and drank without making payment, followed in the route of the young man and girl, returned to the inn *about dusk*, and recrossed the river as if in great haste.[111]

"Now this 'great haste' very possibly seemed *greater* haste in the eyes of Madame Deluc, since she dwelt lingeringly and lamentingly upon her violated cakes and ale—cakes and ale for which she might still have entertained a faint hope of compensation. Why,

---

[111] This passage is based on the *Herald*, Sept. 17, p. 2, col. 3: ". . . On that Sunday afternoon there were a much larger number of fire rowdies, butcher boys, soaplocks, and all sorts of riotous miscreants over at Weehawken, and almost all of them armed with sticks. A great many came in rowboats to the rum hole on the mud bank; and two boats in particular (one with six and the other with nine desperadoes in them) landed. . . . These scoundrels came up to the little shanty by the roadside, next to Nick Moore's House, and there called for drink, seized all the cakes, etc., and ate them—refused to pay anything, and threatened to beat everybody that interfered with them. All these had clubs. They then went toward the hill, and remained prowling about till after dark, when the two boats in question left in a great hurry." It is important that the gang did *not* enter the Nick Moore's House and terrorize Mrs. Loss, nor was Mrs. Loss the source of this part of the *Herald's* story; nor did the "gang" recross the river at "*about dusk*" but "*after dark*." (See notes 112, 114, 115.)

otherwise, since it was *about dusk*, should she make a point of the *haste*? It is no cause for wonder, surely, that even a gang of blackguards should make *haste* to get home when a wide river is to be crossed in small boats, when storm impends, and when night *approaches*.

"I say *approaches*; for the night had *not yet arrived*. It was only *about dusk* that the indecent haste of these 'miscreants' offended the sober eyes of Madame Deluc. But we are told that it was upon this very evening that Madame Deluc, as well as her eldest son, 'heard the screams of a female in the vicinity of the inn.' And in what words does Madame Deluc designate the period of the evening at which these screams were heard? 'It was *soon after dark*,' she says.[112] But 'soon *after* dark,' is at least, *dark*; and '*about dusk*' is as certainly daylight. Thus it is abundantly clear that the gang quitted the Barrière du Roule prior to the screams overheard (?)[113] by Madame Deluc. *And although, in all the many reports of the evidence, the relative expressions in question are distinctly and invariably employed just as I have employed them in this conversation with yourself,*[114] no notice whatever of the gross discrepancy has, as yet, been taken by any of the public journals, or by any of the myrmidons of police.[115]

"I shall add but one to the arguments against *a gang*; but this *one* has, to my own understanding at least,

[112] Mrs. Loss sent her son to drive away a bull "soon after dark." She heard the screams "some time after" that (*Herald*, Sept. 17, p. 2, col. 3).

[113] The question mark is not in the original.

[114] My italics.

[115] Poe at his best: a triumphant piece of chicanery. By deliberately misreading the *Herald* and substituting the words "about dusk" for "after dark," Poe has created a "gross discrepancy" where none existed. There can be no better evidence that Poe's intention in writing this story, originally, was to perpetrate a hoax.

a weight altogether irresistible. Under the circum-stances of large reward offered, and full pardon to any king's evidence, it is not to be imagined, for a moment, that some member of *a gang* of low ruffians, or of any body of men, would not long ago have betrayed his accomplices. Each one of a gang, so placed, is not so much greedy of reward, or anxious for escape, as *fearful of betrayal*. He betrays eagerly and early that *he may not himself be betrayed*. That the secret has not been divulged is the very best of proof that it is, in fact, a secret. The horrors of this dark deed are known only to *one*, OR TWO, living human beings, and to God.

"AND WHO IS THAT ONE? IT WILL NOT BE IMPOSSIBLE—PERHAPS IT WILL NOT BE DIFFICULT TO DISCOVER. Let us sum up now the meagre yet certain fruits of our long analysis. We have attained the idea EITHER OF A FATAL ACCIDENT UNDER THE ROOF OF MADAME DELUC, OR of a murder perpetrated, in the thicket at the Barrière du Roule, by a lover, or at least by an intimate and secret associate of the deceased. This associate is of swarthy complexion. This complexion, the 'hitch' in the bandage, and the 'sailor's knot' with which the bonnet-ribbon is tied, point to a seaman. His companionship with the deceased—a gay, but not an abject young girl—designates him as above the grade of the common sailor. Here the well written and urgent com-munications to the journals are much in the way of corroboration. The circumstance of the first elope-ment, as mentioned by *Le Mercure*, tends to blend the idea of this seaman with that of the 'naval officer' who is first known to have led the unfortunate into crime. WE ARE NOT FORCED TO SUPPOSE A PREMEDITATED DESIGN OF MURDER OR OF VIOLATION. BUT THERE WAS THE FRIENDLY SHELTER OF THE THICKET, AND THE APPROACH OF RAIN—THERE WAS OPPORTUNITY AND STRONG TEMPTATION—AND THEN A SUDDEN AND VIOLENT WRONG, TO BE CONCEALED ONLY BY ONE OF DARKER DYE.

"And here, most fitly, comes the consideration of

the continued absence of him of the dark complexion. Let me pause to observe that the complexion of this man is dark and swarthy; it was no common swarthiness which constituted the *sole* point of remembrance, both as regards Valence and Madame Deluc. But why is this man absent? Was he murdered by the gang? If so, why are there only *traces* of the assassinated *girl*? The scene of the two outrages will naturally be supposed identical. And where is his corpse? The assassins would most probably have disposed of both in the same way. But it may be said that this man lives, and is deterred from making himself known, through dread of being charged with the murder. This consideration might be supposed to operate upon him now—at this late period—since it has been given in evidence that he was seen with Marie—but it would have had no force at the period of the deed. The first impulse of an innocent man would have been to announce the outrage, and to aid in identifying the ruffians. This *policy* would have suggested. He had been seen with the girl. He had crossed the river with her in an open ferry-boat. The denouncing of the assassins would have appeared, even to an idiot, the surest and sole means of relieving himself from suspicion. We cannot suppose him, on the night of the fatal Sunday, both innocent himself and incognizant of an outrage committed. Yet only under such circumstances is it possible to imagine that he would have failed, if alive, in the denouncement of the assassins.

"And what means are ours, of attaining the truth? We shall find these means multiplying and gathering distinctness as we proceed. —PROVIDED THAT OUR PREPARATORY ANALYSIS OF THE SUBJECT HAS NOT GREATLY DIVERGED FROM THE PRINCIPLES OF TRUTH. Let us sift to the bottom this affair of the first elopement. Let us know the full history of 'the officer,' with his present circumstances, and his whereabouts at the precise period of the murder. Let us carefully compare with each other the various communications

sent to the evening paper, in which the object was
to inculpate *a gang*. This done, let us compare these
communications, both as regards style and MS.,
with those sent to the morning paper, at a previous
period, and insisting so vehemently upon the guilt of
Mennais. And, all this done, let us again compare
these various communications with the known MSS.
of the officer. Let us endeavor to ascertain, by
repeated questionings of Madame Deluc and her boys,
as well as of the omnibus-driver, Valence, something
more of the personal appearance and bearing of the
'man of dark complexion.' Queries, skilfully directed,
will not fail to elicit, from some of these parties,
information on this particular point (OR UPON
OTHERS)—information which the parties themselves
may not even be aware of possessing. And let us
now trace *the boat* picked up by the bargeman on
the morning of Monday the twenty-third of June,
and which was removed from the barge office,
without the cognizance of the officer in attendance,
and *without the rudder*, at some period prior to
the discovery of the corpse. With a proper caution
and perseverance we shall infallibly trace this boat;
for not only can the bargeman who picked it up
identify it, but the *rudder is at hand*. The rudder
of a sail boat would not have been abandoned, without
inquiry, by one altogether at ease in heart. And here
let me pause to insinuate a question. There was no
advertisement of the picking up of this boat. It
was silently taken to the barge office, and as silently
removed. But its owner or employer—how *happened*
he, at so early a period as Tuesday morning, to be
informed, without the agency of advertisement, of the
locality of the boat taken up on Monday, unless we
imagine some connection with the *navy*—some
personal permanent connection leading to cognizance
of its minute interests—its petty local news?
  "In speaking of the lonely assassin dragging his
burden to the shore, I have already suggested the
probability of his availing himself *of a boat*. Now we

are to understand that Marie Rogêt *was* precipitated
from a boat. This would naturally have been the
case. The corpse could not have been trusted to the
shallow waters of the shore. The peculiar marks on
the back and shoulders of the victim tell of the bottom
ribs of a boat.[116] That the body was found without
weight is also corroborative of the idea. If thrown
from the shore a weight would have been attached.
We can only account for its absence by supposing
the murderer to have neglected the precaution of
supplying himself with it before pushing off. In the
act of consigning the corpse to the water, he would
unquestionably have noticed his oversight; but then
no remedy would have been at hand. Any risk would
have been preferred to a return to that accursed
shore. Having rid himself of his ghastly charge, the
murderer would have hastened to the city. There, at
some obscure wharf, he would have leaped on land.
But the boat, would he have secured it? He would
have been in too great haste for such things as
securing a boat. Moreover, in fastening it to the wharf,
he would have felt as if securing evidence against
himself. His natural thought would have been to cast
from him, as far as possible, all that had held connection with his crime. He would not only have fled
from the wharf, but he would not have permitted
the boat to remain. Assuredly he would have cast it
adrift. Let us pursue our fancies.—In the morning,
the wretch is stricken with unutterable horror at
finding that the boat has been picked up and detained
at a locality which he is in the daily habit of frequent-
ing—at a locality, perhaps, which his duty compels
him to frequent. The next night, *without daring to*

---

[116] "In contending that the bruises . . . were made by the
ribs of the boat Poe disregards the testimony of Dr.
Cook. Mayor: 'Might or might not those marks . . . have
been caused by the body coming in contact with some
hard substance after death . . . ? Dr. C.: 'They could not.
Because the coagulation was in the cellular tissues.' (*Herald*, Aug. 17, p. 2, col. 4)" [Wimsatt's note.]

ask for the rudder, he removes it. Now *where* is that
rudderless boat? Let it be one of our first purposes
to discover. With the first glimpse we obtain of it, the
dawn of our success shall begin. This boat shall guide
us, with a rapidity which will surprise even ourselves,
to him who employed it in the midnight of the fatal
Sabbath. Corroboration will rise upon corroboration,
and the murderer will be traced."

(For reasons which we shall not specify, but which
to many readers will appear obvious, we have taken
the liberty of here omitting, from the MSS. placed
in our hands, such portion as details the *following up*
of the apparently slight clew obtained by Dupin.
We feel it advisable only to state, in brief, that the
result desired was brought to pass; THAT AN INDIVIDUAL
ASSASSIN WAS CONVICTED, UPON HIS OWN CONFESSION,
OF THE MURDER OF MARIE ROGÊT and that the Prefect
fulfilled punctually, although with reluctance, the
terms of his compact with the Chevalier. Mr. Poe's
article concludes with the following words—*Eds.*)[117]

It will be understood that I speak of coincidences
and *no more*. What I have said above upon this topic
must suffice. In my own heart there dwells no faith
in praeter-nature. That Nature and its God are two,
no man who thinks will deny. That the latter,
creating the former, can, at will, control or modify it,
is also unquestionable. I say "at will"; for the question
is of will, and not, as the insanity of logic has
assumed, of power. It is not that the Deity *cannot*
modify his laws, but that we insult him in imagining
a possible necessity for modification. In their origin
these laws were fashioned to embrace *all* contingencies
which *could* lie in the Future. With God all is *Now*.

I repeat, then, that I speak of these things only as

[117] Of the magazine in which the article was originally
published. [Poe's note.]
More Poe humbug. The author of this paragraph is, of course,
Poe himself. In his 1848 letter to George Eveleth he writes: ". . .
Nothing was omitted in 'Marie Rogêt' but what I omitted my-
self. . . ."

of coincidences. And further: in what I relate it will be seen that between the fate of the unhappy Mary Cecilia Rogers, so far as that fate is known, and the fate of one Marie Rogêt up to a certain epoch in her history, there has existed a parallel in the contemplation of whose wonderful exactitude the reason becomes embarrassed. I say all this will be seen. But let it not for a moment be supposed that, in proceeding with the sad narrative of Marie from the epoch just mentioned, and in tracing to its *dénouement* the mystery which enshrouded her, it is my covert design to hint at an extension of the parallel, or even to suggest that the measures adopted in Paris for the discovery of the assassin of a *grisette*, or measures founded in any similar ratiocination, would produce any similar result.

For, in respect to the latter branch of the supposition, it should be considered that the most trifling variation in the facts of the two cases might give rise to the most important miscalculations, by diverting thoroughly the two courses of events; very much as, in arithmetic, an error which, in its own individuality, may be inappreciable, produces, at length, by dint of multiplication at all points of the process, a result enormously at variance with truth. And, in regard to the former branch, we must not fail to hold in view that the very Calculus of Probabilities to which I have referred, forbids all idea of the extension of the parallel,—forbids it with a positiveness strong and decided just in proportion as this parallel has already been long-drawn and exact. This is one of those anomalous propositions which, seemingly appealing to thought altogether apart from the mathematical, is yet one which only the mathematician can fully entertain. Nothing, for example, is more difficult than to convince the merely general reader that the fact of sixes having been thrown twice in succession by a player at dice, is sufficient cause for betting the largest odds that sixes will not be thrown in the third attempt. A suggestion to this effect is usually rejected by the intellect at once. It does not appear that the two throws which have been completed, and which lie now absolutely in the Past, can have influence upon the throw which exists only in the Future. The chance for throwing sixes seems to be precisely as it was at any ordinary time—that is to say, subject only to the influence of the various other throws which may be made by the dice. And this is a reflection which appears so exceedingly obvious that attempts to controvert it are received more frequently with a derisive smile than with anything like respectful attention. The error here involved—a gross error redolent of mischief—I cannot pretend to expose within the limits assigned me at present; and with the philosophical it needs no exposure.[118] It may be sufficient here to say that it forms one of an infinite series of mistakes which arise in the path of Reason through her propensity for seeking truth *in detail.*[119]

[118] See note 99.

[119] End of third and last installment in Snowden's *Ladies' Companion*, Feb. 1843, pp. 162-167. Publication of Poe's conclusion was postponed from January when, in November of 1842, Mrs. Loss' sons were arrested and charged as accessories in Mary Rogers' murder. The "solution" was published only after the boys were released. Ironically, had Poe known the police theory of a fatal abortion, he could easily have revised his conclusion to accommodate that theory in 1842, and thus built his now exploded reputation as a detective upon apparently unassailable grounds.

Bibliography of Secondary Materials

(I am indebted for most of these titles to the scholarship of William K. Wimsatt. In most cases I merely add to his list those studies printed subsequent to his article.)

Brynes, Thomas, *Professional Criminals of America*. New York, 1886. pp. 334–47.

Clemens, Will, "The Tragedy of Mary Rogers." *Era Magazine*, XIV (1904). pp. 450–63.

Costello, R., "Poe and Mary Rogers." New York *Evening Post*, Jan. 10, 1920, Sec. III, p. 11, col. 4.

Croffut, W. A., "Who Murdered Mary Rogers?" Detroit *Free Press*, June 13, 1885.

Crouse, Russell, *Murder Won't Out*. Doubleday, Doran & Company, Inc., New York, 1932. pp. 52–74.

Duke, Thomas S., *Celebrated Criminal Cases of America*. San Francisco, 1910, pp. 577–82.

Lane, Winthrop D., "The Mystery of Mary Rogers." *Collier's* March 8, 1930, pp. 19, 50, 52.

Levins, Peter, "Rogers Mystery Formed Basis for Poe Short Story." New York *Sunday News*, Sept. 21, 1941, pp. 52–3, 55.

New York *Evening Journal*, June 29, 1897. p. 27, col. 1.

Pearce, Charles E., *Unsolved Murder Mysteries*. London, 1924. pp. 225–45.

Pearson, Edmund, *Instigation of the Devil*. New York, 1930. pp. 177–85; and in *Vanity Fair*, July, 1929, pp. 59, 110.

Poe, Edgar Allan, "The Mystery of Marie Rogêt." *The Ladies' Companion*, New York, XVII, Nov.-Dec., 1842 (pp. 15–20, 93–99.); Feb., 1843, (pp. 162–67.) The same, with revisions, in *Tales of Edgar A. Poe*, New York, 1845.

Radin, Edwin D., "The Mystery of Mary Rogers." *Ellery Queen's Mystery Magazine*, Vol. 14, Nov., 1949. pp. 77–80.

Sun (New York), "The Ghost of Mary Rogers," October 16, 1888.

Tribune (New York), "The Murder of Mary Rogers, a Mystery That Was Never Solved—How Poe preserved it in a story." Oct. 29, 1885.

Trumble, Alfred, *Great Crimes and Criminals of America*. New York, 1881, pp. 7–10; same in *National Police Gazette*, May, 1881.

Van Every, Edward, *Sins of New York*. New York, 1930. pp. 95–104.

Wallace, Irving, *The Fabulous Originals*. New York, 1955. pp. 172–215.

Walling, George W., *Recollections of a New York Police Chief*. New York, 1887.

Walsh, John, *Poe the Detective: The Curious Circumstances Behind "The Mystery of Marie Rogêt."* New Brunswick. N. J., 1968. pp. 5–81.

Wimsatt, William K., "Poe and the Mystery of Mary Rogers." *Publications of the Modern Language Association*, LVI, (March, 1941). pp. 230–48.

———, "Mary Rogers, John Anderson and Others." *American Literature*, XXI (January, 1950), pp. 482–84.

Worthen, Samuel, "A Strange Aftermath of the Mystery of Marie Rogêt." *Proceedings of the New Jersey Historical Society*, LX April, 1942). pp. 116–23.

———, "Poe and the Beautiful Cigar Girl." *American Literature*, XX (November, 1948). pp. 305–12.

Index

Abortion theory of Mary's disappearance
  implausibility of, as cause of death, 143–45, 147
  implication of, in Poe's second version of "Marie Rogêt," 116–21
  lack of, in Poe's first version of "Marie Rogêt," 110–14, 264
  Merritt's suspicion of, 57, 100–2, 125, 143–47, 151, 155–56, 159, 171
  press' discussion of, 125–26
  probability of, 150–51
Adams, Samuel, 72
Advertiser, Jersey City, Kellenbarack hearing reported by, 97, 100
Allen, Hervey, 109, 120–21
American, New York, police defended by, 39, 50
Anderson, John, 177, 181, 183
  abortion arranged by, 150, 156, 161
  abortion mentioned by, 139, 145, 148–49
  accused of publicity stunt, 23
  disputes over estate of, 133–39
  Mary hired by, 20–21, 27, 198
  Mary's ghost heard by, 135, 139, 175–76
  Poe's character of (M. Le Blanc), 198
  possible connection with Poe of, 172
  reward offered by, 40

Anderson, John Charles, 134–36, 138, 177
Anderson, Katherine, 133–34, 136
Applegate, Mary, 177
  Mme. Restell accused by, 128
Appleton, Laura V., 177
  Anderson's will challenged by, 133–34, 138–39

Barnum, P. T., 18
Baudelaire, Charles Pierre, 109–10
Beach, Moses Y., 177
  balloon hoax bought by, 109
  feud with Bennett of, 10, 14
  Sun sold to, 9
Beauvais (A. Crommelin), Poe's character of, 83, 112, 203–5, 207–10, 225–29
Beck, John B., 222
Beck, Theodric R., 222
Benjamin, Park, 177
  feud with Bennett of, 10
Bennett, James Gordon, 1, 123, 138, 177
  attack on police and courts by, 12–15, 40–41, 174–75
  coverage of Jewett case by, 7–9
  feud with New York press of, 9–10
  Herald founded by, 3–5
  theory of Mary's death held by, 36, 65, 86, 142, 174, 241, 249
Benson, Maria (Ellen Jewett), 5
Bernard, Fannie, 133
Bernard, George, 133

267